D1579014

Asian Cinema

A Regional View

Olivia Khoo

EDINBURGH
University Press

This book is dedicated to the memory of my father, Lawrence,
who taught me everything about life and love.

Edinburgh University Press is one of the leading university presses in the UK.
We publish academic books and journals in our selected subject areas across the
humanities and social sciences, combining cutting-edge scholarship with high editorial
and production values to produce academic works of lasting importance. For more
information visit our website: edinburghuniversitypress.com

Edinburgh University Press Ltd
The Tun – Holyrood Road
12 (2f) Jackson's Entry
Edinburgh EH8 8PJ

First published in hardback by Edinburgh University Press 2021

Typeset in 11/13 Monotype Ehrhardt by
IDSUK (DataConnection) Ltd, and
printed and bound by CPI Group (UK) Ltd, Croydon, CR0 4YY

A CIP record for this book is available from the British Library

ISBN 978 1 4744 6176 4 (hardback)
ISBN 978 1 4744 6177 1 (paperback)
ISBN 978 1 4744 6178 8 (webready PDF)
ISBN 978 1 4744 6179 5 (epub)

Contents

Figures

Acknowledgements

This book was written over many years, across multiple places, and with support of family, friends and colleagues from around the world.

I am fortunate to work in the collegial environment of the School of Media, Film and Journalism at Monash University; a big thank you to my friends and colleagues at Monash who make work a better place to be. I am constantly inspired by my amazing graduate students and thank especially Daniel Edwards, Katrina Tan and Teck Fann Goh, who have assisted with the research for this book. Sections of this book that have previously been published in different forms have benefited from the editorial advice and insightful comments of Sean Metzger, Patricia White, Maria Elena Indelicato and David H. Fleming. I also thank my academic mentors and friends Chua Beng Huat, Koichi Iwabuchi, Fran Martin and Audrey Yue.

To my dear friends who have sustained me with shared meals, funny stories and solicitous phone calls and messages; I am grateful to know Larissa Hjorth, Therese Davis, Fiona Camarri, Vince Pacecca, Rozleigh Steffensen, Derreck Goh, Lara Zeccola, Cynthia Seow, Karen Steinburger and Tan Pin Pin.

My family is the source of everything good in my life. Love and thanks to Lee, Alicia, Stuart, Jonathan, Alex and my brilliant nephews and nieces William, Anna, Barnaby, Noah, Lily and Elijah. Thank you Ziggy. And to Sebastian, who lights up my world with his exuberance, kindness, intelligence and generosity of love, I am grateful for you every day.

CHAPTER 1

Introduction: Theorising Asian Cinema as a Regional Cinema

In Abbas Kiarostami's *Like Someone in Love* (2012), a retired professor, Takashi (Tadashi Okuno), meets a young sociology student, Akiko (Rin Takanashi), who works as a high end escort to pay off her tuition. Akiko accompanies Takashi to his apartment where the two engage in a conversation that extends through the night. The next day Takashi encounters Akiko's jealous boyfriend Noriaki (Ryō Kase), who initially believes him to be Akiko's grandfather. The film, a Japanese–French production, screened at the 2012 Busan International Film Festival in the 'A Window on Asian Cinema' category. It represented a marked diversion for Iranian director Kiarostami, known for his Palme d'Or-winning *Taste of Cherry* (1997). Like the film's title and eponymous song, the film is also 'like' an exquisitely crafted work by Japanese master Yasujirō Ozu, reminding us for instance of *Woman of Tokyo/Tokyo no Onna* (1933). This film, together with other examples from the last thirty years featured in the chapters that follow, inspired the writing of this book. They exemplify an ongoing struggle by audiences and scholars, one that enchants as well as frustrates, to define what constitutes Asian cinema given the myriad examples that continually expand, complicate and upend existing categories and conceptual boundaries. While scholarship on Asian cinema has grown exponentially over a corresponding period, the theoretical frameworks for understanding the proliferating categories of this cinema are only catching up, if not quite keeping up. Our understandings of national cinemas from Asia have deepened with new studies, as have our knowledges of the complex production ecologies surrounding particular films; however, coming to terms with Asian cinema as a scholarly field, a marketing category and a spectatorial experience remains unapprehended in a more comprehensive way within academic studies of the cinema. While these demands cannot be fully answered in a single volume, this book provides two analytical frames that are aimed at opening up future studies in this field. The first is to unabashedly study Asian cinema as a regional cinema. Such an approach is not meant to discount the importance of national cinema models or to discourage close analyses of particular films, but to offer an alternative analytical lens through which to approach the complexity of Asian cinema, despite the usual criticisms of the incommensurability of language, cultural, political and economic contexts that attend to such an approach. The second, related, method suggests that a comparative approach to understanding Asian cinema from within Asia is necessary to its analysis. This comparative approach is steadfastly rooted within intra-Asian connections, whatever outside influences and cinemas may also impinge or impress upon it. Retaining Asia as the reference point for Asian cinema might appear to be a theoretical sleight of hand but the aim is to foreground the internal analytical logic of Asian cinema as a regional cinema, a logic that most appropriately manifests the messiness and complexity of language, funding imperatives, fickle audiences and the best (and worst) of scholarly intentions.

From National Cinemas to a Regional Cinema

Since the late 1980s, 'Asian cinema' has become a well circulated term at international film festivals, in academia and among popular cinemagoers. This has been accompanied by an increase in scholarship on cinemas from Asia, from cult and fan-based studies to studies of high profile directors. Asian cinema is a field that now attracts critical attention and avid audiences from around the world, as witnessed by the popular success of Asian genre films (from martial arts to horror), and top prizes awarded to directors such as Apichatpong Weerasethakul, Chen Kaige, Hou Hsiao-Hsien and Hirokazu Kore-eda at the prestigious Cannes Film Festival, and most recently, Bong Joon-ho at the 92nd Academy Awards in 2020.[1] Yet although the term Asian cinema is now widely accepted, it does not constitute 'a unified discursive field' (Yoshimoto 2006: 255). The field of Asian cinema is at present dominated by studies of individual filmmakers representing different national industries (usually male directors such as Hou Hsiao-Hsien (Taiwan), Zhang Yimou (China), Wong Kar-wai (Hong Kong), Hirokazu Kore-eda (Japan), and Park Chan-wook (South Korea)), or readings of individual films or sets of films again predominantly from a national cinema perspective. This overriding national approach represents a missed opportunity for understanding the dynamic industrial and cultural transformations that have occurred in the region over the past thirty years, with greater collaboration and integration between Asia's film industries affecting how films from the region are being made, distributed and viewed.

This book provides a critical study of the development of Asian cinema as a regional cinema in the past three decades. By this, I mean a definition of Asian cinema that is more than a sum of its national constituent parts, and that can account for the growing inter-Asian and pan-Asian films and filmmaking practices being produced out of the intensifying collaborations between Asia's film industries. Although active exchanges have long taken place between film industries in Asia, this book investigates how a period of regional consolidation and cooperation, marked by new models of production, film financing, exhibition and reception, emerged with the development of Asian modernities and economies in the late 1980s, and was again compelled by the collapse of key markets during the Asian financial crisis of 1997.

'Asia', as it is conceived in this book, is not defined in terms of a fixed territory but appears out of particular historical, cultural and economic necessities (Choi and Wada-Marciano 2009), and in the case of regional Asian cinema is predominantly to do with issues of funding and declining audiences. As Ien Ang writes:

> [t]he meaning of the category 'Asian' is thoroughly in flux today, negotiated and contested across multiple dimensions. It is not only a marker of identity (addressing the question: 'Who is Asian?'); it is also, in this twenty-first century, a particular sign of desire ('we want Asia') and a signifier of power (as in the discourse of 'the rise of Asia'). (Ang 2014: 125–6)

From Farah Khan's Bollywood choreography in Peter Chan's pan-Asian hit *Perhaps Love* (2005) to Iranian filmmaker Mohsen Makhmalbaf's *The Gardener* (2012), made with South Korean financing and crew and Kiarostami's *Like Someone in Love* made in the same year in collaboration with Japan, South, Southeast and West Asian players are reinvigorating and reshaping how the more dominant East Asian cinemas are doing business. Regionalisation of Asia's film industries, in the form of collaborative production strategies and cross-border funding, has become an increasing necessity not only for smaller industries, but also the larger production centres in the struggle to compete with Hollywood. Conceiving of the region Asia as not just a geographical space but also as a particular imaginary that nevertheless has a material/economic basis to it is a way of understanding how cinematic productions are constructed within capitalist structures and on cultural grounds.

As yet there has been no sustained study in the form of a monograph of the growing collaborations and connections between film industries in East, Southeast, South and West Asia. Existing scholarship on Asian cinema has been focused on particular national industries, or collected

volumes surveying a range of national cinemas in Asia, with Asian cinema used as an umbrella term for a set of national cinemas (Dissanayake
1994; Grossman 2000; Hanan 2001; Vasudev et al. 2002; Lau 2003;
Ciecko 2006; Eleftheriotis and Needham 2006; Carter 2007; Vick 2007;
Jackson et al. 2006; Yau 2011; Chan et al. 2011; Pugsley 2015; Fang 2017).
Yet another set of works explore the interactions between Asian film
industries and Hollywood or European cinemas (Donovan 2008; Hunt
and Leung 2008; Lim and Yamamoto 2011; Gates and Funnell 2012).
This is not to say that those relationships are insignificant to the myriad
ways in which Asian cinema has been constructed, but that the forms of
inter-Asian referencing occurring today between Asia's film industries
are more urgently in need of attention. More recent collections such
as *The Palgrave Handbook of Asian Cinema* (Magnan-Park et al. 2018)
acknowledge the need for more expansive accounts of Asian cinema. In
their Handbook, the editors include West and Central Asia as well as
Bollywood films. Magnan-Park's chapter 'The desire for a poly-Asian
continental film movement' notes that while pan-African and European
cinemas have long been recognised as regional cinemas, there has been
no equivalent establishment of a 'poly-Asian continental cinematic consciousness' (2018: 15).

Despite this slow yet important shift, to date, existing collections and
studies have not fully examined the integration and transformations occurring within and across the region in recent years, and scholarly approaches
that regard Asian cinema from outside a national cinema framework are
in the minority. While the paradigm of the national as a way of understanding film production and consumption has increasingly been called
into question, the persistence and resilience of national cinema categories
remain.

Darrell Davis and Emilie Yueh-Yu Yeh's *East Asian Screen Industries*
(2008) provides an important model for how to shift scholarship on contemporary Asian cinema from a siloed national cinema approach to an
emphasis on interrelations between East Asian screen industries. Davis
and Yeh argue that the national cinema model cannot encapsulate a region
'as an interconnected whole that is susceptible to global political fluctua-
tions and multinational capitalism' (2008: 1). While avoiding a national
cinema framework, their book concentrates on the film industries of
China, Japan and South Korea, areas that continue to dominate the scholarship on contemporary Asian cinema given the size of these industries
and the strength of their domestic audiences. Since the publication of their
volume over a decade ago, these industries have continued to transform
markedly, with collaborations intensifying across all areas of production,

distribution and exhibition. Stephen Teo's *The Asian Cinema Experience* (2012) expands the geographical reach of Asia to include Bollywood and Iranian cinema. Most of the book's chapters focus on individual national case studies, structured according to thematic concerns. In the book's final section, Teo theorises Asian cinema by setting out to distinguish Asian cinema from the concepts of National Cinema, World Cinema, and Third Cinema. Teo writes:

> Asian Cinema is a concept that outgrows not just National but also Third Cinema, another firmament of film studies that is essentially Western in conception. Thus the theory of Asian Cinema is one that replaces the role played by world-systems theory: Asian Cinema as a unit of analysis that replaces hitherto standard units of largely Western firmaments of film analysis such as National Cinema, World Cinema and Third Cinema. (219)

Teo adds that the 'very idea of Asian Cinema seems . . . to naturally locate itself at the juncture of critical theory lying somewhere between the two concepts of National Cinema and Hollywood, both areas in which Western critics have tended to predominate' (225). Teo seeks to find a specific 'Asian' identity for Asian cinema that allows it to deconstruct these other categories against which it abuts. In *World Cinema: A Critical Introduction*, Shekhar Deshpande and Meta Mazaj (2018) provide a refreshing perspective on cinemas from Asia, recognising that 'Asian cinema has a dual identity, as it constructs an exemplary collective dynamism within the region while interacting with and influencing other components of world cinema' (225). This flexible, dual perspective allows the authors to explore inter-Asian and trans-Asian connections within and outside the region. Peter Pugsley's *Tradition, Culture and Aesthetics in Contemporary Asian Cinema* (2013) takes a thematic approach to locating an Asian aesthetic in films from and about Asia, as does Stephanie DeBoer's *Coproducing Asia* (2014) to the study of film co-productions between China and Japan. These monographs have made significant inroads into how we might approach Asian cinema as a regional cinema and add to a much larger field investigating the transnational dimensions of cinemas from Asia (e.g., Lu 1997; Hunt and Leung 2008; Gates and Funnell 2012). Conceptually and thematically, this book adds to a growing conversation that is constantly evolving.

In the sections of the introduction to follow, the notion of Asian cinema as a regional cinema will be developed firstly from a historical perspective, setting out key historical entanglements that have contributed to the growing industrial collaborations exemplifying contemporary Asian cinema. Secondly, the conceptual basis for Asian cinema as a regional cinema will be developed from critical studies of inter-Asia that can be productively combined with traditional Euro-American film studies approaches. This syncretic model is necessary to account for the growing industrial collaborations in the region and to find new ways of coming to terms with films produced outside of a predominantly national cinema framework. Such an approach opens up a comparative framework that can apprehend national differences while still foregrounding the reality of increasing regional integration.

Asian Cinema as a Historical Category

The kinds of cinematic interconnections characterising contemporary Asian cinema as identified in this book have precursors in premodern regionalism. The conditions of possibility that allow Asian cinema as a regional cinema to emerge over the last three decades are founded in the historical conditions of colonialism and capitalism.

Nick Deocampo's edited collection *Early Cinema in Asia* (2017) takes a dual national and regional perspective to address the diverse historical discourses of Asia's early encounters with cinema. Noting that the 'history of early cinema in Asia remains largely unwritten, perhaps because the region tends to place a strong emphasis on national cinemas' (1), some chapters in the volume take a regional and comparative approach while most trace historical film beginnings in specific national contexts across East, Southeast, South, West and Central Asia. A key point of interrogation in the collection is how the meaning of 'early cinema' in Asia is distinct from the concept of early cinema in Western film scholarship. Deocampo notes, '[w]hen film first appeared, Asia was virtually a continent of colonies' (1). Colonial cinema in Asia, tied to the region's maritime history – with films being distributed along ocean liner routes and through port cities – might not be considered the beginnings of cinema in Asia if Asian cinema is principally defined as being 'indigenously produced or appropriated through a sense of regional belonging' (6). The emergence of national cinemas in Asia, on the other hand, oftentimes marked the independence of the nation state (even though there may be continuous colonial influence), reflecting the importance of the national cinema concept to early Asian cinema. For these reasons, Deocampo only tentatively defines early cinema in Asia as lasting from 1896 until 1918, with the period 1918 to 1941 representing a 'post-early cinema' phase (13) – a transitional time between the continued exercise of colonial powers alongside the increasing domestic ownership of film business.

Deocampo (2017) acknowledges 'prototypically pan-Asian' linkages between countries in Asia, which are precursors to the contemporary forms of pan-Asianism I discuss in the next chapter. However, he notes that efforts were not sustained and did not result in a true pan-Asian cinema:

> Historically speaking, there remains no evidence to show that a collective Asian cinema formed during the early film period. While there were seminal efforts at cross-country market penetration and nascent attempts at financial coproductions, the region's division into colonies and the political divides can be seen as major obstacles for a united continental film industry. (16)

Issues of language, culture, religion, not to mention the region's immense geographical size, are still barriers to further integration, although the latter to some degree is alleviated with greater ease of moving across geographical borders in modern times.

In excavating these incipient (and piecemeal) pan-Asian histories, the important point to highlight is the idea of (early) Asian cinema as 'an aspirational notion, offering us an imagined (though lost) opportunity, when cinema could have galvanized the region into one cinematic institution but did not' (Deocampo 2017: 19–20). This aspirational sense of the term Asian cinema remains key to considerations of national as well as pan-Asian cinematic efforts and influences. Deocampo's collection is significant for its attempt to identify regional commonalities, as well as variances, and to highlight the notion of (early) Asian cinema as an aspirational model.

Taking the period pre-Second World War as her starting point, Kinnia Yau Shuk-ting (2009) traces the origins of the present-day Asian film network to Japan's efforts to develop a Greater East Asian cinema involving China, Hong Kong and Japan during the 1930s and 1940s (171). This Greater East Asian film network (*Daitoa eiga*) is derived from the Greater East Asia Co-Prosperity Sphere (*Daitoa kyoeiken*), a concept advanced by the Japanese government during the 1930s and 1940s to distinguish Asia (and pan-Asian ideals) from the colonial West, while it also set out to promote Japanese superiority over the rest of Asia. In her 2010 volume, Yau explores a range of cinematic interconnections taking place between film companies in Japan, China and Hong Kong following the Second Sino-Japanese War (1937–45) and Second World War (1941–5). As Yau (2009) notes, these interconnections were business-oriented, rather than politically motivated: '[t]he motivation for establishing a network of Asian film-makers was always business-driven: to acquire new markets, to improve the product to make it competitive, and to gain access to the latest industrial technology' (171). Yau's important historical mapping outlines the foundations for collaboration that would continue in the post-war period.

Like Yau, Abé Mark Nornes (2013) similarly notes a 'steady process of interconnection across the region' following a period Japanese colonial occupation during the 1930s and early 1940s (175). Nornes presents a 'tripartite historiography' of the development of Asian cinema (185). In the first period, Nornes turns his attention to one of the earliest books on Asian cinema, Ichikawa Sai's *The Creation and Construction of Asian Cinema* (1941). According to Nornes, Ichikawa's attempt to 'create' and 'construct' Asian cinema in the period just prior to the Second World War provides an early industrial model through which we might think through 'the present-day visioning of Asian cinema' (181). Following nascent imaginings of Asian cinema in the 1930s and 1940s, attempts at pan-Asianism following the Second World War were hampered by the legacy of Japanese imperialism and a focus on bilateral relationships with the United States or the Soviet Union (185). Short lived experiments in regional integration did occur, including the Federation of Motion Picture Producers in Southeast Asia, which was active from roughly 1953 to 1962. Sangjoon Lee (2017) excavates the Asia Foundation's 'forgotten motion-picture projects' in Cold War Asia, including their annual Asian Film Festival. Lee (2017) writes,

> [t]he Asia Foundation covertly supported anticommunist motion-picture industry personnel, ranging from producers, directors, and technicians to critics and writers in Japan, Hong Kong, Burma, and South Korea, as well as American and British motion-picture producers in Malaysia and Thailand through clandestine activities. (108)

Their attempt to construct an anti-communist motion picture producers' alliance in Asia is perhaps the first example of a post-war inter-Asian film producers' organisation. Such ad hoc arrangements are fascinating for the political motivations they reveal at the time. The Asian Film Festival also highlights the growing importance of film festivals to the creation of a modern-day Asian cinema: from the 1970s premiere international film festivals such as Venice and Rotterdam began promoting screenings of films from Asia, and speciality Asian film festivals were being established around the world. Additionally, the development of film festivals within Asia also gathered pace during this period, with the Yamagata Documentary Film Festival, Hong Kong International Film Festival, and later Busan International Film Festival as notable examples.

Thus, it was from the 1980s that a sense of regional dynamism returned, and it is from here that this book takes up the story. Prasenjit Duara (2010) notes that Asian regionalism and interdependence today 'is being managed by ad hoc arrangements and specialised transnational institutions with little possibility of large-scale state-like co-ordination and control. In this sense, region formation in Asia is a multipath, uneven, and pluralistic development . . .' (981). Such a broad and uneven terrain, marked in the cinema by a diversity of language, production and consumption contexts, necessitates the production of what Chris Berry (2016) refers to as a 'history in fragments' (259). In sketching out a historiography of Sino-Korean screen connections, Berry reveals the occluded input of Koreans into Shanghai cinema of the colonial era; the existence of transborder production cultures, such as South Koreans working in Hong Kong in the 1960s and 1970s; and the popular reception of South Korean melodramas in the 1960s. These little-known connections in production, distribution and exhibition provide an alternate and disjunctive history of inter-Asian cinema connections predating the current period of globalisation (248). Berry has acknowledged the value of collective academic efforts in piecing together a fragmented history of Asian cinema emerging from various bilateral and transnational collaborations. Deploying Kim Soyoung's term 'trans-cinema', he calls for a larger transborder cinema historiography composed of 'a collection of distinct transborder projects, each with its own logic' (2016: 248).

Joining the call for a newer paradigm through which to understand film production, distribution and consumption in the Asian region, this book employs a regional, inter-Asian perspective in place of a dominant national cinema approach. The aim is not to displace national cinema frameworks entirely but to consider the processes of consolidation and cooperation occurring on a regional level by examining the various levels of interaction and mutual transformation taking place beyond national boundaries. Regionalism in the book is understood as 'an intermediate zone between the deterritorializing impulses of capitalism and the territorial limits of nationalism' (Duara 2010: 974). Regionalism does not minimise or eradicate marginalisations and oppressions derived from capitalism; as a process complementary with globalisation it also 'replicates, reproduces, and regenerates them' (Berry et al. 2009: 15). Nevertheless, seeing Asian cinema as a regional network, not only of films but also of scholars, offers the kind of transborder or critical transnational approach (Higbee and Lim 2010: 10) that is necessary to combat ideological and methodological nationalism. To that end, the next section acknowledges further scholarly debts in deriving a syncretic methodology that is underpinned by inter-Asia referencing. An emphasis on interdependence and the fostering of a transnational imaginary within Asia is, as Prasenjit Duara puts it, 'not *at* the cost but *for* the cost of our national attachments' (2010: 982; original emphasis). In an era of post-war regionalism 'marked by obstinate and repressive nationalisms' and the 'durability of the national cinema paradigm for film history' (Nornes 2013: 181, 185), a shift towards attending to the regional dimensions of Asian cinema and to modes of encounter and interconnection is vital.

Regional Asian Cinema as a Form of Inter-Asia Referencing

Asian cinema has traditionally been the object of study for film 'connoisseurs' in the West. The national approach that continues to overshadow scholarship on Asian cinema stems from the academic interest in Japanese, Indian and Chinese cinemas existing prior to the introduction of the term Asian cinema within the standard film studies vocabulary. It was only in the late 1980s that Asian cinema as an institutional category began to strengthen, emerging out of political and cultural debates within Western academia that saw a turn towards multiculturalism and with that, a shift in objects deemed worthy of study (Yoshimoto 2006). From the late 1980s and early 1990s international film festivals also began highlighting and promoting art films from different parts of Asia, intensifying the interest in Asian art directors and other Asian national cinemas besides Chinese, Japanese and Indian cinemas. The development of Asian cinema rapidly gained pace from the 1990s. This was a result of the economic rise of East Asia, which played a major role in the globalisation of Asian economies around the world and fostered greater awareness of the so-called 'unique' cultural productions emerging from the region. Together, these factors contributed to the increasing institutionalisation of Asian cinema, albeit an institutionalisation still steeped in national biases.

As yet, within the discipline of film studies, Asian cinema does not exist as an established critical category with its own set of methodologies and frameworks, other than as an alternative to Hollywood filmmaking and to Euro-American film studies critiques. While traditional film studies continues to be shaped in invigorating ways by a transnational 'turn' (Morris et al. 2005; Ezra and Rowden 2006; Yoshimoto 2006; Hunt and Leung 2008; Berry 2010; Higbee and Lim 2010; Gates and Funnell 2012), by global accented cinema studies (Marks 2000; Naficy 2001, 2008), and by recent efforts to 'de-Westernize' film studies (Bâ and Higbee 2012), a critical regionalism recognises that while a regional framework has its problems, it is, for this study, the most appropriate way to view the new, innovative and exciting inter-Asian and pan-Asian work emerging from the area.

Whereas the discipline of film studies has been slow to take up a critical self-examination of the category of Asian cinema, some of the more exciting work to have emerged from the region itself in the last ten to fifteen years has considered the regionalisation of popular culture (television dramas, animation and popular music) under the rubric of the Inter-Asia Cultural Studies movement. The definition of Asian cinema as a regional cinema is indebted to these scholarly developments and from a steadily increasing body of work by Asian cultural studies scholars on the self-conscious rise of the region Asia and the resulting economic and cultural flows between the region's constituents (Sakai 2000; Chua 2004; Iwabuchi 2004, 2010; Chen and Chua 2007; Chen 2010). A key development within the Inter-Asia Cultural Studies movement has been the formation of a regional imaginary and the possibility of a regional cultural identity formed through the flows of popular culture (Chua 2004). The consolidation of a regional cultural identity propounded by Asians themselves marks a historical shift from an externalising discourse of 'You Asians' to a self-asserted 'We Asians' (Sakai 2000). The 'idea' of Asia, while supported by a concrete basis of the movement of capital and cultural flows, is in many ways dependent on a 'structure of sentiment' (Chen 2010: 214) or a 'feeling' (Iwabuchi 2004). As Chen (2010) argues,

> the globalization of capital has generated economic and cultural regionalization, which has in turn brought about the rise of Asia as a pervasive structure of sentiment. As a result, both a historical condition and an emotional basis exist for new imaginings of Asia to emerge. (214)

Kuan-Hsing Chen's (2010) formulation of Asia as method is pivotal to the idea of Asian cinema as a regional cinema and not merely an object of Euro-American film studies. Drawing from a lecture given in 1960 by Japanese Sinologist Yoshimi Takeuchi, Chen's more recent development of the Asia as method idea is put into practice in the form of a series of critical dialogues between sometimes conflicting positions within and outside Asia. In this book, these dialogues take place between Euro-American film theories (on genre, authorship and audience reception, for example) and inter-Asia cultural studies methodologies. Asia as method is not an essentialist formulation but also involves the 'de-Westernisation' or de-colonisation of Western theory (Chen 2010; Hillenbrand 2010; Iwabuchi 2010) so as to maintain a critical or reflexive stance towards 'Asian' theories and thereby avoid a revival of the essentialist discourses on Asian values ascendant in the 1990s. In more specific terms, this methodology aims to shift the point of reference from Asian cinema as an 'object' of Euro-American film studies to open up new possibilities of engagement, including regional interventions to local and national cinemas. As Kwai-Cheung Lo (2014) notes, '"Asia" is a matter of method rather than a matter of content, because we cannot count on having this "object" deduced from previous understandings, perceptions and articulations from either Europe or imperialist Japan . . .' (5). Lo (2014) adds, '[t]he recent rise of some Asian nations, China and India in particular, may create hopes that their successful economic development can lay ground for the emergence of a differential structure of knowledge' (11). This book aims to consider how Asian cinema can be both a critical method *and* object that can intervene into existing knowledge orthodoxies in film studies. In this schema, Asian cinema is its own reference point rather than merely a derivative cinema to be regarded against the cinema of the West.

Although the field of inter-Asia cultural studies has laid important theoretical and empirical groundwork for studies of media and cultural industries in Asia, as yet there has been no sustained research on regional Asian cinema exploring filmic exchanges traversing national boundaries across Asia. This book seeks to bridge work across the fields of inter-Asia cultural studies and Euro-American-dominated film studies to offer an approach that can negotiate between existing national cinema approaches and a regional perspective on Asian cinema. It is only through this syncretic methodology that we can account for and begin to understand the new films and filmmaking practices that have emerged from the region in the last three decades. It should be noted of course that 'Western' theories need not be dismissed entirely as part of a 'de-Westernisation' of film studies. As Koichi Iwabuchi (2014) notes:

> it is unproductive and even absurd to think that the application of theories derived from Euro-American experiences to non-western contexts should be totally rejected. Theory has a translocal, if not universal, applicability. However, being conceptualised and based on the experiences and realities of a particular location in a specific historical situation, theory always requires a subtle spatio-temporal translation whenever we operationalise it to interpret and explain a concrete phenomenon in a specific context. (2)

Another way to understand the practices of de-Westernisation is as a form of inter-Asian referencing. Inter-Asian referencing aims to go beyond the West/ Rest paradigm 'by promoting dialogue among diverse voices and perspectives derived and developed from Asian contexts' (Iwabuchi 2014: 4). It does not represent a narrow form of comparison or a 'closed-minded regionalism' (4); rather the aim is to strategically and self-critically learn from other Asian experiences and contexts and in doing so engender cross-border dialogue and advance knowledge production both within Asia and outside it. 'As such, the idea of Asia as method and inter-Asian referencing must be distinguished from parochial regionalism, as it neither excludes researchers working in and on the contexts outside Asia, nor does it underestimate the significance of transnational collaboration . . .' (4). Inter-Asian referencing is not simply a matter of high theory; it is 'an integral part of people's mundane experiences of consuming media cultures . . . the mundane promotion of mediated transnational dialogue' (8–9).

For Asian cinema to establish itself as a viable critical category and worthy object of film history and criticism, the methods that define it must not only involve a tracing of the 'globalisation' or 'Westernisation' of Asian cinema or a corresponding 'Asianisation' of Western cinema. More often than not, this merely results in critics plotting the exchange of films and culture from Hollywood into Asia, and vice versa. While such an approach can be valuable on its own terms, such a method cannot adequately reflect on the state of the newly formed discipline, since the underlying motivation of such a method is that there is one true origin that can ultimately be traced. In practice, the influences and cross-references between Asia and the West are often endless, messy and open to interpretation, rather than singular and pure.

Bringing film theory to the diversity of Asia's film industries, Ashish Rajadhyaksha and Kim Soyoung (2003) suggest that this task has been 'besieged by an interminable problem: of separating their practices out from those of the "Hollywood mode"; of repudiating categories that Western film theory still considers universal to the cinema without, at the same time, falling into inevitable cultural essentialisms' (7). Rajadhyaksha and Kim (2003) point to three areas in which to imagine Asian cinema anew: questions of distribution, history and spectatorship. In outlining these areas, they emphasise the related textual systems, social practices and narratives of the larger culture industry to which cinema belongs. Attention to these areas can best be addressed by taking a comparative approach to regional Asian cinema. Regionalism is not simply a middle ground between nationalism and globalisation, or an alternative to transnationalism. Regionalism is a particular perspective or positioning that allows us to examine how Asian cinema is constructed in and through capitalism and can therefore be understood primarily through comparative terms.

Comparative Film Studies

The idea of comparative film studies has been developed across a number of publications, albeit in still a fairly nascent form, by film scholar Paul Willemen before he passed away in 2012. In his article 'Detouring through Korean cinema' (2002), Willemen suggests that the basis for comparative work in film studies should not be the same as for comparative literature, but should identify the universality that constitutes the condition of possibility of comparative work in film studies. Given that the history of cinema coincides with industrialisation of culture and the spread and acceleration of capitalism since the end of the nineteenth century, Willemen deduces that there must be a kind of 'universalism' that informs cinema as a cultural form (2013: 97). For Willemen, the

> universalism at issue is not to be defined or conceived in terms of some imagined 'beyond' of verbal language or of national cultures defined according to ethno-linguistic parameters . . . The universalism at stake which enables 'comparisons' to be made is the universal encounter with capitalism. (2013: 97)

As Willemen notes:

> [i]f we jettison the inherited framework of film history that locates a film at the intersection between 'universal values' and 'nationalist' specificity . . . then it becomes possible to reflect on the ways in which the encounter between 'national' histories and the capitalist-industrial production of culture intersect, generating specific ways of 'discoursing'. (2013: 168)

The aim of comparative film studies is to examine the 'modulations of cinematic "speech" or "discourse"' that accompany differential encounters with capitalism (Willemen 2002: 168). Returning to Franco Moretti's essay in *New Left Review* (2000), which seeks to understand the development of the modern novel in different contexts and cultures, Willemen modifies Moretti's triangulated relationship between 'foreign form, local material – *and local form*' in the context of cinema (2002: 168; original emphasis). Whereas for Moretti the modern novel develops as a compromise between foreign form and local materials, which can also be understood as the relationship between foreign plot, local characters and local narrative voice, in the context of film studies, Willemen translates local form as narrative voice. For Willemen, comparative film studies constitutes 'not an alternative discipline, but a detour in order to re-arrive at a better model of cinematic functioning' (2013: 98).

Taking Korean cinema as a point of departure, Willemen (2002) sought to identify the 'particularities of [Korea's] encounter with capitalism' by focusing on the technique of the freeze-frame ending, which appears across several of the film examples examined (168). Willemen argues that the tendency to use the freeze frame as a way to conclude films signifies a blockage of Korean cinema, which can be understood in terms of the difficulty of exporting Korean cinema, anxieties about international recognition and how to insert Korean cinema into the arena of international art cinema, as well as the requirement of competing with Hollywood (2002: 173). Willemen has also explored the use of the zoom shot as another technical operation that can be read in a similar way (Rajadhyaksha and Kim 2003).

In film co-productions with China, differential encounters with Chinese capitalism ('capitalism with Chinese characteristics') can be seen for example as a form of verticality in film aesthetics or in the use of changing aspect ratios (Chapter 2). Comparative film studies differs from other attempts to shift the (national) discourse in film studies because, as Mitsuhiro Yoshimoto (2013) puts it, Willemen 'radically put into question the fundamental assumptions underlying film studies' (54). Comparative film studies is not a method of comparing films from different national traditions to one another: '[t]he essential core of comparative film studies is not any specific method of comparison, but the ground that makes the act of comparison possible in the first place' (Yoshimoto 2013: 54). Following Willemen, filmmaker and scholar Kim Soyoung also writes in what Kim refers to as a 'comparative film studies mode' (2013: 45; see also Kim 2008). Kim notes that while this mode of analysis is not new, 'comparative film studies is a crossroads misguided by a demon of comparison and illuminated by detours and dislocative fantasy. It is still a highly uncharted, oblique, and asymmetrical site demanding and waiting for transformation as Paul Willemen has predicted' (2013: 52).

Regional Asian cinema is conceptualised in this book in the spirit of comparative film studies, understood as shaped by the capitalist structures that underpin the films emerging from Asia in the contemporary period regardless of their national origins. Film history and film theory as they currently exist are presented with difficulty when seeking to understand the workings of non-Euro-American cinemas. By emphasising the universal encounter with capitalism and yet the particularities of that encounter – local attempts to advance, resist or negotiate it, and how these play out discursively – shows up the shortcomings of the Euro-American mode of cinema as a frame for all cinemas, especially as it relates to the study of form, aesthetics and technology. Comparative film studies is not an 'alternate' discipline but a radical and critical intervention into the discipline of film studies and its Euro-American basis. This book identifies Asian cinema as a form of inter-Asian referencing that is framed by a comparative context.

The Book

Given the breadth of the geographical area covered, the book is designed to focus on key transformations in Asia's film industries that will be delineated according to the main analytical categories of production, distribution, exhibition and reception/criticism. My aim is not to be exhaustive but to provide key examples or case studies that will illuminate the field through a twin focus on shifting industrial and cultural contexts over the past thirty years. Admittedly, this is an idiosyncratic charting. This introductory chapter has explored the key industrial and cultural developments that have resulted in greater co-operation and integration between Asia's film industries over the last three decades. The following chapters will provide an account of changing production practices, distribution patterns, exhibition sites and modes of engagement for audiences that are a result of the increasingly collaborative nature of Asia's film industries today.

Chapter 2, 'Pan-Asian Filmmaking and Co-Productions with China: Horizontal Collaborations and Vertical Aspirations', considers how new funding models and production practices have been developed by Asia's film industries in response to declining theatrical audiences and changing consumer trends. Competition from pirated discs, digital downloads and television, coupled with the ongoing struggle to compete with big budget Hollywood films for domestic and regional audiences, has led to greater pan-Asian financing and co-productions. New business models, however, have not been universally successful; for example, Chen Kaige's big budget pan-Asian production *The Promise* (2005) failed to appeal to a wider regional audience despite employing star power from across Asia. The chapter revisits Emilie Yueh-yu Yeh's assertion that pan-Asian filmmaking has been 'deferred' (2010: 198) in favour of transnational Chinese co-productions. Taking Hong Kong/China co-production *Office* (Johnnie To, 2015) as its study, the chapter employs a comparative film studies framework to examine transnational Chinese co-productions as a model of regional Asian filmmaking.

Chapter 3, 'Re-making Asian Cinema', examines remakes and omnibus films as specific forms of 'pan-Asian' production and explores ways of rethinking genre in relation to Asian cinema. Although consideration has been paid to remakes of Asian cinema from Hollywood and vice versa, less attention has been given to remakes from within Asia as a form of inter-Asian referencing. Specifically, the chapter investigates CJ Entertainment's business strategy of producing localised Asian remakes of its original Korean hit comedy *Miss Granny* (2014) for different regional markets. This strategy of remaking provides an alternative to the co-production model discussed in the previous chapter and highlights questions of a more comparative or horizontal nature. The chapter also explores the phenomenon of Asian omnibus films, of which an increasing number have been made in Asia in recent years, and how this format fosters the development of cultural regionalism in the form of aesthetic and generic transformations targeted towards regional audiences.

Chapter 4, 'From Film Festivals to Online Streaming: Circuits of Distribution and Exhibition', explores new circuits of distribution and exhibition for Asian cinema from film festivals to online streaming. The international distribution and exhibition of Asian cinema has become an important industrial concern given the rapid growth in the popularity of the cinema not just in areas external to the region (Europe, the United States and Australia), but also in the context of intra-regional consumption (Crisp 2012). The chapter considers the rise of digital distribution and exhibition of Asian cinema through the Internet, including online models such as Viddsee, which focuses on intra-regional distribution. The chapter will investigate how alternative circuits of distribution respond to and in turn precipitate different audience consumption practices as filmmakers continue to seek ways of making films that will cross national markets.

The chapter will also examine how the growth of specialised Asian film festivals (e.g., Vesoul Asian Film Festival in France), international film festivals in Asia (e.g., Busan International Film Festival and Hong Kong International Film Festival) and key international film festivals promoting Asian cinema outside the region (e.g., Venice and Rotterdam) participate in the development of a regional Asian cinema. While there is a growing body of scholarship on film festivals in Asia (see Knee 2009; Iordanova and Rhyne 2009; Teo 2009; Iordanova and Cheung 2010, 2011; Ahn 2011; Pugsley 2013), most of these focus closely on a single festival and do not approach the film festival as a site of exhibition for regional Asian cinema. The chapter will consider issues of specialised programming and non-theatrical exhibition and consumption.

Chapter 5, 'Queer Asian Cinema, Female Authorship and the Short Film Format', notes that some of the most vibrant and politicised work being created in Asian cinema today is in the realm of queer cinema. The chapter considers the relationship between queer Asian cinema and the short film format given the important role the short film has played in raising the profile of Asian cinema, particularly Southeast Asian cinema, internationally. Unlike new queer cinema, which was gradually co-opted by the mainstream as US independent filmmaking gained popularity, queer Asian cinema still exists primarily as a festival category representing a collection of films produced out of particular national and industrial contexts: queer films from Indonesia, queer films from China, queer films from the Philippines, etc. The dominance of this national cinema approach is reflected in the (admittedly limited) critical scholarship on queer Asian cinema. What such an approach ignores, however, are the active exchanges (sometimes explicit, sometimes subterranean) taking place between these filmmakers and their films, marking a period of regional consolidation and transformation in the cinema. This regional development of queer Asian cinema is, for better or ill, proceeding along gendered lines. The contribution of women filmmakers to queer Asian cinema (who have had long careers making television, documentaries and short films) has not been as visible as that of their male counterparts unless or until they break onto the scene with a first feature film. As a corrective to the customary devaluation of non-feature film production, this chapter seeks to examine the importance of the short film format to an understanding of women's contribution to queer Asian cinema. The chapter examines how the short format work operates as a form of minor transnationalism that participates in the formation of queer Asian cinema as a category that can and should incorporate the efforts of women filmmakers. It pays attention to how unique qualities of the short film format allow women filmmakers to actively engage with each other's work within and across the region, and how this transnational connection is redefining how we might come to understand the figure of the individual 'auteur' of women's filmmaking.

Chapter 6, 'Archiving Asian Cinema', explores issues of archiving and digital preservation in light of changing exhibition strategies, with a focus on the important roles played by the Southeast Asia-Pacific Audiovisual Archive Association (SEAPAVAA) and the Asian Film Archive in the creation and maintenance of a regional Asian cinema. The chapter considers the issue of archiving broadly, to encompass not only the physical preservation of films from Asia but also journals, societies and other forums that have sought to preserve scholarly interpretations of those films. Thus, a central component of the chapter will be an investigation into the state of Asian cinema scholarship both in terms of its development as a discrete object of study and also as it is situated within the disciplinary context of film studies internationally. In 2012, the journal *Asian Cinema*, associated with the Asian Cinema Studies Society (ACSS) and edited by John A. Lent for seventeen years, was transferred to British commercial publisher Intellect, marking a new era in the publication of Asian cinema scholarship. In 2011, the Busan International Film Festival held its inaugural Busan Film Forum, a unique academic and industrial forum focused on new developments in Asian cinema scholarship. Alongside these newer developments, longer-running associations such as the Network for the Promotion of Asian Cinema (NETPAC), which has been in existence for thirty years, mark the significant changes that have occurred in the advancement of Asian cinema during that time. Given this rich field of criticism, it is surprising that consolidated research on the changing landscape of Asian cinema scholarship and its archiving, that draws together historical and more recent developments in research and criticism, is virtually non-existent.

Chapter 7, 'Asian Cinema in 3D: Regional Technical Innovation', considers changing consumer trends, including a resurgence of interest in stereoscopic 3D formats in Asia. Singapore, South Korea and Hong Kong have invested heavily in 3D filmmaking, infrastructure and training to build regional technical centres in this area, attracting collaborations with Thailand, Malaysia and Australia (MDA 2010b). However, the development of 3D filmmaking in Asia as a distinctive production strategy has not been addressed in any detail in the scholarly literature. This chapter explores the burgeoning technical developments in 3D filmmaking in Asia, focusing on Australia-Asia co-productions, as practitioners aim to situate themselves as part of a regional hub for stereoscopic pre- and post-production and innovation.

Exploring new ways of imagining film studies transnationally, each chapter of the book examines a different facet of the interconnections and collaborations between Asian film industries and together build a picture of Asian Cinema from a regional view.

Note

1. Chen Kaige won the Palme d'Or (the highest prize at the Cannes Film Festival) for *Farewell My Concubine* in 1993; Apichatpong Weerasethakul won the same prize for *Uncle Boonmee Who Can Recall His Past Lives* in 2010; and Hirokazu Kore-eda won it for *Shoplifters* in 2018. Hou Hsiao-Hsien won the Best Director award at the Cannes Film Festival in 2015 for *The Assassin*. Bong Joon-ho made history when *Parasite* won the Best Picture Award at the 2020 Academy Awards, the first film not in the English language to do so. Bong also took the Best International Feature Film (formerly Best Foreign-Language Film) and Best Director awards that night.

CHAPTER 2

Pan-Asian Filmmaking and Co-productions with China: Horizontal Collaborations and Vertical Aspirations

Introduction

Pan-Asian filmmaking, the practice of pooling talent and financial resources from across Asia to target a wider regional audience, has a long history and can be traced to as early as the 1930s and 1940s (Davis and Yeh 2008: 88; Yau 2009: 171). After the Second World War, advances in technological communications and changing levels of international cooperation, combined with the decline of national audiences across East and Southeast Asia, saw an acceleration of post-war collaboration. Film co-productions in Asia of this period include the Hong Kong/Thailand crime thriller *Flame in Ashes/Di xia huo hua* (Wang Tian-lin, 1958), the Hong Kong/South Korean collaboration *Love with an Alien* (Jeon Chang-geun and Tu Gwang-qi, 1958), and the Hong Kong/Japan co-production *A Night in Hong Kong/Honkon no yoru* (Yasuki Chiba, 1961; HK/Japan), shot in Macau. Following the Asian financial crisis of the late 1990s, the push towards regional co-productions intensified, with political and industrial barriers to co-production gradually being removed and co-production strategies further developed and formalised. *Crouching Tiger, Hidden Dragon/Wo hu cang long* (Ang Lee, 2000), a Hong Kong, Taiwan, China and United States collaboration, was an early success that had widespread appeal beyond Asia, reaching a global audience.

Inter-Asian filmmaking can take many forms, from bilateral agreements under official state treaties to pan-Asian conceived projects involving multiple countries. Some of the more prominent examples of the latter include *Perhaps Love/Ruguo Ai* (Peter Chan Ho-Sun, 2005), *The Myth/Shen hua* (Stanley Tong, 2005), *The Promise/Wu ji* (Chen Kaige, 2005) and *Red Cliff/Chi bi* (John Woo, 2008). Gina Kim's *The Final Recipe* (2013) is a more recent pan-Asian example, produced with input from

Thailand, China, Singapore and Korea, and aimed at global audiences while emphasising a pan-Asian subject. Peter Chan Ho-Sun's Applause Pictures, responsible for *Perhaps Love* and other pan-Asian projects such as *Jan Dara* (Nonzee Nimibutr, 2001, Thailand/Hong Kong), *The Eye* (Pang Brothers, 2002, Hong Kong/Singapore), and *Three . . . Extremes* (Fruit Chan, Takashi Miike and Park Chan-wook, 2004, Hong Kong/Japan/South Korea) was established to advance the strategy of pan-Asian production. The potential audience pool to be tapped by creating films for a regional market is by far the greatest incentive for pan-Asian filmmaking. However, beyond the economic imperative, co-production benefits can also be creative, cultural and/or diplomatic. As Dal Yong Jin and Wendy Su (2019) note, 'inter-Asia cultural exchanges and regional film collaboration, as well as cross-regional collaboration in the Asia-Pacific area, are demonstrating new dynamics' (1). Stephanie DeBoer suggests that the importance of film co-production in the early 2000s lay

> not only in its convergence with a region opening to new intensities in capitalist exchange and widening markets. Co-production's significance also lay in its function as a technology – that is, as a mode of production that potentiated new forms of encounter, expression, and ultimately, identity for the region. (2014: 2)

The question of whether it is possible to imagine an East Asian identity based on the consumption of popular cultural products, including film, has been considered by Chua Beng-Huat in his seminal essay 'Conceptualizing an East Asian popular culture' (2004). In the context of film co-productions, one of the key debates has been around the issue of local content; of how to retain cultural specificity in any of a film's home countries in the face of an imperative to regionalise or globalise. In aiming to appeal to several markets a film may end up appealing to none. Taiwanese director Hou Hsiao-Hsien has spoken of how the Taiwanese film industry needed to find new directions for its survival including becoming more genre oriented and opening up to the Asia-Pacific market without losing its 'local colour'. Hou (2003) comments: '[a] cinema cannot be merely local within the Chinese-speaking region. It has to be Asian-Pacific.' But how does a film achieve 'localness' as well as project an 'Asian-Pacific' identity?

The ideal of pan-Asian cinema, of creating a regional production culture and engaging several markets across Asia, has largely not been fulfilled. The critical and commercial failure of several big-budget pan-Asian films such as *The Promise* has led some critics to reassess the optimism surrounding pan-Asian filmmaking. In her essay 'The deferral of Pan-Asian: a critical appraisal of film marketization in China' (2010), Emilie Yueh-yu Yeh argued that the pan-Asian strategy would need to be 'deferred', if not postponed indefinitely, in favour of sub-regional groupings such as transnational Chinese collaborations based on a shared cultural identity. Yeh suggests that 'before the pan-Asian strategy reached maturity, it was derailed by the allure of the China market' (198). The question of what kind of 'market' the Chinese market is becomes relevant. Yeh distinguishes corporatisation – the transformation of state-owned enterprises into shareholder operations – from China's approach to a market-oriented managerial approach, or 'marketisation' (183). Within the processes of marketisation, 'pan-Chinese – not pan-Asian [filmmaking] – is the dominant order. As long as market entry remains regulated by the Chinese state, pan-Asian cinema will be deferred until there is a better integration between China and the rest of East Asia' (Yeh 2010: 198). It is this evolution (or perhaps devolution) of pan-Asian cinema towards pan-Chinese filmmaking that provides the greatest hope in terms of appealing to the vast Chinese market. It is this that Yeh calls 'the initial promise and the eventual compromise of pan-Asian co-production' (198). Successful pan-Chinese (or transnational Chinese) co-productions, including *The Warlords/ Tau ming chong* (Peter Chan Ho-Sun and Wai Man-yip, 2007) and *The Mermaid/Mei ren yu* (Stephen Chow, 2016), appear to carry out this promise of the future of pan-Chinese filmmaking in the region, although they must 'work through' China to get there (V. Lee 2011a: 235).

Questions of Scale and Perspective: 'Working through China'[1]

As Emilie Yeh (2010) comments, 'No longer just a stylistic device or cost-efficiency strategy, pan-Asian cinema has turned to China in hopes of amplifying production scale and market prospects of big-budget movies' (194–5). The notion of amplifying production scale and marketising blockbuster films has been central to changing power dynamics in the region in the last twenty years as nations have sought to find ways of collaborating with China. In their collection *Asia-Pacific Film Co-productions: Theory, Industry and Aesthetics* (2019), Dal Yong Jin and Wendy Su categorise film co-productions in Asia according to three major historical periods. The first, between the late 1980s and early 1990s, was driven by Japan, and in particular Japanese investment in the American motion picture business; the second, from the mid- to late-1990s, followed the easing of cultural and political tensions in East and Southeast Asia and strongly featured partnerships with South Korea (27). The third and most recent phase is associated with China's emergence as a major economic power (29). China has recently signed official film co-production agreements with partners in Asia–Pacific countries including Singapore (2010), New Zealand (2010), Australia

(2012), India (2014) and South Korea (2014). There have been in-depth studies on historical film collaborations between various Asian partners and China (see Davis and Yeh 2008; N. Lee 2012; Shim 2012; S. Lee 2017 for South Korea/China collaborations; Kim 2005a on South Korea/Hong Kong connections in action cinema; and DeBoer 2014 for Japan/China collaborations; Yue 2014 has written about Australia/China co-productions, characterising Australia as a 'junior partner' that has successfully leveraged a minor position against China). The Closer Economic Partnership Agreement (CEPA) between Hong Kong and China, signed in 2004, has been significant in terms of facilitating greater collaboration between Hong Kong and China in the last decade. Co-productions with China are of course not a new phenomenon. Hong Kong–China co-productions, in particular, have been a key form of inter-Asian filmmaking from the 1970s through to the implementation of CEPA and beyond. From 2002 to 2012, 68.5 per cent of China's co-productions were with Hong Kong (Peng 2016: 298). And for Hong Kong, co-productions with China are the dominant mode of film production, with more than half of Hong Kong films produced in partnership with China (Bettinson 2017: 25).

With its small domestic market, Hong Kong cinema has long relied on Southeast and East Asian markets for its audience. The reception of Hong Kong cinema within Asia, and the localisation of its forms and genres, have been the subject of numerous enquiries: Srinivas (2003) has traced the circulation of B-grade Hong Kong action cinema in India; Davis and Yeh (2002) have considered Hong Kong-Japanese bilateral connections using the rubric of 'Japan Hongscreen'; Lee (2006a, 2006b) has explored South Korea's fascination with films from Hong Kong; Hwang (2012) discusses the 'epic mode' in South Korea's East Asian co-productions; and Teo (2008) has examined the circulation of Hong Kong films among the Chinese diaspora in East and Southeast Asia. Adam Knee (2006) has surveyed the representation of Thailand and Thai characters in Hong Kong cinema, and Kwai-Cheung Lo (2009) has explored Hong Kong cinema's relationship with Japan, including through cross-racial performances. In recent years, however, the success of locally produced films in these traditional markets, most notably in South Korea, Thailand, Taiwan, Singapore and Malaysia, has led to shrinking audience shares for Hong Kong films. This decline in regional audiences has been accompanied by a shift in industrial strategies towards greater regional collaboration. Of these Hong Kong–China collaborations and the changing dynamics of film production, particularly for Hong Kong, Laikwan Pang has remarked that the 'Hong Kong film industry's difficulties since the 1990s can be characterised by Hong Kong cinema's painstaking attempts to come to terms with China' (2010: 140). Mirana Szeto and Yun-Chung

Chen have regarded the situation as constituting the 'mainlandization' of Hong Kong cinema (2012). What these various considerations have grappled with is a situation that Vivien P. Y. Lee characterises as 'working through China' (2011b: 235), or how to negotiate a capitalist economy 'with Chinese characteristics' (Yeh 2010: 187).

Developing this notion of 'working through China', Stephanie DeBoer (2014) suggests that 'desire for China', as a site of new sources of finance, production resources and technologies, has driven the continued push towards co-production, although these have not been fully realised with trade restrictions, differences in production styles and censorship concerns (18).[2] In this sense, China has been 'less a location of progress and actual development for the region than the very site and spectre of its *desire* for progress and development' (DeBoer 2014: 19).

For DeBoer, 'working through China' is a question of scale: '[f]ilm co-productions, in their most general and material sense, are technologies of production whereby creative and cultural capital can be accumulated to exploit the contingencies of regional production, whether by taking advantage of cross-border economies of scale or by fostering new markets' (2014: 4). Echoing Yeh, DeBoer refers to the production of blockbuster films in East Asia within the logic of 'scaled convergence': 'the transformation of local or regional cinemas towards wider transnational markets, both across East Asia and beyond, has been sought in the production of large-scale, "big" blockbuster panregional films' (2015: 215). The question of scale is, however, also one of perspective, and as DeBoer puts it scale is a 'multivalenced *relational* and *practised* term' (DeBoer 2015: 216; original emphases). Perhaps then, in the context of film co-productions the question is not so much one of 'working through China', but of 'working *with* China' in terms of how relationships with China are practised or practically managed. Taking as a case study Johnnie To's *Office/Hua li shang ban zu* (2015), this chapter provides a relational perspective on China as a site of desire when it comes to co-productions with its Asian neighbours. Through a framework of comparative film studies, the chapter will address how differential modulations of capitalism are represented through scale and perspective (verticality contra horizontality) in the 'deferral' of pan-Asian cinema towards pan-Chinese blockbuster filmmaking.

Office/Hua Li Shang Ban Zu (Johnnie To, 2015): Working with China

Johnnie To's *Office* is based on Sylvia Chang's stage production *Design for Living*, and is set in 2008 just prior to the fall of the Lehman Brothers global financial services firm. To directed and co-produced the film, a Beijing

Hairun Pictures and Edko Films production, with Sylvia Chang. The film centres around the dealings of a mainland China-based trading company, Jones and Sunn, which is preparing for its public launch (or IPO). A long-term affair between the company's Chairman Ho Chung-ping, and CEO Winnie Cheung, played by Chow Yun Fat and Sylvia Chang, respectively, is mirrored in a budding romance forming between two young interns, the CEO's daughter Kat (Lang Yueting), and another new intern, Lee Xiang (Wang Ziyi), who explains that his name is 'Lee for Ang Lee, and Xiang for dream': bringing together the name of a well-known director and a dream for what turns out to be a transnational Chinese collaboration. This motif of aspiration – 'the dream of Ang Lee' – is central to the film and references the regional, indeed global, success of Lee's films, in particular *Crouching Tiger, Hidden Dragon*. In *Office* the 'dream of Ang Lee' is realised *through* China. Johnnie To, a director closely associated with the Hong Kong film industry, exemplifies the process of working with and through China to sustain his craft.

Johnnie To is perhaps most well-known for his Hong Kong-based action and thriller films, including *PTU* (2003) and *Election* (2005). As an auteur, To's films are well regarded for their dedication to the portrayal of Hong Kong identity in its myriad forms. To's first film as a director was in fact a co-production with China, *The Enigmatic Case* (*Bishui hanshan duomingjin*, 1980), and he has also co-produced (as director) at least ten further films with China including *Love for All Seasons* (*Baak nin ho hap*, 2003, co-directed with Wai Ka-Fai), *Don't Go Breaking My Heart* (*Danshen nan nu*, 2011), *Drug War* (*Du zhan*, 2012), and *Three* (*San ren xing* 2016). To's production company, Milkyway Image, which he co-founded with producer, director and screenwriter Wai Ka-Fai, was launched in 1996 just prior to Hong Kong's handover to China, and the company completed its initial public offering in 2001. In preparation for going public, Milkyway scaled up its production, with most films from 2003 being released in both Hong Kong and mainland Chinese markets. To has commented in an interview with Gary Bettinson (2017) that his collaborations with China are a way of keeping his production company, Milkyway Image, afloat, while he balances a desire to produce local Hong Kong films with the need to make a profit from Chinese co-productions. To remarks,

> [m]aybe eighty percent of my films are personal. If the movie is not a co-production with China, the movie belongs to me – it is a personal film. But if the movie is a co-production, then this is a film that is compromised. (Bettinson 2017: 25)

Office joins an ongoing industrial strategy of Milkway to 'work through' and with China since CEPA in order to gain a wider share of the regional

market. This balancing act between censorship, artistic vision, and business imperative, has reconfigured the terms of what a 'Chinese' film, or
even an 'Asian' film might be. To referred to his 2001 film *Fulltime Killer/
Chuen jik sat sau*, as an 'Asian' film because most of the dialogue is in Japanese (with some English) and the film was shot outside of Hong Kong. To
notes that this linguistic hybridity and reliance on English is a reality for
many in Asia: '[f]or people in Asia, from all regions, the common means
of communication is always English . . . So it makes sense in the movie
that the main characters, working in different countries in Asia, are using
English' (Leary 2004). To continues: '[i]f there's a Hong Kong movie that
can be called an "Asian movie", I think something has changed then in
Hong Kong cinema' (Leary 2004). *Office* occupies a complex position in
this Hong Kong/transnational Chinese/pan-Asian film matrix. The film
is a musical, with the musical numbers a collaboration between Taiwanese
songwriter Lo Tayu and Hong Kong lyricist Lin Xi. The musical genre
is hybridised with lyrics and tunes that are locally specific, yet with a performance style that is reminiscent of Hollywood classics. As with Peter
Chan's *Perhaps Love* (2005), To utilises the musical genre to reference
'Hollywood . . . [as] the universal, global ideal of filmmakers' (Teo: 352).

Revisiting Stephen Teo's key question from his 2008 essay on *Perhaps Love* and *The Promise*: '[w]hat is China's role in the phenomenon
of Pan-Asian production?' (341), ten years on *Office* appears to eschew
attempts to produce an 'Asian movie', turning instead to a transnational
Chinese collaboration between China, Hong Kong and Taiwan. Through
its generic hybridity, *Office* references Hollywood through the musical
genre, yet ultimately rejecting the association in favour of a transnational
Chinese perspective.

Central to understanding this collaboration is a consideration of how
co-productions function as a form of technology within a networked Asia,
and a mode of production that potentiates new forms of encounter, expression, and, perhaps, identity for film in the region (DeBoer 2014: 2). *Office*
allegorises a dynamic of economic polarisation between China and Hong
Kong, manifest in the striking verticality of the film's elaborate set design.
William Chang, best known for his collaborations with Wong Kar-wai, is
the film's production designer. The set has been described by reviewers as
recalling Fritz Lang's *Metropolis* (1927) and Jacques Tati's *Playtime* (1967)
(see Dargis 2015; Sweeney 2015). Both these films, set forty years apart,
employ vertical lines in their set design as a way of representing the aspirations of the time. Vivian Sobchack (1989) regards the New York of Lang's
Metropolis as 'a vertical veil, shimmering, almost weightless', with the city
'concretized in an architecture of "aspiration"' (8). *Office*, made almost

fifty years after *Playtime* and referencing a very different economic and cultural context, showcases vertical set design as part of a different technology of co-production, one where verticality, allegorising a condition of extreme economic disparity or polarity, forms part of the film's expressionistic *mise-en-scène* of hypercapitalism. Skyscrapers, office blocks and an elevator straight to the top of the building represent forms of mobility that lead into a bright new future just as they emphasise the ever-widening chasm between the powerful and the powerless. The express elevator in *Office* functions as a central motif, standing in for the fantasies and desires of those who seek to 'rise to the top' of the corporate ladder. This new, digitally enhanced verticality participates in (and extends) a very long pictorial tradition that has made use of the vertical axis of the frame (or page) to emblematise the rise and fall of mythological figures (Whissel 2014: 2).

This representative function of verticality has been described by Kristen Whissel (2014) as 'The New Verticality' in her book *Spectacular Digital Effects: CGI and Contemporary Cinema*. Whissel's writings on this topic examine the spatial dialectics and allegorical significance of contemporary cinema's vertical imagination – the vertical staging of action in effects sequences to express the dynamic relationship between power and powerlessness in post-1996 blockbusters. Whissel argues that digitally enhanced verticality is an effects emblem that naturalises the ways in which social and economic power are embedded in culture: 'verticality often functions allegorically to give dynamic, hyperkinetic expression to power and the individual's relation to it – whether defiant, transcendent, or subordinate' (22).

Whissel (2014) examines how verticality operates in two Hong Kong/China co-productions: *Hero* (Zhang Yimou, 2002) and *Crouching Tiger, Hidden Dragon* (Ang Lee, 2000), in addition to Hollywood films such as *Titanic*, *Avatar* and *The Matrix*. In the case of *Hero*, verticality emblematises the spectacular end of an era – the ending of the King of Qin's conquest of the region's warring kingdoms – and represents the 'aesetheticization of acquiescence' (35). In *Crouching Tiger, Hidden Dragon*, digitally enhanced visual effects are used to dramatise a struggle for power, whereby 'upward verticality is linked to insurgency against ongoing tradition and the past' (38).

Whissel's description of the new verticality in cinema can be contextualised within wider calls to prioritise verticality in film production and exhibition against an ongoing bias towards the horizontal film image throughout the history of cinema (Bordwell 2009). The rectangular 4:3 aspect ratio of the early twentieth century has been stretched lengthways in ever expanding widescreen formats that began in the 1950s (for example, CinemaScope and Panavision). Within a shot, figures usually move laterally, with the camera following accordingly. Critics have argued that this horizontality was a natural consequence of the way human vision works, with our eyes mounted side by side, making it easier to follow movement along a horizontal axis (Bordwell 2009). Very basic changes in human perception have occurred since the nineteenth century, linked to urbanism and transportation. Hot air balloons and urban developments like glass elevators and the skyscraper, emphasise vertical movements over horizontal panoramas. Within film studies there have been various rethinkings of the horizontal bias over the years. As early as 1930, Sergei Eisenstein proposed that we rethink the 4:3 framing in his lecture 'The Dynamic Square'. He pointed out that Asia had strong traditions of vertical imagery, especially in Chinese scrolls and Japanese woodblock prints. Eisenstein wanted to restore verticality to the cinema in a 'dynamic square' that would grant both axes equal weight (Bordwell 2009). 'It is my desire to intone the hymn of the male, the strong, the virile, active, *vertical* composition!' (Eisenstein, 1930). Eisenstein speculated that there was also an economic factor, claiming it is possible to fit more people in a theatre with decent sight lines if the image is horizontal. In 1953, at a symposium on 'Poetry and the Film', Maya Deren described 'horizontal' film structure as affiliated with drama, 'one circumstance – one action – leading to another'. Alternatively, 'vertical' film structure, or 'poetic structure': 'probes the ramifications of the moment, and is concerned with its qualities and its depth, so that you have poetry concerned, in a sense, not with what is occurring but with what it feels like or with what it means' (Deren in Sitney 1970: 173–4). David Bordwell (2009) has pointed out that film technology itself is vertical, with the film strip moving from top to bottom, feed reel to take-up reel.

More recently, proponents of vertical cinema have sought to intervene in the prevailing horizontal orientation of traditional film projection and exhibition. Vertical Cinema presentations have been held since 2013 at locations across Europe, the USA and Australia. The movies are projected using a custom-built 35 mm film projector in vertical CinemaScope (G. Edwards 2015). Form dictates content to some degree and the type of stories you can tell with vertical cinema are limited. Shorter films, shot with mobile phones, are also more inclined to be in portrait orientation, rather than landscape, as another example of how technology is shifting the axis of perception.

Instead of taking vertical cinema literally, if we think about verticality in cinema in its broadest terms, we can see that filmmakers since the 1990s have been utilising the screen's vertical axis more and more through the aid of new digital technologies, and this is having an impact on how new spatialisations of power and time are imagined. Kristen Whissel (2014) writes, '[t]he resulting spatialization of power and time allows the new

Figure 2.1 Vertical aesthetics in *Office* © Milkyway Image

verticality to map spatial transience onto historical transition, and radical forms of mobility onto the possibilities and perils of change such that the new verticality becomes an emblem for (desired or thwarted, social or political) transformation' (2014: 29–30). In the case of *Office*, the theme of 'going public' – on a literal level the company's IPO, and on a more figurative level the exposure of personal secrets under the guise of corporate intrigue – corresponds to China's moves toward greater marketisation. As reviewer Amy Taubin (2016) comments, '[t]he multilevel Jones and Sunn Tower looks as if it is made entirely of oversized pick-up sticks. The double metaphor: the new Chinese capitalism is anything but solid, and its secrets and lies take place in plain sight of everyone on the take and also those left out in the cold.'

Examined in this light, what kind of region do co-productions like *Office* imagine, or produce, through their representation of verticality? While verticality in *Office* can be said to mirror the structure of how co-productions with China often work in material terms – a dominant financial power others seek to gain access to – if we look at co-productions as a technology within the 'sustainability network' of Asian cinema, to use Prasenjit Duara's (2015) term, co-productions are a way to survive in a changing global film industry, despite other forms of vertical integration and territorialisation of power that exist across the region, including issues of language, religion, ethnicity and colonial histories.

In a chapter entitled 'The horizontal spread of a vertical malady: cosmopolitanism and history in Pernambuco's recent cinematic sensation', Lucia Nagib (2017) analyses Kleber Mendonça Filho's *Neighbouring*

Sounds/O Som ao redor (2012). Nagib argues that the film integrates its form and content through a 'vertical figuration that crystallizes the devastating effects of global capitalism' (346). In Nagib's example it is the effect of rapid urban development (in particular property development) on Pernambuco, a north-eastern state of Brazil. Nagib suggests that there is a 'two-way drive within this vertical motif: a movement off the ground, resulting in global cosmopolitanism; and another into the ground, in search of the social history and film history at its base' (346). Despite the characters' disconnect from local context and history, they are also connected to regional and national history, to Brazilian and world cinema (346).

In the case of *Office*, the vertical set design and the vision of capitalist excess that it represents might look very similar to other vertical displays of power in cinema, for example in *Metropolis*. However, *Variety* reviewer Justin Chang (2015) commented that although *Office* is '[a]n elaborate construct and a stylish treat for To's fans, [the film] may prove too singular an operation to earn high profits outside Asia'. Despite the film's use of the global generic form of the musical and its recognisable vertical display of aspiration, the film has held very little appeal outside the region, and indeed outside the transnational Chinese context. I suggest that in the case of this, and indeed other, transnational Chinese co-productions, any critique of verticality and aspiration (the 'dream of Ang Lee') might be better served by a more 'horizontal' form of thinking. This requires a networked, or regional approach, which Paul Willemen began formulating in his call for a comparative film studies. This model can help us account for the new interconnections in film production taking place in Asia.

Changing the Aspect (Ratio)

As we recall from the introduction, Paul Willemen suggests that the basis for comparative work in film studies should not be the same as for comparative literature but should identify the universality that constitutes the condition of possibility of comparative work in film studies. For Willemen (2002), '[t]he universalism at stake which enables "comparisons" to be made is the universal encounter with capitalism' (167). Capitalism is an 'equalising' force but it can also be contextualised by the various political revolutions that accompanied its rise in different settings. More precisely, the aim of comparative film studies is to examine the 'modulations of cinematic "speech" or "discourse"' that accompany differential encounters with capitalism (Willemen 2002: 168).

In relation to co-productions with China, I have argued that understanding a shift towards verticality in representation through a horizontal or comparative approach is one way to apprehend differential encounters with capitalism in the Chinese context. Another modulation in cinematic discourse that registers China's differential encounter with capitalism in transnational Chinese co-productions is the use of changing aspect ratios within a film. Within videographic terminology, aspect ratio refers to the proportional relationship between the width and the height of an image, that is, its horizontal by vertical ratio. There have been several high profile transnational Chinese film co-productions that have experimented with changing aspect ratios part way through a film in recent years.

In Hou Hsiao-Hsien's *The Assassin* (a Taiwan/China/Hong Kong/France co-production, 2015), most of the film unfolds in the square 4:3 (or 1.33:1) aspect ratio, except for two flashback sequences, which are shot on slightly grainier film stock and are in the 1.85:1 aspect ratio. Shifts between black and white and colour stock also register the film's thematic and temporal modulations (the film begins with a prologue in black and white in the 4:3 aspect ratio before opening up to 1.85 in colour).

There is a similar change of aspect ratio in Jia Zhangke's *Mountains May Depart* (a China/Japan/France co-production, also from 2015). The film is set over three different time periods across two countries (1999 and 2014 in China, and 2025 in Australia). Like other films by Jia Zhangke, *Mountains May Depart* documents China's rapid economic and social development over the last two decades and into the future. The first segment, New Year's Eve, 1999, is shot in the 4:3 aspect ratio with a narrow depth of field. As the film moves into different time zones and locations the aspect ratio opens up (the year 2014 is projected in 1.85:1), and by the time of the final segment – a futuristic Australia in 2025 – the film is in full widescreen (2.35:1). Not only has the film's geographic scope widened, concluding with the economic migration of the Chinese diaspora to Australia, the technological changes accompanying film's development have also progressed. The young protagonist of the film, named 'Dollar' by his aspirational parents, inhabits this expansive space with a physical and emotional distance from his parents that has also grown.[3]

Feng Xiaogang's *I Am Not Madame Bovary/Wo bu shi Pan Jinlian* (2016), which won Best Achievement in Directing at the 2016 Asia-Pacific Screen Awards, is also highly stylised in its radical play with aspect ratios. The film moves between 4:3, anamorphic widescreen shot on 35 mm film (2:35:1), and, predominantly, a circular aspect ratio. Recovering from a somewhat jarring and 'gimmicky' feel at the start of the film, the shift between the three different aspect ratios seems to make perfect sense by the end. The film is written by Liu Zhenyun, based on his 2012 novel *I Am Not Pan Jinlian*, referring to an adulterous woman from Song dynasty literature who plots with her lover to murder her husband (the film's Chinese title is literally *I Am Not Pan Jinlian*). Gustav Flaubert's

Figure 2.2 Circular aspect ratio in *I Am Not Madame Bovary* © Huayi Brothers Media

Madame Bovary, published in 1856, provides the most recognisable version of this story in the Western world, hence the English translation of the film's title. Most of the film's action occurs in the circular aspect ratio, which has been described as reminiscent of Song Dynasty paintings (Hans 2017) but is also suggestive of the voyeurism associated with the peephole. However, when the action shifts from rural Jiangxi to Beijing the aspect ratio changes to the square 4:3 ratio. Shelley Kraicer (2017) writes,

> Feng and his cinematographer Luo Pan establish the changes between circle and square frames very cleverly: square objects within the circle set up the transition to the Beijing/urban square format; a round tunnel within the square later sets up the retransition back to the rural/Jiangxi circle.

Kraicer (2017) continues:

> Roundness in this film has associations with nature, female-gendered subjects, community, wholeness, and humanity. The square frame, on the other hand, is Feng's evocation of central authority. Derived from Beijing's almost square concentric grids, it suggests the Forbidden City at Beijing's centre, courtyards, structured power and authority, and masculine-gendered discourse – a rigid, defining, and imprisoning space. Lian lives in her rural landscaped circles, but ventures out into power's square space twice, where she achieves a temporary victory, then a final defeat.

The final scenes play out in widescreen, representing a further rupture in perspective.

The relationship between circular and square aspect ratios in *I Am Not Madame Bovary* has a similar function as the relationship between horizontal and vertical in *Office* and in the other transnational Chinese co-productions discussed. The displays of verticality in *Office*, and the changing aspect ratios in other co-productions are examples of 'the discursive knots where the particularities of the encounter with capitalism . . . may be traced' (Willemen 2002: 168) in the Chinese context. These pointed technical and aesthetic shifts alert us to the changing economic and political modulations that have manifest different versions of capitalism 'with Chinese characteristics'. Willemen's nascent theory of comparative film studies is useful to understanding a nascent regional Asian cinema because it does not involve a literal comparison between two different national cinemas or types of cinemas but rather a questioning of 'how socio-historical dynamics impact upon and can be read from films' (Willemen 2005: 110).

In film co-productions with China, I argue that differential encounters with Chinese capitalism have been rendered as a form of verticality in film aesthetics. The displays of verticality in *Office*, specifically, are an example of how we can use a comparative film studies framework to understand the function of co-productions as a technology in the Asia-Pacific, a technology that helps us produce knowledge about China's role in a regional film network as 'less a location of progress and actual development for the region than the very site and spectre of its *desire* for progress and development' (DeBoer 2014: 19). Thus transnational Chinese co-productions allow us to map out a cultural regionalisation that includes imaginaries, histories and legacies that are often uneven between different sites of production, and that are horizontal as much as they are vertical and integrated through an encounter with capitalism (Jin and Lee 2007: 31). The implication for Asian cinema studies is that it allows us to better account for the new interconnections in film production, including co-productions, taking place across Asia-Pacific, in which China is but one important node.

Seeking strategies for growing co-productions in Asia, KOFIC (the Korean Film Council) organised an industry forum on 'International Co-Productions in Asia' at the Busan International Film Festival in October 2012. Representatives from major production companies in Asia were invited to discuss ways of growing inter-regional co-productions in Asia, while offering possible keys to success. Korean producer Eoh Ji-Yeon, director of production at Sopoong Film, pointed to Hur Jin-Ho's China/South Korea/Singapore co-production *Dangerous Liaisons* (2012) as a notable example of a successful strategy. Hur Jin-Ho's film of Pierre Choderlos de Laclos's eighteenth-century novel *Les Liaisons dangereuses* stars Zhang Ziyi, Jang Dong-gun and Cecilia Cheung (from China, South Korea and Hong Kong, respectively). Hur's version is set in Shanghai in the 1930s with the film's dialogue in Chinese. Producer Eoh suggested that star power, Chinese dialogue, an 'exotic' (historical) background and emotional sentiment were the main reasons for the film's success across Asia. Another interpretation of de Laclos's novel was the 2003 Korean film *Untold Scandal/Seukandeul – Joseon namnyeo sang'yeoljisa*. This version, directed by Je-yong Lee (also credited as E J-yong), was set in late eighteenth-century Korea during the Joseon dynasty and was extremely popular in South Korea although *Dangerous Liaisons* is an arguably more interesting example for how it unashamedly sets out to imagine a transnational or regional audience. The ability to transport an eighteenth-century French story across time and space and sustain its relevance points to the importance of film co-productions in raising questions of location and localisation that tend not to be addressed in the valorisation of an emergent capitalist 'rise' of Asia enabling pan-Asian productions and audiences. The co-production offers a set of practices – from the imperialist to the market-driven – that in its various manifestations can be used to investigate and interrogate meanings of place and the contestations of economic and cultural production within different locations. Co-productions are a form of technology; however, technological and aesthetic shifts within co-productions themselves, for example through changing aspect ratios and the foregrounding of verticality in representation, provide new opportunities for apprehending how differential encounters with capitalism in transnational Chinese contexts manifest in cinema through scale and perspective across a networked Asia. The next chapter, on remakes and omnibus films, explores alternatives to the co-production model discussed in this chapter.

Notes

1. Part of this chapter was originally published as 'Another day at the *Office:* Huallywood co-productions, verticality, and the project of a comparative film studies', *Transnational Screens*, 2019, 10:170–83. My thanks to the journal special issue editors, Maria Elena Indelicato and David H. Fleming, for their invaluable editorial insights.
2. Co-productions with China involve scrutiny and censorship from the scripting stage to post-production.
3. Bong Joon-ho's films consistently play with horizontal and vertical imagery and highlight the significance of a film's aspect ratio. The horizontal imagery of *Snowpiercer* (2013), set on a train, can be contrasted to the vertical imagery of class stratification in *Parasite* (2019), set across a multi-level house and a sub-basement apartment. *Parasite* production designer Lee Ha Jun comments that he designed a house structure that is 'wide and has depth rather than height so that the house suits the 2.35:1 aspect ratio'. The window wall in the main house is also constructed to exactly match the dimensions of the 2.35:1 aspect ratio (O'Falt 2019).

CHAPTER 3

Re-making Asian Cinema: Inter-Asian Remakes and Asian Omnibus Films

In the autumn of 2019, sitting in a cramped New York City apartment in front of a rented smart TV, I found myself repeatedly entering a spectatorial position where I went from cantankerous elderly lady to a young, brash twenty-year-old and back again, watching multiple remakes of the South Korean hit feature *Miss Granny/Soosanghan Geunyeo* (Hwang Dong-hyuk, 2014). *Miss Granny* is a comedy-drama about a woman in her seventies who is returned to the body of her twenty-year-old self after having her photograph taken at a magical portrait studio. The film was a box office hit, with a cumulative box office gross of ₩62.5 billion (US$61.8 million) (Cremin 2014). It has been remade eight times for film – in China, the Philippines, Japan, India, Vietnam, Indonesia and Thailand, and in English and Spanish for the US – and once as a television series.[1] Each remake has been carefully handled by the same South Korean producer, CJ Entertainment, in collaboration with local talent. This chapter explores CJ Entertainment's business strategy of producing localised Asian remakes for different regional markets as an alternative to the co-production model discussed in the previous chapter.

In the Korean original, Na Moon-hee plays Oh Mal-soon, a seventy-four-year-old widow who lives with her son and his family. Mal-soon has a strained relationship with her daughter-in-law Ae-ja (Hwang Jung-min) but dotes on her son Hyun-chul (Sung Dong-il), a professor of gerontology, and her grandson Ji-ha (Jinyoung). Following the collapse of Ae-ja one day from stress, Mal-soon is reluctantly sent away to live in a nursing home. She passes the 'Forever Young' portrait studio and, feeling wistful, has her photograph taken. When she emerges, Mal-soon is surprised to find that she now inhabits the body of her twenty-year-old self (played by Shim Eun-kyung). Mal-soon renames herself Oh Door-ri after her favourite actress, Audrey Hepburn, and has a makeover to look like Hepburn in *Roman Holiday* (William Wyler, 1953). The literal English translation of

the Korean title is 'suspicious girl', and Door-ri's family is initially mis-
trustful of her anachronistic ways of talking and behaving. After some
amusing misunderstandings, Doo-ri confides in Mr Park (Park In-hwan),
an old friend who has had romantic feelings for Mal-soon for years. One
day, while singing at the cafeteria where she used to work, Doo-ri captivates
an audience of seniors and also gains the attention of a record producer,
Han Seung-woo (Lee Jin-wook), and her grandson Ji-ha, who convinces
Door-ri to join his band. Ji-ha's band becomes successful with Seung-
woo's support, and Seung-woo and Door-ri begin to develop romantic
feelings for one another. On his way to a concert Ji-ha is hit by a truck
and seriously injured. Doo-ri decides to sing Ji-ha's song before rushing
to the hospital. She is the only member of the family who is a match for
Ji-ha's blood type, although she has discovered that any blood loss will
result in her reverting to her actual age. Her son Hyun-chul finally realises
that Doo-ri is his mother and touchingly urges her to live the life she has
always wanted and now has a second chance at, but Doo-ri proceeds with
the blood donation. In the final scenes of the film, the family is reunited
and Mal-soon has an improved relationship with her daughter-in-law
Ae-ja. The film ends with Mr Park arriving at a bus station to pick Mal-
soon up on a motorcycle. He has found the same magical portrait studio
and is transformed into a handsome young man looking like James Dean.
The two drive off together.

Before attending to the variations of the different remakes of *Miss
Granny* and CJ Entertainment's strategy of producing local language
remakes of original hit movies, it is important to consider the cultural
politics of transnational film remakes in general.

The Cultural Politics of Film Remakes

A film remake can be defined as a new version of an existing film that has
taken on aspects of the plot, characterisation or setting of the original.[2]
In industrial terms, making another version of a film which has proven
successful in one market makes sense. Constantine Verevis (2006: 23) posits that remakes can be viewed from a number of perspectives: as (1) an
industrial category, able to be 'pre-sold' to audiences; (2) a textual category,
understood through categories of genre, narrative invention, homage and
updates; and (3) a critical category, located in audience expectations and
knowledge. In the case of *Miss Granny*, with the same production company involved in each remake, every iteration of the film functions within
a discernible web of intertextuality, referencing a shared artistic enterprise

(of generic and thematic citations) at the same time as they collectively constitute a remake 'franchise' of regional local language filmmaking.

The scholarly field of remakes is extensive. Key texts on Hollywood remakes of Asian films include Kenneth Chan's *Remade in Hollywood: The Global Chinese Presence in Transnational Cinemas* (2009), Yiman Wang's *Remaking Chinese Cinema: Through the Prism of Shanghai, Hong Kong, and Hollywood* (2013), and Jinhua Li's *Transnational Remakes: Gender and Politics in Chinese Cinemas and Hollywood* (2011). Notable films from Asia that have been remade in the West span from *The Seven Samurai* (Kurosawa, 1954), remade as a Western, *The Magnificent Seven* (John Sturges, 1960), to more recent examples *Ringu* (Hideo Nakata, 1998)/*The Ring* (Gore Verbinski, 2002), *Infernal Affairs* (Andrew Lau and Alan Mak, 2002)/*The Departed* (Martin Scorsese, 2006) and *Oldboy* (Park Chan-wook, 2003)/*Oldboy* (Spike Lee, 2013). Writing in 2005, Gang Gary Xu suggests, '[t]he current remaking trend corresponds to East Asia's new status as the world's production centre'. Xu's remarks are directed towards what he refers to as Hollywood's 'outsourcing' to Asia, 'making Hollywood leaner, stronger, more efficient, more profitable, and more dominant than ever' (2005).

From the successes to the flops, the high-profile examples to those lesser known, there has been scant attention paid in the critical literature to inter-Asian remakes. Why is this category of film remakes interesting or important? In an exploration of inter-Asian remakes, the focus is arguably not so much on questions of appropriation or media imperialism as it is on inter-referencing and intertextuality and how these facilitate a broader conception of a regional Asian cinema.

In their edited collection *Transnational Film Remakes*, Iain Smith and Constantine Verevis ask:

> What happens when a film is remade in another national context? To what extent can a film embedded within one cultural context be adapted for another? How might a transnational perspective offer us a deeper understanding of a specific socio-political context, and of the politics underpinning film remaking more generally? (2017: 2)

While the examples in their volume traverse film remakes between and outside Asia, these questions are useful in thinking about inter-Asian remakes through a framework of comparative film studies. As explored in the previous chapter in relation to co-productions, the vertical or hierarchical relationships that are often implicit in discussions about an 'original' film text and its remake are better served by a more horizontal approach and way of thinking. Verevis questions how 'textual accounts of remaking risk essentialism, in many instances privileging the "original" over the remake' (2006: 2). This is especially true of critiques that plot the exchange of films and culture from Hollywood into Asia, and vice versa. While such an approach can be valuable on its own terms, often the underlying motivation of such a method is that there is one true origin which can ultimately be traced in any remake. In practice the influences and cross-references between Asia and the West are often endless, messy and open to interpretation, rather than singular and pure. This is especially so when considering existing political and economic power imbalances and questions of appropriation in cross-cultural remaking.

Inter-Asian remakes, on the other hand, involve a form of internal referencing, or intertextuality. They are fertile ground for considering the development of cultural regionalism in the form of generic transformations targeted towards both particular national audiences within Asia and to a broader regional audience through the (re)circulation of storylines, themes and aesthetics. The *Miss Granny* franchise is a key case in point, having achieved success and popularity across Asia. This is very different from the pan-Asian strategy of a company like Applause Pictures, for example, in that it involves localisation while remaining focused on the region in terms of its (cumulative) audience.

Miss Granny was the first film chosen for CJ Entertainment's local language remake strategy

> because it has a very universal concept: A grandmother wants to be young again, and she gets a chance to chase the dream she was forced to give up when she had kids. Everyone wants to be young again, and everyone has a dream they wish they could go back and fully pursue. (Jeong Tae-Sung, CJ Entertainment's CEO, in Brzeski and Lee, 2017)

The use of the comedy genre is key here, and particular genres, including martial arts and horror, have been more successful in Asia as remakes. Fernández Labayen and Martín Morán (2019) note that film comedies are especially suitable for the strategy of local language remakes and are the most commonly adapted film genre used in this business model (284). Not only is the industrial strategy of the remake trade connected to generic trends but remake rights representatives actually 'mold generic trends through their interaction with local producers' (Fernández Labayen and Martín Morán 2019: 285). Film comedy is not a genre that travels easily, with humour being culturally specific. However, universal situations that may lend themselves to comedy can be effectively adapted using local cues, performance and language (Fernández Labayen and Martín Morán 2019: 285).

The comedy genre, while in this case conveying a 'universal' story, also requires a dedication towards localisation of production in cases where humour cannot easily be translated across cultures. Jeong adds:

> successful local production entails a serious commitment. We were the first to open a foreign production office in Vietnam to make local films. Then we launched the first major joint venture in Thailand [with Major Cineplex, the country's dominant local exhibitor], the first foreign production office in Indonesia and now one in Turkey, too. We didn't just send teams to do some co-productions; we've opened physical offices as legal local business entities. And that's not easy to do in some of these countries. Legally, you have to go through a lot of complicated government approval and licensing. But it shows our commitment. And now we have dedicated teams working very hard on developing localized content in these markets, communicating closely with our experienced development team in Seoul. (Brzeski and Lee 2017)

The practice of producing local language remakes of the same film, targeted at different national audiences, makes sense, with the market share of local language films increasing. Roxborough and Brzeski (2018) note, '[a]nnually, the theatrical market share of local-language films has reached or exceeded 90% in India, 60% in Japan, 55% in China, Turkey and Korea, 40% in France, 30% in Denmark and 25% in Germany, Italy and Poland'.

From the perspective of European cinema, Miguel Fernández Labayen and Ana Martín Morán (2019) analyse the phenomenon of the global remake rights trade through case studies of remake rights representatives, trade intermediaries and intellectual property (IP) agents involved in licensed remakes. The largest of their case studies, Globalgate Entertainment, provides an interesting example of an institutional model 'which rests mostly on the construction of film remaking as culturally proximate for different territories' (Fernández Labayen and Martín Morán 2019: 284). Globalgate, established in 2016, 'sources and curates intellectual properties and remakes, with priority access to its Consortium Partners' libraries of over 20,000 titles'.[3] Consortium partners include Lionsgate (US/UK/Canada), Lotte (Korea), Kadokawa (Japan), Viva Communications (Philippines), TME (Turkey), TF1 (France), Tobis (Germany), Rai Cinema (Italy), Belga Filmes (Belgium, Netherlands, Luxembourg), Nordisk Film (Scandinavia), Televisa/Videocine (Latin America) and CineColombia/Dynamo (Colombia), with offices in Los Angeles, New York, London, Mumbai and Beijing representing a global enterprise.

This network model operates beyond the dominant Hollywood set-up and is instead reliant on intermediaries' knowledge of popular films in local language contexts, collaboration on the production and distribution of local language film remakes, and sharing the IP and distribution rights of a vast film library between consortium partners (Fernández Labayen and Martín Morán 2019: 290). Drawing on notions of cultural proximity (Straubhaar 1991), Fernández Labayen and Martín Morán (2019) refer to Globalgate's process as 'manufacturing proximity': remaking local language hits in other territories with their own stars, languages, and talent (285). 'The balance between local flavor, popular success, and universal appeal is the formula that all remake intermediaries and producers try to find' (Fernández Labayen and Martín Morán 2019: 291). These remakes are then presented 'as originals for national audiences' (Fernández Labayen and Martín Morán 2019: 284). Such an alliance of remake rights and IP distributors is potentially extremely powerful, providing a horizontal structure that operates globally.[4]

On a more confined and predominantly regional scale, CJ Entertainment follows a similar model of producing film remakes that mobilises local talent, language, settings and style to 'manufacture proximity'. The next section looks more closely at CJ Entertainment's strategy of local customisation through the remake formula.

CJ Entertainment: Localisation and Regionalisation

Established in April 2000 by brother and sister team Jay and Miky Lee, CJ Entertainment is South Korea's largest entertainment company, encompassing film production, distribution and exhibition, as well as cable networks, music performance and distribution, and online games. The Lees initially paid $300 million for an 11 per cent equity stake in the new DreamWorks studio, giving CJ Entertainment exclusive distribution rights to Paramount and DreamWorks films in East and Southeast Asia, excluding Japan (Kil 2015). From this platform, CJ Entertainment launched a distribution and exhibition business. The first CGV multiplex opened in 1998 (Kil 2015).

CJ Entertainment forms part of the larger media company CJ E&M, which is a subsidiary of CJ Corporation.[5] In 2010, CJ Corporation integrated five media holdings – CJ Entertainment, CJ Media, M-net Media, On Media and CJ Internet – into CJ E&M (Kim 2016b: 103). In July 2018 CJ E&M was merged again with CJ O Shopping, becoming CJ ENM.[6] (For the purposes of consistency in this chapter, I will continue to refer to the company as CJ Entertainment despite the various name changes over time.) As Kim (2016b: 96) notes, the growth of CJ Corporation in the entertainment markets was linked to financial liberalisation in South Korea. This background to the company reveals a high degree of horizontal as well as vertical integration – across production, distribution, exhibition – and indeed CGV multiplexes were fined by South Korea's competition regulators for favouring films that had CJ Entertainment involvement (Kil 2015). Nevertheless, while other Asian nations were still in the grip of a financial crisis, CJ Entertainment managed to participate in a revival of the Korean film industry following the success of *Shiri* (Kang Je-gyu, 1999).

CJ Entertainment was involved in some of the key Korean films of the early 2000s, including *Joint Security Area* (Park Chan-wook, 2000), *Memories of Murder* (Bong Joon-ho, 2003) and Park Chan-wook's *Sympathy for Mr. Vengeance* (2002) and *Sympathy for Lady Vengeance* (2005). Following its success in South Korea, CJ Entertainment looked overseas, particularly to other parts of Asia, for its growth (Kil 2015: 101). CEO of CJ Entertainment Jeong Tae-sung notes: '[t]he South Korean market is already highly saturated. Expanding overseas is not a choice but a necessity' (H. Lee 2017). The domestic film market in South Korea has remained stagnant at about ₩4 trillion (US$3.55 billion) since 2014 (Doo 2017).

South Korea has a long history of interconnection with other Asian nations, especially Hong Kong and Japan. Nikki J. Y. Lee (2012) points to examples of these connections from the silent movies made in Chosun in the 1920s by Japanese filmmakers, to war propaganda movies made by Korean and Japanese filmmakers in the 1940s, to international co-productions of martial arts action movies with Hong Kong companies in the 1970s, and beyond into pan-Asian productions such as *Seven Swords/Qi jian* (Tsui Hark, 2005), *Red Cliff/Chi bi* (John Woo, 2008), *Red Cliff II/Chi bi xia: Jue zhan tian xia* (John Woo, 2009) and *The Promise/Wu ji* (Chen Kaige, 2005) (82). With its strong domestic film market, combined with a desire to expand into regional and international markets, South Korean cinema is supported by a broader appeal for South Korean popular culture from other Asian countries as part of the Korean Wave or *hallyu*. Nikki J. Y. Lee (2012) writes that what distinguishes Korean cinema's current phase of Asian connections from past trajectories is that the emphasis has shifted 'from simply exporting Korean movies to other international territories to becoming a transnational producer/provider of titles customized for particular local audiences in different countries' (2012: 82). This encapsulates one of CJ Entertainment's core business strategies precisely.

CJ Entertainment's 'one source, multiple territory' strategy of taking an original film and remaking it into several different localised versions has been highly successful (Noh 2016; Soh and Yecies 2017: 79). The company's CEO Jeong Tae-sung remarks:

> Hollywood studios have a global distribution channel and face little cultural barriers in any given territory. Korean films, however, must overcome linguistic and cultural differences when they sell to foreign markets. The number of sales for remake rights

also remains low. We cannot model ourselves after China either, and buy out major exhibitors and production companies. There is much more added value in creating localized content that is tailored to the culture codes of a given territory. This will also create more opportunities for Korea's pool of creative talent. (Lee Hyo-won 2017)

This central aspect of CJ Entertainment's international strategy uses remakes of genre films that can travel well and that are able to be inflected with national characteristics. CJ Entertainment remains involved in overseas local productions and retains intellectual property, and does not simply sell off remake rights. Where other remakes have failed because of lack of cultural sensitivity or engagement (including the use of the English language in whitewashed remakes such as *Ghost in the Shell* (Rupert Sanders, 2017) and *Oldboy* (Spike Lee, 2013)), this strategy of localisation with a hands-on company has resulted in greater success than simply selling remake rights.

CJ Entertainment's Head of US productions Francis Chung adds:

In the past we sold a lot of remakes to studios and none of them have gotten made. And so over the past few years we've taken a more hands-on approach in terms of our remakes, where we develop . . . and we work with the writers directly. One of the things that we've learned from all of these sort of failed remakes in the past is that a lot of U.S. producers and writers, they failed to sort of bring over the more core essence of why these movies were good in the first place. They feel like they have an obligation to change a lot of things to fit their culture . . . The setting can change, the actors can change, but keep the core story telling. (Bui 2019)

The various remakes of *Miss Granny* do not veer substantially from the original, although some have incorporated cultural variations more than others in an effort to localise. The Chinese remake of *Miss Granny*, *20 Once Again* (2015), produced by CJ Entertainment in collaboration with China's Beijing Century Media, C2M and Huace Film and TV, was hugely successful, topping the box office for eight consecutive days and earning over US$59 million in China in the first month of its release (Shim 2016: 42). Since late 2005, CJ Entertainment has sought new markets in China, including the opening of a Beijing office and co-producing films such as *Sophie's Revenge* (Eva Jin, 2009) and *A Wedding Invitation* (Ki-hwan Oh, 2013). 'CJ E&M's modus operandi is to work closely with Chinese actors and local production crews while reserving core creative positions (and IP) for Korean nationals' (Yecies and Shim 2015: 166).[7]

The Chinese version of *Miss Granny* has a more serious and dramatic tone than the original. The film begins with a family portrait, in sepia tones, with accompanying soft piano music creating a sense of nostalgia. Shen Meng Jun (Gua Ah-leh) spends her days playing mah-jong with her friends and does not work or cook. The film has lost much of the comedy and slapstick nature of the original Korean. There is also reduced physical and emotional connection between the characters. In the final scene, when the son tells his mother to live her life, they do not embrace. There is no romantic reunion with her old friend, in this case a former childhood servant, Li Dahai (Deshun Wang), and he does not become young again at the end of the film. Doobo Shim explains how these changes in the Chinese version resulted in box office success. In a personal interview with an anonymous employee in charge of film distribution at CJ Entertainment's China office, Shim reports:

> In order to better connect with the sensibilities of Chinese audiences, *20 Once Again* focused on the love affairs between the protagonist and three male characters, a different emphasis than in the original *Miss Granny*, which underlined the comic character of the heroine. This adaptation was made because the kinds of jokes that Korean and Chinese audiences find humorous are different, and because a young woman's romantic involvement with men from different age groups is more socially acceptable in China than in Korea. The main setting was changed from a café to a mah-jongg club, and the television drama that the heroine used to enjoy was changed from a typical Korean drama which revolved around birth secrets to the famous *My Fair Princess* . . . Taken as a whole, *20 Once Again* was not simply a translation of the Korean original, but in the process of adaptation it became a Chinese film. (2016: 42)

Shim (2016) notes that because of the pervasiveness of the Korean Wave in the region, many Chinese viewers would have already watched *Miss Granny* through illegal downloads, thus greater differentiation was necessary in the Chinese context (42).

The Japanese remake of *Miss Granny*, *Sing My Life/ Ayashii Kanojo* (Nobuo Mizuta, 2016), co-financed by CJ Entertainment, Shochiku Films and Nippon TV, also has a different opening scene, beginning with a flashforward to the grandson in hospital and his grandmother beside him, while the other remakes have humorous beginnings. Perhaps the biggest departure in the Japanese version is that the seventy-three-year-old grandmother, Katsu Setayama (Mitsuko Baisho), has a daughter, Yukie Seyama (Satomi Kobayashi), instead of a son, and only one grandchild, Tsubasa Seyama (Takumi Kitamura); in the other remakes, even in the Chinese version, there are two grandchildren, a boy and a girl. The daughter Yukie Seyama is also divorced, and like her mother, she is also a sole parent. The film highlights discourses of ageing through its dialogue, which are pointed in the context of Japan's well-documented crisis around its ageing population. Katsu comments, 'for women of this country youth rules supreme', although she is far more fit and sprightly as a grandmother than her regional filmic counterparts. Her daughter Yukie is employed as the editor-in-chief of a high-profile magazine until she is considered too old to occupy this role and is removed from the editing team. There are not as many scenes of the twenty-year-old Katsu, Setsuko Otori (phonetically similar to 'Audrey' [Hepburn], played by Mikako Tabe) and Jiro, which may have been viewed as culturally inappropriate.

The more recent Telugu version from India, *Oh! Baby* (B. V. Nandini Reddy, 2019) has a longer running time than the other remakes at 2 hours and 26 mins. The opening sequence echoes the original, with Shekhar (Rao Ramesh), a university professor in gerontology. His mother, Savitri (Lakshmi Bhupala) works at the university cafeteria and is referred to by her friends, including her oldest friend Chanti (Rajendra Prasad), as 'Baby'. Religion plays a central role in this remake. Instead of visiting a portrait studio, Baby meets a mystic at a fair who gives her a Ganesha idol and tells her 'Goddess Saraswati will bless you'. Baby's twenty-year-old self (played by Samantha Akkineni) sings songs with religious lyrics and her musical talents are discovered at a prayer service for Ganesha. Instead of Audrey Hepburn, Banumathi Ramakrishna, the first female superstar of Telugu cinema, becomes the role model for her makeover. Song is used to convey the narrative, especially its religious overtones, and the music is composed by award-winning Indian composer Mickey J. Meyer, known primarily for his work in Telugu cinema. The film ends with a credit sequence featuring the two lead actresses together; through these various gestures towards the filmmaking process, *Oh! Baby* foregrounds the film's production processes and the fact that this is a remake in the particular context of Telugu cinema.[8]

As C. S. H. N. Murthy (2013) notes:

> Remakes have been well accepted by the Indian audience since the beginning of the talkie era (1931). Film-makers in India have remade films from different cultures to reflect their local culture and vice versa, thus rendering the films both local and global. Furthermore, remakes within a national context (e.g., from Bengali to Hindi or Telugu or from Telugu to Hindi and Tamil) also have cross-cultural significance when it comes to local adaptations. It does not seem academic to underrate the remakes as mere copies or to describe them as the outcome of a dearth of ideas (20).[9]

My analysis of the various remakes of *Miss Granny* is not directed at power imbalances between the different national contexts, but rather seeks to highlight questions of a more comparative or horizontal nature. While still retaining the core story line, what is considered culturally significant to one national context may be very different to another's. This approach allows a comparative analysis to be made.

For instance, in *Oh! Baby*, religion, class and caste are highlighted. Baby was the chief's daughter. Her husband was a soldier who left to fight a war with China but does not return. In the Korean original, Mal-soon's husband left when she was pregnant to work in a coal mining company and is reported to have died in Germany. In the Japanese remake, Katsu's husband dies in a construction accident. The explanations for the death and absence of the husband and father are revealing of the political contexts of each Asian nation. The relationship between the lead actress and her oldest friend and love interest is also illuminating. In the Japanese remake, Katsu's good friend Jiro Nakata (Kotaro Shiga) was a war orphan with Katsu and they scavenged on the streets together and kept each other alive (compare this to the Chinese version where Li Daihai was a former servant of Shen Meng Jun's). The transformation of the portrait studio is also noteworthy. In the Korean version, the portrait studio has disappeared and been replaced by a Chinese restaurant. In the Chinese version the portrait studio has become an adult erotic shop. A comparison of the scene in which each elderly woman contemplates her rejection from her family before entering the portrait studio also reveals interesting variations played out through the advertisements at the bus stop. In the Chinese version, a Korean beauty advertisement is prominent. In *Oh! Baby*, local advertisements (in English) are instead displayed (see Figures 3.1 to 3.4).

Figures 3.1 and 3.2 Bus stop scene in China's *20 Once Again* © CJ ENM

Figures 3.3 and 3.4 Bus stop scene in India's Telugu-language *Oh! Baby* © CJ ENM

These variations in the *mise en scène*, while altering seemingly only minor details, provide a subtle backdrop to shifting cultural relations between the various Asian nations. This balance between a 'universal' story and its local inflections is key to the films' success.

CJ Entertainment's *Miss Granny* remakes are a strategy that supports the domestic film industry while addressing the need to expand internationally, first within the region and then beyond it. This 'Asianisation' of the film remakes is itself a form of localisation. 'Whilst "Asianization" as a particular phase of regionalization concurs with the growing sense of coevalness . . . it invokes and reproduces a multitude of different and often conflicting cultural imaginations of Asia within Asian film and media markets' (N. Lee 2012: 90). *Miss Granny* is a transnational product that is produced for regional audiences 'that are defined not by national allegiance but by taste and sensibility' (Higson 2011: 89). In this case, the advertisements on the bus stop billboards preceding the transformation from elderly grandmother to young woman represent ideals of beauty, femininity and youth tied up with consumerism and middle-class values that have spread across East Asia, to a modernising South and Southeast Asia.

Expanding into Southeast Asia and Beyond

Patrick Frater (2019a) notes that CJ Entertainment has been so aggressively promoting productions overseas that 'it is now producing more movies outside Korea than at home'.[10] In 2016, CJ Entertainment created nine foreign titles from Thailand, Indonesia, Vietnam, Turkey and the United States, almost double the five films it produced the year before. In addition to the *Miss Granny* remakes, the CJ Entertainment film *Sunny* (2011) has also been remade in Vietnam and Japan (and is in production in Indonesia). *The Classic*, another Korean blockbuster, is being remade in Thailand as *Classic Again* (directed by Thatchaphong Suphasri). In Indonesia, CJ Entertainment is producing *Death Whisper* (with Pichouse Films), a remake of the South Korean horror film *Whispering Corridors* (Frater 2019a).

These film remakes are providing CJ Entertainment the opportunity to experiment with different production and marketing techniques in different territories. In Vietnam's *Sweet 20* (Phan Gia Nhat Linh, 2015; CJ Entertainment with K+ and HK Entertainment), CJ Entertainment took a risk with local talent, employing a first-time feature film director and rising star Miu Le. It also tried new marketing strategies not commonly employed in Vietnam at the time, such as premiere events before release (Noh 2016). Kini Kim, head of CJ Entertainment's International Department, said: '[o]ur first localisation strategy was to make the project suit well to the local audience. That is, to bring up the family-loving sentiment and emphasising on the comedy code, which the Vietnamese audiences are much fond about' (cited in Noh 2016). As a result of these modifications, *Sweet 20* became the country's highest grossing local film (Noh 2016). Mothers-in-law meddling with their daughter-in-law's cooking, and the raising of grandchildren, is universal, and also central to the Thai remake *Suddenly Twenty* (Araya Suriharn, 2016; CJ E&M and Thai Major Cineplex Group), the Indonesian remake, *Sweet 20* (Ody C. Harahap, 2017; CJ Entertainment and Starvision), and the Philippines remake *Miss Granny* (Joyce Bernal, 2018; CJ Entertainment and Viva Films).[11]

CJ Entertainment's practice of making genre films is solidified with the launch of the company's new genre label, 413 Pictures, which specialises in thrillers and supernatural horror films in both English and local languages in Asia. The label hopes to produce four or five Asian titles each year, both remakes and original projects. The first films to be released under the 413 Pictures label in the United States were English-language remakes of Korean film *Hide and Seek* (Huh Jung, 2013), and Vietnamese horror film *The Housemaid* (Derek Nguyen, 2018) (Lee Hyo-won 2018). CJ Entertainment has also entered into a partnership with Singapore media entertainment company, mm2 Entertainment, to co-produce six Southeast Asian films (two Indonesian films and four Thai films), mainly horror and romance, both original films and remakes (Marketing-Interactive 2018).

In addition to film remakes, CJ Entertainment has also expanded into East and Southeast Asia through distribution and exhibition. In Thailand, CJ Entertainment has established True4U, a terrestrial entertainment channel that airs local remakes of CJ Entertainment's hit shows. Since 2015 CJ Entertainment has been selling formats of its hit programmes in Thailand. In 2016, it established True CJ Creations, a joint venture with a broadcast provider in Thailand, allowing it to create local productions. Riding on the success of *hallyu*, CJ Entertainment plans to open new channels to air Korean content in Malaysia, Vietnam and Hong Kong. The company will launch a Korean movie channel 'tvN Movies' in Malaysia and Singapore and 'TV Blue' in Vietnam. In Hong Kong, CJ Entertainment will provide the 'CJ Korean Entertainment Pack' on the set-top platform 'myTV SUPER' (Korea Bizwire 2017).

Following the acquisition of leading Turkish exhibitor Mars Entertainment by CJ-CGV, in May 2017, CJ Entertainment established a regional office in Turkey. Mike Im, head of international at CJ Entertainment, noted that Turkey is one of the few countries in the world, along with Korea, where local films outperform Hollywood imports (Kil 2017). A Turkish-language version of *Miss Granny* is also in production (H. Lee 2017).

CJ Entertainment's collaboration with other Asian partners in the *Miss Granny* franchise presents the best example of the regionalisation of its activities. While this strategy was born from economic necessity (and a desire for growth), it is fuelling the development of a regional Asian cinema. Local remakes are a horizontal strategy because there are no significant power differentials involved in these collaborative encounters (although there is vertical integration in CJ Entertainment's case). The horizontal nature of this strategy draws on the creative talent of other local Asian film industries, while relying on core storytelling from the original. I began this section by outlining slight cultural variations between the remakes, but the control held by CJ Entertainment means that the differences are really only at the surface of a much larger regional imaginary as the promotional posters of the various *Miss Granny* remakes illustrate in their almost identical layout, colour palettes and poses.

CJ Entertainment's localisation strategy through remakes is contributing to the development of a regional imaginary for Asian cinema. It utilises the creative talent of other Asian film industries, while relying a core story that appeals across the region, remaking it anew with each iteration as a shared space where local differences can be not only celebrated, but also contained by a broader regional imaginary.

Omnibus Films

The second half of this chapter shifts focus from a consideration of remakes to the practice of making omnibus films, also referred to variously as anthology films, compilations, portmanteau films and collective films. Defined as:

> a feature-length motion picture comprised of two or more discrete narrative sketches or vignettes, each separated from the others by way of interstitial gaps . . . the omnibus film is a decidedly undecided form, one whose dialogic capacity to combine multiple voices and visions makes it difficult to pin down yet also conducive to a rethinking of narrative formulas and spectatorial solicitations. (Diffrient 2012: 109)

Similar to remakes, omnibus films also operate on a strategy of containment, consisting of a number of short(er) films, usually with a shared theme or concept, within a feature length format.

Mark Betz (2001) notes that 'omnibus films tend to occupy a marginal status within the field of film studies: most international histories all but ignore them as a particular type of filmic product' (58; see also Diffrient 2014a: 32). While the omnibus film remains a minor mode of production (similar to the short films discussed in Chapter 5), marginalised throughout the history of cinema, there is something about the format of multi-director, episodic cinema that has been particularly appealing to contemporary filmmakers in Asia.[12] The predominance of omnibus films in Asia has been noted by several scholars. Stephanie DeBoer (2014), for instance, observes that omnibus films were a 'significant mode of production for Japanese industries to engage with the region in the early to mid-1990s' (117). Diffrient (2012) examines the place of human rights discourses in South Korean omnibus films in the context of the post-Cold War political climate. In their section on Asian cinema as world cinema, Deshpande and Mazaj (2018) comment on how 'a collection of films by different directors and from different contexts is bound to be uneven, but in their intertextual, collective identity, they project an internal dynamism different from other forms of co-production ventures' (246).

It is the melding together of these multiple voices into an 'internal dynamism' that makes omnibus films such an interesting model for (re)thinking a regional identity for Asian cinema, formed through the 'gaps' in between (national, cultural and authorial) difference; in this case the whole is greater than the sum of its parts. While the format has been around since the 1930s (with an example recorded in 1910 (Betz 2001: 59)), the omnibus film did not feature more significantly in Europe or Asia until the 1960s. 'Beginning in that turbulent decade, omnibus films increasingly lent themselves to collaborative, cooperative efforts to shore up a sense of solidarity in the face of historical, political and social changes' (Diffrient 2012: 111). In the contemporary period, omnibus films not only call for solidarity but also conjure a form of collectivity or collective identity. It is through the interstices between the constituent parts that audiences are proffered 'spectatorial solicitations' and invited to make links between the two or more episodes (Diffrient 2012: 109).

Diffrient (2012) writes:

> In transiting from one setting to another, the viewer not only engages in a kind of inter-subjective cosmopolitanism, increasing his or her capacity to see similarities among the text's visible differences, but also metaphorically enacts, at the 'local' level, the kind of border-crossing movement inscribed in transnational flows. Indeed, the omnibus film is the most 'trans' of all transpositional cinematic-cultural forms, collapsing transmedial, translinguistic, transgeneric, translocal and transnational modes in the space of a single feature that unites multiple voices and visions. (Diffrient 2012: 122)

In a later article, Diffrient (2014a) elaborates on omnibus films as a kind of 'transauthorial cinema', where the 'trans-' signifies movement:

> Meaning 'across', 'between', and 'through', the prefix *trans-* tells us that an omnibus film is a motion picture containing both movement and borders, permeable though the latter might be. In fact, the permeability of those internal divisions is what facilitates transit from one episode to another, not only during the actual viewing of a film but also after that experience is officially over, when spectators have the opportunity to reflect back on a motion picture's formal properties, narrative structure, and thematic motifs *as a whole* while 'moving' themselves, mentally, back and forth across the boundaries separating *the individual segments*. (2014a: 3; original emphases)

Writing specifically on human rights-themed films such as *If You Were Me* (*Yŏsŏtgae ŭi sisŏn*, 2003), Diffrient (2014a) notes that this sense of movement, of being emotionally moved, is also an ethical form of spectatorial engagement (3).

I am interested in how omnibus films foster the development of a regional identity for Asian cinema in films that deliberately seek the involvement and collaboration of filmmaking talent across national borders within Asia. It is this intertextual, inter-Asian referencing within the format of one film that operates rather differently to both local remakes of films and film co-productions. Stephanie DeBoer (2014) writes,

> the omnibus is a particular technology of film and media coproduction . . . In this sense, *omnibus* is also a term through which we can gain understanding of the tensions of regional coproduction – as it is produced in disjuncture with, but often imagined and mobilized under, a shared horizon of 'Asia'. (DeBoer 2014: 119)

DeBoer continues:

> as a production technology, the omnibus sought not simply to address commercial interests; it was also a production technology that was regarded as a means for taking on broader public concerns. Such projects were ostensibly concerned with introducing 'Asia' to a Japan that was only then, in the postwar moment, becoming popularly conscious of itself as a part of the region in the face of the rising significance of its neighbors. (DeBoer 2014: 117)

In light of the trans-authorial nature of omnibus films, genre is accorded as much significance as authorship, if not more, in the commercial success of these films. Nikki Lee (2011) examines how Asian horror operates as a 'brand of taste distinction' in regional and global markets (105). Lee comments that Asian horror is 'an intraregional and also a transregional product' (114). For example, *Three/Saam gaang* (2002), an omnibus film directed by Peter Chan Ho-Sun (Hong Kong), Kim Jee-woon (South Korea) and Nonzee Nimibutr (Thailand), was 'initiated by Asian producers with the aim of establishing intraregional industrial networks' (Lee 2011: 105). The sequel, *Three . . . Extremes/Saam gaang yi* (2004) combines the Asian horror and Asian extreme genres, consisting of Fruit Chan's *Dumplings* (Hong Kong), Park Chan-wook's *Cut* (South Korea) and Takashi Miike's *Box* (Japan). Both *Three* and *Three . . . Extremes* were produced by Peter Chan's Applause Pictures. Lee (2011) notes that what differentiates these omnibus projects from others is that their '*raison d'être* lies in developing intraregional industrial networks rather than celebrating a certain occasion or cause or evoking public interest in a given social issue' (107). Lee describes how the films, while consisting of quite disparate elements, consolidate as well as extend the regional genre of 'Asian horror'. She writes, 'the irony is that such an attempt to tame the omnibus movie's conflicting generic elements results in the strengthening and extension of given generic horizons. Ultimately, the relatively multilayered and incoherent format of the omnibus movie may not hinder so much as facilitate new forms of genre-branding' (2011: 114).

Asian horror circulates as a regional genre only as an alternative to Hollywood and to other local horror movies. 'Asia' then, becomes the referent to which both genre and authorship are subsumed.

Other examples of regional omnibus films include *Letters from the South* (Aditya Assarat, Royston Tan, Midi Z, Tan Chui Mui, Tsai Ming-liang, Sun Koh; Myanmar/Singapore/Thailand/China/Malaysia, 2013), which reflects on experiences of the Chinese diaspora, and *Breakfast, Lunch, Dinner* (2010), featuring contributions from three female directors, and set in China (directed by Wang Jing), Thailand (directed by Anocha Suwichakornpong) and Singapore (directed by Kaz Cai) respectively. Each story occurs at a specific mealtime, with the theme of love drawing them together, tied to the question, 'Will you marry me?'

An omnibus film explicitly tied to a film festival for its distribution and exhibition is *Asian Three-Fold Mirror*, the product of a collaboration between the Tokyo International Film Festival (TIFF) and the Japan Foundation Asia Center. In 2014, these two institutions launched a film culture exchange initiative to 'deepen mutual understanding within Asia, by showcasing Asian films in Japan, Japanese films in Asia, and by bringing Asian talent to the world through TIFF'.[13] The project is described thus by its creators:

> The directors portray people living in Asia from their own viewpoints and project the society and culture of their own countries, like a three-fold mirror. These films have been produced with an aim to deepen mutual knowledge, understanding and empathy, and to provide opportunities to explore the Asian identity and ways of living. The project framework requires the directors to include a character who is connected in some manner to another Asian country, and to shoot on location in an Asian country. The rest is left to each director's unique style.[14]

The films premiered at the Tokyo International Film Festival, using the festival site as a platform. Omnibus films so far produced out of this initiative are *Reflections* (Brillante Mendoza (Philippines), Isao Yukisada (Japan) and Sotho Kulikar (Cambodia), 2016), and *Journey* (Degena Yun (China), Daishi Matsunaga (Japan) and Edwin (Indonesia), 2018). Using generic titles such as 'journey' and 'reflection' invite an open canvas on what life is like across contemporary Asia from different perspectives. There is not a great deal of internal coherence to the films, with the broad themes attempting to tie quite diverse cultural stories together. What is interesting about the *Asian Three-Fold Mirror* initiative from TIFF and the Japan Foundation is the effort being made by these institutions to further integrate Japan into the newly developing regional film consciousness and connections in Asia. *Asian Three-Fold Mirror* appears to be a contemporary resurgence of earlier projects that sought to 'organise' Asia under the direction of Japan (Tokyo), this time by the Japan Foundation in light of its new Asia-Pacific initiative. As DeBoer (2014) noted in her discussion of Tokyo-initiated omnibus projects of the late 1980s to 1990s that operated to 'organise' or 'conduct' Asia:

> [t]he linking of Asian experience across the borders of a diverse and unevenly developing region has been a central mode through which such production has largely been promoted for Japan. But rather than pulling together a coherent geography, omnibus projects made under the name of Asia display the 'tensions and contradictions essential to the mapping' of regional film and media, to use the words of Mark Betz, who has made a similar argument for Europe . . . [Tokyo becomes] a locus against and through which the tensions of regional coproduction might be made visible. (DeBoer 2014: 118)

Projects such as *Asian Three-Fold Mirror* can be considered alongside other collaborative works that consciously endeavour to produce a regional consciousness from the position of a shared marginality. *Vai* (2019) is an omnibus film directed by nine South Pacific women: Nicole Whippy, 'Ofa-Ki-Levuka, Guttenbeil-Likiliki, Matasila Freshwater, Amberley Jo Aumua, Mīria George, Marina Alofagia McCartney, Dianna Fuemana and Becs Arahanga. The film was shot in seven different Pacific countries – Fiji, Tonga, Solomon Islands, Kuki Airani (Cook Islands), Samoa, Niue and Aotearoa (New Zealand), and in each location, a different indigenous actress plays Vai at a different stage of her life, from childhood to old age. *Vai* means water in each of the Pacific locations and the stories are connected via an archipelagic imaginary.

There are, of course, significant nationally based omnibus films in Asia, such as Taiwan's *The Sandwich Man* (Hou Hsiao-Hsien, Tseng Chuang-hsiang, Wan Ren, 1983), Hong Kong's *Triangle* (Tsui Hark, Ringo Lam, Johnnie To, 2007) and *Trivisa* (Jevons Au, Vicky Wong Wai-Kit, Frank Hui, 2016), and Singapore's *7 Letters* (2015), an omnibus film directed by Eric Khoo, Boo Junfeng, Jack Neo, Kelvin Tong, K. Rajagopal, Tan Pin Pin and Royston Tan to celebrate Singapore's 50th anniversary. Hong Kong's *Ten Years* (2015), a controversial film envisaging Hong Kong ten years in the future, in 2025, was a box office success, with a political message critical of the Chinese government. The film inspired *Ten Years Thailand* (2018), *Ten Years Taiwan* (2018) and *Ten Years Japan* (2018). Even though each omnibus collection is national, together they form a (political) project of (re)imagining the future of the nation within the broader context of the region. For *Ten Years Japan*, thirty filmmakers were asked to submit ideas, with only five making it into the final film. The project was mentored by Hirokazu Kore-eda and, because it fell outside the expectation of commercial distributors in Japan, had to be released in Japan by the producers themselves. *Ten Years Thailand* was also self-distributed (Ramachandran 2018). The difficulties of releasing an omnibus film, much less a political one, are significant. Without its collaboration with the Tokyo International Film Festival, distribution would have been far more difficult for *Asian Three-Fold Mirror. Sincerely Yours, Dhaka/Iti, Tomari Dhaka*, a recent Bangladeshi omnibus film by eleven directors that was shown at the Busan International Film Festival (2019), has aspirations towards greater commercial success.[15] Producer Abu Shahed Emon is optimistic about its prospects: '[t]his is a major ensemble cast with 33 major actors. We've also recorded a rap song specially for the film. It should be popular' (Ramachandran 2018).

Conclusion

Writing on Taiwan's *The Sandwich Man*, Diffrient (2014b) notes, '[i]t is *in* and *through* its seriality that we experience this Taiwanese motion picture' (87). Diffrient's term, 'horizontal depth' is useful for understanding the spectatorial positions that potentially arise out of watching an omnibus film, including when choosing to view only one episode in isolation. Diffrient (2014a) writes that omnibus films 'move beyond the temporal-historical markers of vertical depth to point toward the spatial-textual coordinates specific to what [he calls] *horizontal depth*, which extends signification across an array of narrative environments or social milieus, segmentally organized and transtextually linked' (22). Rather than the kind of 'intersubjective cosmopolitanism' Diffrient (2014a: 22) suggests, I recast this spectatorial experience of horizontal depth in the context of comparative film studies as a way of attaining a broader regional view of Asian cinema. The next chapter, which plots movements of distribution and exhibition, continues this discussion to explore the circuits of international film festivals and online streaming.

Notes

1. A twenty-six-episode series, *Twenties Once Again/Chong Fan Er Shi Sui*, aired in China on iQiyi in 2018.
2. See Denison (2014) on adaptations more broadly (including remakes, serial production, and franchising), and in particular their importance to Japanese and Korean film cultures. Denison's examples traverse adaptations from literature to film, historical texts to contemporary contexts, and are not necessarily confined to inter-Asian remakes.

3. See <http://www.globalgate.world/about/> (last accessed 12 September 2020). My thanks to Constantine Verevis for bringing the Globalgate example to my attention and for supplying me with this reference.

4. These observations are limited to official film remakes, and not any number of possible adaptations, homages, or unlicensed copies.

5. In 1997 the CJ group separated from the Samsung group and diversified both vertically (CJ Entertainment owns CJ CGV and Primus (now merged with CGV)) and horizontally (into related cultural industries including cable TV, music, online and gaming), consolidating into the audiovisual industries and establishing a media empire of production, distribution and exhibition in South Korea. The CJ group also operates across industries (construction, leisure, pharmaceuticals) (Kim 2016b: 94).

6. See <http://www.cjenm.com/index_en.html> (last accessed 12 September 2020).

7. Following a diplomatic feud over South Korea's deployment of the THAAD missile defense system in 2016, China boycotted South Korean films. Some South Korean films were again being released in 2018 (Yonhap 2018).

8. *Oh! Baby* is streamed on Netflix and the Netflix Delivery Fulfilment Partner is Vista India Digital Media.

9. There are numerous examples of Indian films that have looked towards South Korea for inspiration. In 2016, two Korean films were remade: *The Man From Nowhere* (2010), which became *Rocky Handsome* in India, and *Montage* (2013), remade as *TE3N* in its Bollywood version. *Rocky Handsome* was produced by Azure Entertainment, which has also planned a Bollywood remake of *Infernal Affairs* in collaboration with Warner Bros. Azure Entertainment founder and CEO Sunir Kheterpal says, 'Indian producers are being drawn to Korean films for remakes because of two factors: action and emotional quotient' (Bhushan 2018). A list of Bollywood movies that are remade (either officially, or unofficially) from South Korean films includes: *Prem Ratan Dhan Payo* (2015) from *Masquerade* (2012); *Ek Villain (Mohit Suri)* (2014) from *I Saw The Devil* (2010); *Zinda* (2006) from *Oldboy* (2003); *Ugly Aur Pagli* (2008) from *My Sassy Girl* (2001); *Murder 2* (2011) from *The Chaser* (2008); *Jazbaa* (2015) from *Seven Days* (2007); *Awaarapan* (2007) from *A Bittersweet Life* (2005); *Rocky Handsome* (2016) from *The Man From Nowhere* (2010); *Bharat* (2019) from *Ode To My Father* (2014) (official remake); *Jayantabhai Ki Luv Story* (2013) from *My Dear Desparado/My Gangster Lover* (2010); *Singh is Bliing* (2015) from *My Wife is a Gangster 3* (2006), and *Te3n* (2016) from *Montage* (2013).

10. The company is planning to produce at least twenty titles in more than ten languages per year beginning in 2020 (currently, the company funds and distributes approximately ten to fifteen films in Korea each year) (Frater 2019a).

11. The young protagonist in the Philippines remake (played by Sarah Geronimo), is also modelled after Audrey Hepburn, in this case named Audrey De Leon.

12. Mark Betz (2009) notes that omnibus productions have been associated with the beginning of film movements around the world, including Italian neorealism (*Giorni di Gloria/Days of Glory*, 1945), Brazil's Cinema Nôvo (*Cinco*

vezes favela/Slum Times Five, 1962), the Czech New Wave (*Perlic ̆ky na dne ̆/ Pearls of the Deep*, 1965), and the Taiwanese New Wave (*Guangyin de gushi/In Our Times*, 1982 and *Erh-tzu te ta wan ou/The Sandwich Man*, 1983) (215; see also Diffrient 2014b: 72). The key point about the amenability of this form to new cinematic movements is how they facilitate collaboration and engagement with filmmakers wanting to do something different when feature filmmaking remains a more costly and time-consuming form.

13. Asian Three-Fold Mirror, available at <https://asian3mirror.jfac.jp/en/> (last accessed 12 September 2020).

14. Asian Three-Fold Mirror, available at <https://asian3mirror.jfac.jp/en/> (last accessed 12 September 2020).

CHAPTER 4

From Film Festivals to Online Streaming: Circuits of Distribution and Exhibition

Okja (2017), by acclaimed South Korean director Bong Joon-ho, is a remarkable film aesthetically and thematically, but industrially the film also raises interesting questions about film distribution and exhibition within Asia and beyond. At the level of narrative, *Okja* is a fantastical film about a genetically modified pig that brings to the foreground issues of animal rights, factory farming and environmental concerns in the Asian context. Okja, the eponymous 'superpig', is the product of experiments conducted by the Mirando Corporation, led by eccentric CEO Lucy Mirando (Tilda Swinton). Along with twenty-six other super piglets sent out to be raised by farmers in different countries, Okja is being lovingly tended to in the mountains in South Korea by a young girl named Mija (Ahn Seo-hyun), and her grandfather Hee Bong (Byun Hee-Bong). Okja is deemed the most successful superpig by size and will be showcased at an event in New York City. Mija's grandfather accepts payment from the Mirando Corporation allowing Okja to be released back to the company, unbeknownst to Mija. A distraught but determined Mija follows Okja first to Seoul and then to New York where he is freed by the Animal Liberation Front (ALF), narrowly escaping slaughter for food.

Okja has been at the centre of debates concerning the relationship between online streaming (in this case on Netflix), theatrical exhibition and the role of film festivals. Bong's films, including *Memories of Murder* (2003), *The Host* (2006), *Mother* (2009), *Snowpiercer* (2013) and *Parasite* (2019), have all performed well at international film festivals, with *Parasite* winning the Palme d'Or at the Cannes Film Festival. Described as 'the first great Netflix movie' (Tiffany 2017), *Okja* challenges the singular portrayal of Bong as 'festival auteur'. During *Okja*'s screening at the Cannes Film Festival in May 2017, the film's Netflix title card was reportedly booed (Tiffany 2017). Although *Okja* did not win the Palme d'Or, Kaitlyn Tiffany (2017) notes that what the film achieved instead 'was arguably better: weeks of conversation around the egalitarian spirit of cinema'. Crystallising around the film's screening at Cannes was a set of new rules laid down by the festival to exclude films without a theatrical release in France. Cannes director Thierry Frémaux declared that any producer that would not commit to a theatrical release in France would have their films barred from main competition at Cannes, effectively meaning that Netflix films are disqualified from being in competition in future years. Shortly after, major movie chains in South Korea announced they would be boycotting *Okja* in protest against a simultaneous release on Netflix (on 29 June 2017) without a theatrical hold back. Bong has said: 'I fully understand the multiplexes asking for a minimum three-week hold back. Netflix's principle for a simultaneous release should also be respected. The film is, after all, financed by Netflix users and I don't think we should deprive them of their privileges' (Lodderhose 2017). Defending the value of online platforms, Bong told the *Los Angeles Times*, '[t]he best way to watch a film is in the theater. But for directors who make weird films like mine, the digital studio platforms are a great creative opportunity. I do believe that the two [modes] can coexist' (Chang 2017).

Bong's statements reflect a changing media landscape that, while applying to transforming film and media industries globally, has particular significance to Asian cinema. The important role that international film festivals – including Venice, Berlin, Cannes and Rotterdam – have played in the circulation and exhibition of Asian national cinemas since the 1980s is well noted (Yoshimoto 2003: 453; Lee and Stringer 2012b: 245). What has been less scrutinised are the multitude of streaming sites for films from Asia, which have mushroomed since the late 1990s. Beyond the vast landscape of national and regional platforms, including Youku Tudou (China), Iqiyi (China), Tencent Video (China), iflix (Southeast Asia), HOOQ (South and Southeast Asia), Viu (Southeast Asia), Viki (based in San Francisco, Singapore, Tokyo and Seoul, and operating globally), Hotstar (India), Tving (South Korea), Pooq (South Korea), dTV (Japan) and others, international providers such as Netflix and Amazon Prime have also significantly increased their catalogue of Asian films. This chapter first considers the contribution of international film festivals to the formation of Asian cinema's regional identity, followed by the rise of Asian cinema's digital distribution through online platforms. It examines how alternative circuits of distribution respond to and in turn precipitate different audience consumption practices (including downloading and streaming) as filmmakers continue to seek ways of making films that will cross national markets.

The Fates of the Festivals

This section provides an overview of the film festivals inside, and to a lesser degree, outside Asia dedicated to the promotion, exhibition and circulation of Asian cinema. While there is a growing body of scholarship on film festivals in Asia (see, for example, Knee 2009; Teo 2009; Iordanova and Rhyne 2009; Iordanova and Cheung 2010 and 2011; Ahn 2011; Wong 2011; and Goh 2020), many of these works focus closely on a single festival and do not approach the film festival as a site of exhibition that contributes to the formation of a regional Asian cinema. This section explores the changing fortunes of festivals in the region that have contributed to the emergence of a regional Asian cinema.

Film festivals began as a distinctly European phenomenon, with major festivals such as the Venice International Film Festival, Cannes Film Festival and Berlin International Film Festival representative of the key international film festivals originating in Europe.[1] In recent years, however, 'it is the Asia region that has emerged as especially important to the continual advancement of the film festival' (Stringer 2008: 46).

Historically, a pan-Asian film festival, organised by the Federation of Motion Picture Producers in Asia-Pacific (FPA), existed from the mid-1950s. This event was established in 1954 under the title of the Southeast Asian Film Festival and was renamed the Asian Film Festival in 1957 and then the Asia-Pacific Film Festival in 1982 (Stringer 2008: 47). It continues today, holding the awards ceremony of its fifty-ninth edition in Macau in 2020. The festival travels from country to country as an industry-sponsored competitive event (Wong 2007; Baskett 2014; S. Lee 2017). This is quite different in format and function to the contemporary film festivals discussed below.

From the late 1970s to the early 1990s, Asia started developing its own film festivals, which have been instrumental to the regionalising processes I have emphasised throughout this book. The Hong Kong International Film Festival was founded in 1977, the Shanghai International Film Festival in 1993 and the Pusan International Film Festival in 1996 (with its name changed to the Busan International Film Festival in 2011 following the adoption of the Revised Romanisation system). Dina Iordanova (2011) points to a two or three tier structure of film festivals in Asia, with the Busan International Film Festival and Hong Kong International Film Festival at the top tier; Tokyo, Shanghai, Taipei Golden Horse, Yamagata International Documentary Film Festival and Tokyo FILMeX occupying the second tier; and below that local and national festivals or smaller identity and theme based festivals (2). Only the festivals in the top two tiers form part of the broader international festival circuit.

Film festivals are an important space in conceptualising what 'Asian cinema' is both for the region itself, and outside it. Within the region, film festivals are 'a key transnational and infrastructural node that makes new networks and alliances possible' (Iordanova 2011: 17). This is especially the case for the Hong Kong International Film Festival, which provided an important meeting place for filmmakers from Hong Kong, China and Taiwan to promote Chinese cinemas. From outside the region, the Hong Kong International Film Festival served as an important link between filmmakers, producers and distributors in Europe and America, and films from Asia, helping to 'place Asian films . . . into the international film festival circuit' (Wong 2011: 194).

Hong Kong International Film Festival

The oldest film festival in the region is the Hong Kong International Film Festival (HKIFF), established in 1977. At a time when Hong Kong cinema was booming, this festival was extremely important both locally and regionally. As a major port city, Hong Kong was the nexus for film traffic between East and West.[2] Stephen Teo (2009) notes, '[t]he first edition of HKIFF . . . was devised as a festival organised by cinephiles for cinephiles' (109). The HKIFF soon gained a reputation as an important platform for Asian films and the most prestigious film festival in Asia (Teo 2009: 109; Deshpande and Mazaj 2018: 230). It was an important forum, particularly in Asia, when there was not a lot of attention being paid to films from Asia, and it quickly became a place of discovery, showing films from the Hong Kong New Wave, the Chinese Fifth and Sixth Generation, and New Taiwan Cinema.

By the 1980s, the festival was becoming increasingly well known for its programming of films from across East and Southeast Asia. The festival also became involved in film production as well as distribution, through the Hong Kong-Asia Film Financing Forum. An acknowledgment of the regional identity it was establishing for itself and for Asian cinema came in the form of the inaugural Asian Film Awards (AFA) on 20 March 2007. As the first such award, the ceremony was, unsurprisingly, uncontentious and diplomatic. Reflecting the ascendancy of *hallyu* at that time, the South Korean film *The Host* (2006) won four of the ten available awards (for Best Actor, Best Cinematographer, Best Visual Effects and Best Film). The other awards were spread fairly evenly among other countries in the region.[3] Jia Zhangke won the Best Director award for *Still Life* (2006); Iran won the award for Best Screenplay, Thailand for Best Editor, Indonesia,

Best Composer and Japan, Best Actress. The most surprising award of the event was for 'Excellence in Scholarship in Asian Cinema', presented to Professor David Bordwell, in recognition of not only the industrial, but also the academic and institutional development of Asian cinema. The AFA later became a joint venture with the Busan and Tokyo International Film Festivals. From 2020, the Asian Film Awards will be run out of the Busan International Film Festival (Frater and Kil 2019). As Cindy Hing-Yuk Wong (2011) notes, events like AFA sought to attract new audiences to the HKIFF: '[t]he festival took up a pedagogical function for Asian cinema in the early years and later its archival projects shaped long-term strength for the cinema of the region' (Deshpande and Mazaj 2018: 230). HKIFF became an important model and inspiration for other film festivals in Asia, including the Busan International Film Festival (BIFF) and the Singapore International Film Festival (SIFF). With strong domestic film cultures, similar to Hong Kong of the 1980s and 90s, these festivals emerged in large part from the economic and cultural development of these cities.

Busan International Film Festival

Film festivals exist in a network or circuit and the fortunes of individual festivals are always in a state of flux. Iordanova (2011) notes in particular that 'the "Asian circuit" is in constant flux' (2). In the late 1990s, the Busan International Film Festival began to overshadow the Hong Kong International Film Festival as the premiere film festival in Asia.

The Busan International Film Festival was established in 1996 and rapidly grew to be the most prominent film festival in Asia over the next several years. Capitalising on the rise of the Korean New Wave, the festival played an important role in allowing the expression of cinephilia (or cine-mania as it is referred to in Korea) in the country (Kim 2005b). SooJeong Ahn (2011) contends that Busan managed to promote a strategy of cultural and industrial regionalisation while keeping the interests of Korean cinema central at the same time. In fact, Ahn argues that the strength of BIFF's regionalisation strategy goes hand in hand with its close links to the national film industry (2011: 54). The strong domestic film culture in South Korea provided the foundation that initially allowed the festival to conceptualise a regional identity for Asian cinema and to actively build up regional networks (Ahn 2011: 2).

Ahn (2011) examined BIFF's efforts at regionalisation over the period 1996 to 2005 in order to explore how BIFF sought to differentiate itself from its regional counterparts, in particular the Hong Kong International

Film Festival and Tokyo International Film Festival (145). BIFF's 'strategy to survive the highly competitive global film industry is not only to link its festival identity to its city identity, but also to develop this identity so as to integrate the region of (East) Asia through industrial links' (Ahn 2011: 72). Beyond promoting the city and showcasing Korean national cinema, Busan began creating a 'self-reflexive regional identification' for itself as an important platform for Asian cinema, becoming a hub for films in the region (Ahn 2011: 72).

Thus, while the rapid growth of cultural industries in South Korea, in particular its film industry, led the initial success of BIFF, the festival began creating a process of negotiating roles and identities at national, regional and global levels through programming and the establishment of different schemes aimed at promoting Asian cinema as a regional cinema (Ahn 2011: 145). These include the Pusan Promotion Plan (PPP), a co-financing and co-production market for Asian films launched in 1998 and renamed the Asian Project Market in 2011; the Asian Film Market (launched in 2006), providing investors an opportunity to be introduced to film projects in pre-production; and the Asian Cinema Fund, to support independent film production.[4] The festival has also participated in research and education on Asian cinema in addition to its industry focus. BIFF brings the industrial and the critical together through the Asian Film Academy, 'an education program modelled on the Talent Campus at the Berlin Film Festival and the Sundance Lab', designed to train a new generation of filmmakers (Ahn 2011: 121). Together, these initiatives 'support regional industries and collaboration and provide infrastructures for development and distribution of Asian cinema' (Neves 2012: 236).

BIFF is not a competition festival, it is a market-oriented festival, and its regionalisation strategy, and success, need to be understood in light of this. Rules of the International Federation of Film Producers Associations (FIAPF) state that festivals classified as competitive are not allowed to accept or exhibit films previously in competition elsewhere.[5] 'As a new festival, in a non-Western region, the BIFF had to consciously position itself as non-competitive to survive in the competitive global festival world' (Ahn 2016: 271).

In terms of the programming of films, BIFF's regionalisation strategy is apparent through its non-competitive programme 'A Window on Asian Cinema', a showcase of new and/or representative films by Asian filmmakers, and its international competition section, 'New Currents', which features first or second feature films by Asian directors.[6] These programming sections provide a regional and comparative frame for viewing Asian films, strengthened by the fact that European and North American films are marginalised through their programming (on a lesser scale) in the 'World Cinema' and 'Open Cinema' categories, in the same way that Asian cinema is usually relegated to either a broad 'World Cinema' section or a very specific and narrow category at other international film festivals. BIFF defines Asian cinema expansively, including films from Kyrgyzstan, Turkmenistan, Tajikistan and Syria, to Bangladesh and India, beyond the usual East and Southeast Asian locations.

Dina Iordanova argues that Busan 'gained a competitive advantage' over Hong Kong

> both because it had a better budgetary provision and because it had been launched at an opportune political moment, just as Hong Kong was plunged into a period of political insecurity leading up to the 1997 handover of Hong Kong from the UK to China. BIFF's smart moves included the decision to brand itself early on as 'a window for Asian cinema' rather than as a national showcase. (Kim et al. 2015: 82)

However, Iordanova more recently revisited her statement on BIFF's position as the premiere festival in Asia in light of events involving 'interference in programming decisions, excessive financial scrutiny, and pressure on the festival's leadership' (Kim et al. 2015: 82). While the festival has benefited from the safety of having government financial support, this has also come at a cost.

In 2014, the Busan International Film Festival screened the documentary *Diving Bell (The Truth Shall Not Sink with Sewol)* (co-directed by Lee Sang-ho and Ahn Hae-ryong, 2014). The film was critical of the Korean government's handling of the Sewol ferry disaster that claimed 304 lives. The programming of the film resulted in the removal of the festival chairman Lee Yong-kwan. Kim asks, '[s]hould a film festival be virtuous?', when considering BIFF's crisis that resulted with the screening of this documentary. BIFF refused the request by Seo Byeong-soo, Busan's city mayor, to remove the documentary from the festival's programme, which brought greater attention to the film's screening than it might otherwise have had (Kim et al. 2015: 80). Since this period, in which the festival was beset by scandal and controversy, BIFF's position within the international circuit has been blemished, although it remains important to the regional circuit within Asia.

Ahn (2016) notes that

> [s]ince the BIFF intensified its efforts to be the hub of the Asian film industry, it has impacted neighboring markets. In 1999, a year after the first APM [Asian Project Market], the Tokyo International Film Festival established the Tokyo Film Creators' Forum . . . [and the] Hong Kong Asia Film Financing Forum (HAF), the project market that runs concurrently with the HKIFF, was organized in 2000. (Ahn 2006: 270)

Joshua Neves (2012) writes:

> In short, the BIFF has created a regional structure that relies on Asian filmmak-
> ers, audiences, judges, funding, retrospectives, marketing, distribution, and the like,
> building manifold sites of exchange that need not be legitimized by Euro-American
> festivals and where Asian cinemas, urbanisms, and modernities operate as blueprints
> and not exceptions. (236)

BIFF represents a model that other film festivals in Asia have either sought
to emulate or distinguish themselves from, while collectively operating as
part of a growing network of regional film festivals.

Other Film Festivals in Asia

Other film festivals in Asia[7] that operate within a regional framework include
the Singapore International Film Festival (SIFF), established in 1986, and
balancing Singaporean films with other regional and international films.
In 2019, SIFF launched the Southeast Asian Producers Network, a three-
day industry event that brings together producers and speakers to further
provide opportunities for funding, dialogue and networking.[8] SIFF also
includes a dedicated Asian Film Focus programme.

The Japanese Film Festival: Asia-Pacific Gateway Initiative (JFF Initiative) aims to raise interest in Japanese films and attract a larger audience
from ASEAN countries. As it is described on their website, '[t]he JFF Initiative provides opportunities for people to gather offline and online, under
the vision of building a system for an extensive bridge between the Asia-
Pacific film market and the Japanese film industry'.[9] The Japanese Film
Festival online platform includes a website and social networking services,
initially in English but with the aim to roll this out in the local languages
of ASEAN countries, as a platform for the discussion of Japanese films.[10]

Taipei's Golden Horse Film Festival, established in 1962, is another
significant and long-running event in the circuit of inter-Asian film festivals.[11] As Neves (2012) notes, this inter-Asian circuit operates on a principle of exchange, rather than on the basis of Western conceptions of
promoting or 'discovering' new Asian cinemas. Neves writes, 'Asian film
festivals provide a material and analytic space for thinking about inter-
Asian practice and theory, especially as Asia-Asia correspondences and
becomings' and refers to these connections as 'media archipelagos', which
foreground 'marginalized zones of interaction' (233). For Neves, the idea
of archipelagos looks 'beyond the mainland and the sea and to chart new
and old regional constellations as sites of interreferencing, as models and
not exceptions' (238).[12] Lee and Stringer's (2012b) conceptualisation of

port city film festivals supports the conception of media archipelagos and sites of fluid connection between and among these festivals.

Asian Film Festivals outside Asia

There are a number of film festivals outside Asia that are dedicated to the programming of Asian films, including the Montreal Asian Film Festival, New York Asian Film Festival (NYAFF), Asian Film Festival (Filmasia) in the Czech Republic, and the Udine Far East Film Festival in Italy. The Vesoul International Film Festival of Asian Cinemas (*Festival international des cinémas d'Asie*) held in Vesoul, France, was created by Martine and Jean-Marc Thérouanne in 1995 and runs annually. In 2018, the mayor of Vesoul announced the establishment of a resource centre for Asian cinema (Lijano 2018). This is in addition to festivals such as the International Film Festival Rotterdam (IFFR), whose director Hubert Bals had a personal interest in Asian cinema, with the result that 'Rotterdam still maintains a strong reputation for bringing in new films from Asia to Europe' (Chan 2011: 254).

While international film festivals tend to focus on Asian art cinema, the Udine Far East Film Festival (FEFF), held annually in Italy's northeast, has been a significant showcase for Asian popular cinema. As Hannah McGill notes, Udine sits somewhere between a major international film festival and a 'specialist fan convention targeted at devotees of genre cinema' (cited in Lee and Stringer 2012a: 303). Dalla Gassa and Tomasi (2016) add, '[t]he basic criterion of the FEFF selection and its "anti-festival" vocation is that it privileges – although not exclusively – the so-called "popular cinema", in other words, those films that earned a particular success in their home country' (127).

Writing on Udine's pioneering 'counter-programming practices', Lee and Stringer note that the festival has set new trends in the international distribution of Asian cinema. 'By proclaiming itself susceptible to regional developments, it has been able to lead rather than merely follow the trends of the globalized festival circuit' (Lee and Stringer 2012a: 306). The first few editions of the festival were organised with Derek Elley, *Variety* film critic, as chief programmer. The festival sought to incorporate the tastes of the local audience into the festival through the establishment of an Audience Award (Lee and Stringer 2012a: 305). Udine's 'anti-festival' identity is also established through the fact that the award for Best Film – the Golden Mulberry – is decided not by a jury but by the audience itself (Dalla Gassa and Tomasi 2016: 128). The classification of films in the festival programme also highlights genre, without necessarily privileging national cinema origins. 'Country of origin has always been explicitly stated, but type of premiere and generic classification has been provided as additional information since 2006 and 2007 respectively. Indeed, genre has come to play an increasingly important role in facilitating Udine's counter-programming strategies' (Lee and Stringer 2012a: 305). Genre films, from martial arts and horror to science fiction and melodramas 'prevail against what is commonly considered "auteur cinema"' (Dalla Gassa and Tomasi 2016: 127). The importance of genre is also highlighted through the fact that genre classifications themselves are 'subdivided to an unusual degree' (Lee and Stringer 2012a: 305).

> Many commentators claim that national cinema circulates as a genre on the globalized festival and art house circuits, functioning as 'a distinctive brand name' within international distribution networks. FEFF has moved to prioritizing genre over nationality when contextualizing films, and it highlights the popular commercial genres of respective countries rather than the 'nation-as-genre'. (Lee and Stringer 2012a: 305)

Film festivals like Udine cannot compete with the speed of circulation of films online or with DVD releases (where the window between theatrical and DVD release is ever decreasing, especially in some Asian territories). In this environment Udine has carved a space for itself as a festival event, and also by stressing a 'shared contemporaneity – that is, the ability to consume popular films that Asian audiences themselves have enjoyed watching over recent months' (Lee and Stringer 2012a: 308–9). Returning to Bong Joon-ho's comments sympathising with both the mulitplexes' desire for theatrical hold back while understanding the online streaming platforms' insistence on simultaneous release, this notion of 'shared contemporaneity' takes on new meaning in the context of online streaming as the new 'festival' arena.

New Circuits of Distribution and Exhibition: Online Streaming

In this book I have considered various sub-regional groupings of Asian cinema, which are an integral part of the broader conceptualisation of Asian cinema as a regional cinema. Many significant studies of Asian cinema have focused on East Asian cinemas, often grouping together Japanese, South Korean and Chinese (PRC, Taiwan and Hong Kong) cinemas as an area of study. Southeast Asian cinema, in particular its independent cinema, has gained increasing prominence internationally in the last three decades. Part of this growth can be attributed to the success of Southeast Asian films on the international film festival circuit, which has led to the exposure of filmmakers, stories and styles from the region. While there have been a few high profile feature film examples that have been successful on the festival circuit, such as Apichatpong Weerasethakul's *Uncle Boonmee Who Can Recall His Past Lives* (2010, Thailand), which won the Palme d'Or at the Cannes Film Festival, and Anthony Chen's *Ilo Ilo* (2013, Singapore), which won the Camera d'Or at Cannes, it is predominantly short films (films under sixty minutes running time) that have achieved widespread success, with many winning awards internationally. I return to this in more detail in the next chapter to discuss Asian queer women filmmakers' use of the short film form specifically.

The production, distribution and exhibition of short films from Southeast Asia have been especially impacted upon by technological developments that have democratised filmmaking in the region. Empowered by easy and cheap access to digital video (DV) technology, digital filmmaking has had a major impact on film cultures in Asia, democratising the 'art' of filmmaking to those not professionally trained, and providing a greater range of potential distribution channels, including the Internet and mobile phones (Marchetti 2008: 414; Baumgärtel 2011: 62). The production of short films using smartphones has been an exciting area of development in the field of mobile media creative practice, and recent work has reflected on the new forms, practices and formats of mobile media making that are enabled in an age of smartphones (see Berkeley 2014; Schleser 2014).[13] Much of the aesthetic and formal concerns of mobile media making, for example their pedestrian quality, their personal nature, and their portability, are reflected in other forms of DV short film culture in Asia (see Ito et al. 2005 in relation to Japan).

Neves and Sarkar (2017) also focus on video as 'a cultural form and practice across Asia' in facilitating trans-Asian encounters (1). While their book *Asian Video Cultures* concentrates on local practices, as a project it envisages a broader regional landscape of Asian video and media cultures. They write, '[v]ideo's plasticity across lo-fi and high tech, on-and offline networks, social groupings, and diverse geographies is crucial to its ubiquity and irrepressibility' (Neves and Sarkar 2017: 6). Online videos can be downloaded, sold on various forms of discs, cards and drives, and in the local Asian grocer store – a form of social media, made up of 'diverse circuits, informal practices, and bazaar atmospherics' (Neves and Sarkar 2017: 8). These practices operate between formal and informal networks. To turn to one example of an online platform for the circulation of short films and videos from Asia, the next section explores the case study of Viddsee.

Viddsee and Online Publics[14]

While the exhibition of short films from Southeast Asia has grown on the major international film festival circuit, what is far less examined is the formation of a regional viewing community that is growing in parallel, online. I examine the role played by Singapore start-up company Viddsee, which promotes itself as an 'online social watching' platform, in growing this community. Co-founded by engineer/filmmakers Ho Jia Jian and Derek Tan in September 2012, Viddsee was built when Ho and Tan struggled to find distribution for their own short film productions. I evaluate how online distribution and exhibition sites like Viddsee are responding to and in turn precipitating different audience consumption practices as filmmakers in Asia continue to seek ways of making and marketing films that have relevance beyond local audiences while at the same time building an active (online) community in the region.

Writing specifically in the context of China, where issues of censorship and state control are ever-present, Paola Voci (2012) suggests that smaller screens such as the DV camera, the computer monitor – and, within it, the Internet window – and the cellphone display screen have created new public spaces where many long-standing divisions between high-brow and low-brow, mainstream and counterculture, conventional and experimental are dissolving and being reinvented (xx). Voci notes that movies made by and for smaller screens are marked by a 'lightness'; 'light' movies are characterised by 'small production costs, distribution ambitions, economic impact, limited audiences [and] quick and volatile circulation' (xx).

These factors outlined by Voci foster the development of new publics, including an emerging online public. Although smaller-screen practices tend to be personal and individual (it is difficult to share a mobile phone or laptop screen with another viewer or viewers), the viewing practices associated with smaller screens also tend to be collectively shared, even though the actual watching experience may be individually experienced (Voci 2012: 12). This is because the short format film, often downloadable or streamed through the Internet, is more 'portable' in the sense of being able to be shared online, through Facebook, Twitter and blogs, as well as emailed or sent via SMS messaging. Their portability (and digital nature) means that they can also be edited or remade by other viewers. That is, the 'lightness' of short films, which in digital form are often made to accommodate smaller screens, defines both their production *and* distribution contexts.

While Voci refers to small-screen practices as marking a form of individualised or personal viewing ('viewers *appropriate* smaller-screen movies [download, save, carry and transfer, gift them] at a very personal level'

(2012: xxi; original emphasis)), and indeed many viewers take individual control and ownership of the films outside of major institutions and industries, I suggest that the online distribution of short format films within Southeast Asia opens up another kind of sociality tied to the increasing interactivity of the cinematic form, one that was previously associated with the festival arena and audiences meeting face to face. The films that are shown on Viddsee are not necessarily *public*, in the sense of being widely consumed, but the viewing practices associated with watching these films can be described as social. To reconceive of this kind of individualised viewing experience as social and interactive, it is useful to consider the strategies through which Viddsee seeks to engender or foster a sense of 'social viewing' online.

Online film distribution in Asia has tended to be associated with piracy – that is, the illegal download of film and television programmes through the Internet in tandem with the physical circulation of pirated DVDs and VCDs. I would like to focus on the more productive (and legal) aspects of online film distribution and exhibition to consider how online viewing forms part of the sociality of everyday life in Southeast Asia and how independent filmmakers from the region are actively participating in the creation of an online community and network.

Viddsee: Curating Southeast Asia through its Short Films

Rated as one of the top fifty start-up companies at the Echelon Asia Summit 2013, Viddsee is a video content hosting site launched in February 2013. It sits below much larger Euro-American dominated video services like YouTube and Vimeo, and other national and regional services showing predominantly Asian content. For example, China has its own video-sharing websites, including one of the largest, Youku Tudou, which targets mainly local Chinese audiences, with content ranging from South Korean TV dramas, Japanese animation and music videos to user generated content in the form of original videos and videoblogging. Viki, a video streaming website based in Singapore and founded by Razmig Hovaghimian, Changseong Ho and Jiwon Moon in 2007, and AsiaPacific-Films.com (originally run by members of the Network for the Promotion of Asian Cinema (NETPAC) and sold to Alexander Street, an imprint of ProQuest, in 2012), are two other examples based in Asia that offer on-demand streaming of movies, TV shows and music videos.[15] The landscape of online content hosting and distribution sites on the Internet is diverse and constantly proliferating. Two things set Viddsee apart. The first is its focus on short format films, and the second is the element of curation, with films on Viddsee being vetted and organised into channels by the founders Ho Jia Jian and Derek Tan.

While the content on sites such as YouTube and Youku Tudou is not necessarily 'short', Viddsee, in contrast, hosts films usually under thirty minutes (and on average between six and ten minutes long), with a focus on Southeast Asian short films.[16] Dedicated channels stream films from Singapore, Indonesia, Malaysia, the Philippines, Cambodia and Thailand, with a range of films from other Southeast Asian nations, such as Myanmar, scattered throughout other channels. Viddsee does host films from across East Asia, including Japan, Hong Kong, South Korea and India, through dedicated channels. Not all of the channels are organised according to country of origin; many are compiled according to regional or subregional groupings. Viddsee has also partnered with the ASEAN International Film Festival and Awards, the Busan International Short Film Festival, the Singapore Short Film Awards, the Asian Film Archive and Tropfest Southeast Asia to create dedicated channels.

Being a 'niche content platform' (Wong 2013) filmmakers are more easily able to reach their target audience and audiences do not have to surf through large amounts of content to find what they are looking for. Viddsee's founders have said in an interview, '[w]hile content is readily available over the Internet today, it's still hard to find culturally contextual content from Singapore and around Southeast Asia' (Xu 2015). Ho explains,

> I explored the option of putting my film on Vimeo and YouTube, but the problem for filmmakers is that just getting their work online doesn't guarantee that it'll be watched by a large audience. Good short films get drowned among Gangnam Style parodies on YouTube, and discovery of Asian films is hard on Vimeo. (Russell 2013)

Viddsee is distinctive as a site focused on short films from Asia.

The second element that distinguishes Viddsee from other content hosting sites is the fact that material on the site is curated. Viddsee has been described as a 'targeted platform [that] . . . curate[s] an audience for short films' (Xu 2015), and as 'a socially-equipped site with a light touch of curation' (Millward 2013). Each film is vetted by Ho and Tan for quality and suitability with no cost charged for putting videos on the site (the company was funded by a Startup Grant from Singapore's 'Action Community for Entrepreneurship'). With other video hosting sites, there is usually no content curation, and minimal effort made to build a community for either audiences or filmmakers. It is this dual aspect of curation and community that form the most distinguishing features of the site.

In its first year, 5 million people watched at least one short film on Viddsee, with roughly a third being active (repeat) users from over ninety-eight different countries (Racoma 2013; Bischoff 2014). Some 70 per cent of Viddsee's viewers are from Asia, but English subtitles on most of the films means that they are also readily accessible by US, Australian, and UK-based viewers (Bischoff 2014).

A sense of community emerging from the use of this site is integral to the company's ethos, which describes itself as an 'online social watching service' (Viddsee.com). Viddsee's founders have a motto, 'short films are the new movies of the social web age' and the company's logo is a video screen within a chat bubble, encapsulating the site's desire to provide social interaction about Southeast Asian short films. Viddsee's model is heavily reliant on interaction between viewers and the site actively encourages ongoing discussion, engagement and exchange about each film posted, for example by providing colourful editorial descriptions and synopses of films, or by occasionally posing questions on Facebook as provocations for viewers to respond to. Indeed, the company's distribution strategy is closely integrated with social networking sites like Facebook and Twitter, with users given the option of logging in via their Facebook account to provide comments and ratings.[17] Viddsee refers to these ratings as micro-ratings, relating to elements such as story, acting, camera and sound production, thus providing feedback on technical aspects also benefiting the filmmakers.[18]

In this way, Viddsee genuinely seeks to include filmmakers in the community it seeks to build. While the dominant model for Southeast Asian films is to try to be shown at prestigious international film festivals and then to receive DVD distribution, Viddsee provides an alternative avenue with a very different kind of community based audience.[19] The site includes not only films by emerging filmmakers that would otherwise receive little or no distribution by other means, but also films by well-known, successful festival filmmakers, including Anthony Chen, Royston Tan and Tan Pin Pin, in support of this model.[20] These elements together create a model that actively seeks to foster the creation of a social community of viewers (and filmmakers) in Southeast Asia.

Although there is some content curation on Viddsee, because films are vetted and also because they are organised according to tags and channels, viewers also have freedom to choose what they want to watch and are able to discover films based on shared parameters such as country, genre, or topic, or to follow 'trending' films (a 'Viddsee Buzz' link, described as a 'discovery guide', features highlighted films under the tagline 'Your daily dose of awesome stories'). This sense of 'discovery' is important to creating ownership and a sense of individuality, as well as fostering the social aspect of the site – wanting to share and discuss short films found with those sharing similar interests and tastes. Through this model, Viddsee has 'transferred the power of discovery from film buyers and distributors to audiences' (Tan 2013).

Engineering Social Viewing through Social Message Films

Viddsee's unique features – a focus on Southeast Asian short films (which are more portable, and sharable), and the element of curation combined with an encouragement of social interaction, have seen it grow rapidly in a short space of time. After seven years, how successful has Viddsee's model been in fostering 'online social watching' in Southeast Asia? While the site may have a community of viewers that are 'connected' through Facebook and Twitter, this is not necessarily a community in conversation or dialogue. While a small number of films on Viddsee have a high amount of 'likes' on Facebook, some in the hundreds of thousands, only a very small percentage of individual films have any comments, and if they do it is usually only a handful of comments at most. How do we gauge participation or measure community building: through 'likes', comments or shares on social media? Perhaps a better frame of analysis for what the site seeks to do is to contemplate how it imagines Southeast Asia, and Asia more broadly, as a regionally connected community of viewers.

Viddsee's project of fostering a regional community through a shared visual archive can be regarded as a means of encouraging viewers within Asia (and Southeast Asia in particular) to talk to one another, aligning it to some extent with Kuan-Hsing Chen's notion of Asia as method. Chen writes in his book *Asia as Method: Toward Deimperialization*:

> the implication of Asia as method is that using Asia as an imaginary anchoring point can allow societies in Asia to become one another's reference points, so that the understanding of the self can be transformed, and subjectivity rebuilt. Pushing the project one step further, it becomes possible to imagine that historical experiences and practise in Asia can be developed as an alternative horizon, perspective, or method for posing a different set of questions about world history. (2010: xv)

To consider Asia as method is to rethink how we might conceive of Asia not as an object deduced from the understandings, perceptions and articulations of either the Euro-American West or imperialist Japan, but as its own reference point. On perhaps a smaller scale of ambition, the founders of Viddsee pose similar questions about the value of regional integration, in this case through local communities of viewing. Arguably, watching, sharing and curating digital short films from Asia online foster the formation of a new kind of sociality and the possibility of new pedagogical practices tied to 'social watching' of films from across the region. One way that Viddsee has sought to engender community formation and interest has been through the use of the site to promote a relationship between 'social viewing' and 'social message' films. For Viddsee, social viewing also carries some responsibility towards conveying a social message.

Kamil Haque, an actor and festival consultant for the ASEAN International Film Festival and Awards (AIFFA), which has collaborated with Viddsee to host a channel, says, 'I see distribution platforms like Viddsee as great big soapboxes for the ASEAN community-at-large to collaborate, to create, to share, to entertain and most importantly to educate' (Budiey (Admin) 2013). In terms of this 'educational' function, the site foregrounds 'social message' films as part of the act of social viewing and community building. A short film added to the site in June 2014, *Purple Light* (directed by Javior Chew, Cecilia Ang and Charlene Yiu), is based on a true story about a gay army recruit to the National Singapore Army and his exploration of his sexuality with one of his fellow cadets and best friend. It is one of several films on Viddsee tagged with the topic 'LGBT' (lesbian, gay, bisexual, transgender). Viddsee also hosts a channel called 'Our Better World', an initiative of the Singapore International Foundation, which aims to share stories 'to inspire good'.[21] The channel includes films such as *They Should Be at the World Cup* (directed by Anshul Tiwari) on Singapore's cerebral palsy football team, *Deaf, Loud and Proud* (also directed by Anshul Tiwari), on the deaf percussion band, ExtraOrdinary Horizons, and *Paraplegic's Dream Bike Ride* (directed by Peter Wall), a short film about a woman left paralysed after a motorcycle accident who rides again in a modified motorcycle that accommodates her wheelchair in a trip from Jakarta to Bali. Viddsee also hosts short films about street kids in Mumbai and South Asian migrant workers to Singapore, amidst comedies and animation and, most recently, original web series.

Perhaps it is these 'social message' films that allow viewers to engage more actively in what Carter and Arroyo call 'participatory pedagogy' (2011: 291). The forms of participation that the site offers are not necessarily those of political action or activism, but rather operate on a more subtle level of persuasion by exposing viewers to alternative forms of identities, stories and experiences, opening up the potential for a slow changing of attitudes. In brokering potential forms of interaction between viewers, Viddsee is promoting the value of dialogue between Southeast Asian neighbours through a shared contemporary cinema.

Conclusion

In this chapter I have been interested in how the act of curation and the forms of social interaction engendered by Viddsee allow us to contemplate the use of digital media, in this case digital short films, in the building of an online community of viewers in Southeast Asia. Through social interaction and participation, filmmakers and audiences engaging through Viddsee provide a critique of the individualised act of viewing on 'small screens'. Combined with the site's elements of curation and audiovisual archiving, Viddsee also structures our viewing choices to produce certain pedagogical and emotional outcomes. Viddsee's social watching platform facilitates, in however limited a way, the coming together of Southeast Asia as a region that is constituted both on and offline by local viewing communities that are not reliant upon an external perspective or source of 'curation' for their existence or validation but participates in a form of sociality that more closely resembles the forms of inter-Asia referencing that are called for in the Asia as method project.

New digital distribution practices and models like Viddsee are a way for the industry to respond to and in turn precipitate different audience consumption practices (including online streaming) as filmmakers continue to seek ways of making films that will cross national markets and audiences seek new avenues of content discovery and ways of being social, without leaving their homes, computers or mobile phones. The international distribution and exhibition of Asian cinema has become an important industrial concern given the rapid growth in the popularity of the cinema not just in areas external to the region (Europe, the United States, and Australia), but also in the context of intra-regional consumption – from path breaking distributors such as Fortissimo Films to newer online exhibitors such as Viddsee.[22] As the case of *Okja* demonstrates, a nimble approach in negotiating the international film festival circuit and the new streaming landscape is a necessity for filmmakers both established and emerging.

Notes

1. The Venice International Film Festival was founded in 1932, Cannes Film Festival in 1946 and Berlin International in 1951.
2. See Lee and Stringer (2012b) on the significance of port city film festivals in their survey of Chinese films at Cannes, Venice, Tokyo, Rotterdam and Busan.
3. Eligibility is for films from across East, South, Southeast and West Asia. To be eligible, films must be feature length (more than sixty minutes), in 35 mm or 70 mm film format or digital format suitable for exhibition in cinemas, and be fiction films from Asia. The films must have English subtitles.
4. Busan International Film Festival website, available at <http://www.biff.kr> (last accessed 12 September 2020).

5. The International Federation of Film Producers Associations, or *Fédération Internationale des Associations de Producteurs de Films* (FIAPF), was founded in France in 1933 and is the regulatory body for film festivals around the world.

6. Busan International Film Festival website, available at <http://www.biff. kr> (last accessed 12 September 2020).

7. Julian Stringer (2008) discusses the advantages of using the term 'film festivals in Asia' over 'Asian film festivals', in large part to be more mindful of the diversity of the festivals (49).

8. Singapore International Film Festival, available at <https://filmacademy. sgiff.com/seapn/> (last accessed 19 September 2020).

9. Japan Foundation Asia Center, available at <https://jfac.jp/en/culture/ dictionary/japanese-film-festival/> (last accessed 12 September 2020).

10. Japan Foundation Asia Center, available at <https://jfac.jp/en/culture/ dictionary/japanese-film-festival/> (last accessed 12 September 2020).

11. In 2019 China's Golden Roosters Awards was set for the same date as Taiwan's Golden Horse Awards, the result of a controversy that occurred when pro-Taiwan independence filmmaker, Fu Yue, won the award for Best Documentary for her film *Our Youth in Taiwan* and made an acceptance speech calling for the world to recognise Taiwan as an independent country. Chinese authorities banned mainland Chinese film industry professionals from attending the Golden Horse Awards that year (Davis 2019).

12. See also Katrina Tan on Cinema Rehiyon and the idea of an 'archipelagic imagination' in regional cinema from the Philippines (PhD, Monash University, [forthcoming 2021]).

13. Park Chan-wook and his brother Park Chan-kyong made the fantasy horror short film *Paranmanjang/Night Fishing* in 2011, shot entirely on an iPhone 4.

14. Part of this chapter was originally published as 'Short Circuits of Southeast Asian Cinema: Viddsee and the Project of Online Social Viewing' in Larissa Hjorth and Olivia Khoo (eds), *The Routledge Handbook of New Media in Asia*, London and New York: Routledge, 2016, pp. 229–37.

15. The name Viki is a combination of video and wiki since, like Wikipedia, the site also relies on volunteers, including subtitlers, for content management. AsiaPacificFilms.com was founded in 2009 by Jeannette Hereniko. The site houses more than 600 historically significant films from Asia and the Pacific, many of which struggled to gain distribution outside their home country.

16. The site does stream a limited number of feature films (the first feature, *S11*, directed by Gilbert Chan and Joshua Chiang, 2001, was posted on 25 May 2013). The company quotes that 40 per cent of Viddsee's audiences view their films on mobile phones (Racoma 2013), and Viddsee launched a mobile app in June 2013. The short format film is particularly suited to these users accessing through their mobile phones using Internet connections, and caters to bandwidth requirements, shorter attention spans, and distracted viewing contexts.

17. As of March 2020, Viddsee has over 595K 'Likes' on Facebook and 9800 followers on Twitter.

18. Jean Burgess and Joshua Green (2009) have commented on the generative nature of video sharing, suggesting that participation is crucial to YouTube's structure. Being 'literate' on YouTube is about how to navigate it 'as a social network' (72). The comments attached to videos are a 'crucial part of YouTube participation and social interaction' (Lange 2010: para 28); users come to expect a sense of reciprocity with other participants in the shared online video culture.

19. In October 2013, with Singapore's fifteenth DigiCon6, Viddsee organised for viewers to watch and vote for the top eighteen finalist animations on their DigiCon 6 channel. Viddsee was the official digital partner of the ASEAN International Film Festival and Awards 2013, which expanded its inaugural short film festival beyond Malaysia to audiences around ASEAN countries online. Viddsee is not just a place for the discovery of new films, but also participates in the archiving of these short films. It does not completely disregard the desire of filmmakers to find success on the film festival circuit, partnering with film festivals in order to improve the visibility of both the site itself and the films on it.

20. Kelvin Sng, director of *The Gang*, says, 'Viddsee is a new platform for short films, and having my film on it is also a way of showing my support to it . . . I was actually planning to release *The Gang* on DVD together with another mid-length film that I executive-produced called *Steadfast* (2010). But, I decided to share it through Viddsee to thank everyone with *The Gang* made available for viewing free of charge to all' (Xu 2015).

21. The Singapore International Foundation (previously called Singapore Volunteer Overseas) is a not-for-profit organisation established on 1 August 1991. Its vision is described as 'Making Friends for a Better World'. 'We build enduring relationships between Singaporeans and world communities, and harness these friendships to enrich lives and effect positive change across the world' (<https://forum-ids.org/member/singapore-international-foundation-sif/>).

22. Founded in 1991, Fortissimo Films was known for twenty-five years as a leading international distribution company, with a focus on independent filmmakers from Asia and elsewhere around the world. Fortissimo played a key role in launching the careers of several Asian auteurs, including Wong Kar-wai, Wang Xiaoshuai and Tian Zhuangzhuang, and grew the audience for Asian art house films worldwide. On 17 August 2016 the company filed for bankruptcy. It was restarted under new management in 2017 after being brought back from receivership by China's Hehe Pictures (Frater 2019b). While Fortissimo's head office will still be in Amsterdam, company decisions will be made from Beijing.

CHAPTER 5

Queer Asian Cinema, Female Authorship and the Short Film Format

This chapter examines the relationship between authorship, gender and film form in the context of queer Asian cinema.[1] As mentioned in the introduction, Asian cinema's rise as an international marketing category has been predicated on the successful promotion of the figure of the male auteur – Zhang Yimou, Hou Hsiao-Hsien, Wong Kar-wai, Park Chan-wook, Bong Joon-ho, Hirokazu Kore-eda and Apichatpong Weerasethakul, for example – and his success in the international arena, which privileges modernist, 'art house' cinema. As Lingzhen Wang (2011) argues, the films that are valued on the international circuit 'endorse depoliticization, aesthetic transcendence, and an indifferent cosmopolitan style, and dismiss the significance of gender and alternative histories' (22). Critical approaches to Asian women directors within the evolving disciplinary formation of Asian cinema are shaped by this dominant framework that privileges auteurism as a way of defining the cinema against Euro-American counterparts. Although there have been, and continue to be, important works recuperating 'lost' or marginalised female auteurs throughout the history of Asian cinema, much of this work has been conducted in the context of national film histories, making it difficult to draw meaningful connections outside such a framework.

Queer cinema constitutes a more politicised international dimension of contemporary Asian cinema, and some of the most vibrant and interesting work currently produced by women in Asia today can be located within queer cinema. Yet, again, most of the high profile directors associated with queer Asian cinema are men (e.g. Stanley Kwan, Tsai Ming-liang and Cui Zi'en), in part because they have made feature films. The contribution of women filmmakers – many of whom who have had long careers making television, documentaries and short films – to queer Asian cinema has not been as visible as that of their male counterparts unless or until they break onto the scene with a first feature film.

Thus the female director within queer Asian cinema is marked by an 'in-betweenness' that in many cases renders her invisible. She is caught between national cinema formations and the institutional flows of 'world cinema' (the desire to attract a local audience while also aspiring to the film festival circuit), and between commercial and independent imperatives (the requirement to make a career out of filmmaking despite carrying the limiting labels of 'Asian', 'woman' and/or 'queer'). These tensions are registered in the format of filmmaking, with feature film production regarded as a primary marker of critical and/or commercial success. Far from devaluing non-feature film production, this chapter seeks to examine the importance of the short film format for an understanding of women's contributions to Asian cinema generally, and queer Asian cinema in particular. It pays attention to how unique qualities of the short film format allow women filmmakers to actively engage with each other's work within and across the region, and how this transnational connection is redefining how we understand the figure of the individual 'auteur' of women's filmmaking.

In this chapter I examine the particular industrial and institutional contexts for a commissioned short film from Singapore, Sun Koh's *Dirty Bitch* (2009), tracing the production and circulation of this film to explore how female authorship might be productively reconceptualised in a regional framework drawing upon the 'in-betweenness' that has so far rendered it invisible. Although Singapore itself provides a 'minor' or small nation context, I explore how this particular local, authorial example highlights the need to make regional connections from production to reception, situating this discussion within women's film culture and Asian queer culture as a form of minor transnationalism.

The Short Film Form and Singapore's Minor Cinema

The contemporary film industry in Singapore experienced a revival in the 1990s following a period of dormancy between 1973 and 1991, when not a single feature film was recorded as having been made on the island. After independence from Malaysia, the country was consumed in the process of rapid industrialisation, turning only in the 1990s to supporting a local film culture again. Some forty-five feature films were made in the period between 1991 and 2004, a marked increase from the previous decade. Singapore's film revival was the product of a combination of public and private initiatives: state-sponsored scholarships for Singaporeans to study film abroad, funding for training at local polytechnics, and the establishment of the Singapore Film Commission and production company, Raintree Pictures, both in 1998. Since the revival, an important area of success for Singapore cinema has been in the realm of short filmmaking.

Singapore's short film production has grown since 2000 as a result of government financial support through the Singapore Film Commission and by allowing short films to feature in a competitive category at the Singapore International Film Festival, which in turn has paved the way for the success of Singapore shorts at other major international festivals, including Cannes and Rotterdam. Film scholars Jan Uhde and Yvonne Ng Uhde (2004) note that 'short films have significantly contributed to the development of Singapore cinema as a whole' (18). Whereas in some national film industries it is difficult to obtain funding for short films because of low prospects for a return, in Singapore short films receive funding because they are seen as a stepping stone to success in the feature film industry, and thus a way of nurturing local talent to achieve success internationally.[2]

A short film is generally classified in terms of its length, usually under sixty minutes in running time. However, the temporal aspect of characterising the short film does not account for the range of techniques, styles and themes that can be created, nor for the variety of short films and the diverse professional and institutional functions for which they are made: from calling card shorts and commissioned shorts, to independent, avant-garde experiments for alternative exhibition circuits.

Nick Deocampo outlines the short film's shared characteristics of '*brevity*, *unity* (or singularity of theme, character or technique), *variety of form*, and a *large degree of creative freedom*' (Deocampo 1985: 1; original emphasis). Uhde and Uhde (2004) add, 'As the short is not a format used for general commercial release, it is less subject to censorship control and therefore allows for greater artistic freedom and experimentation, an advantage especially important in tightly controlled Singapore' (20). Short films enable filmmakers to debate issues in Singaporean society that might otherwise remain unremarked upon. Young Singaporean-born filmmaker Sun Koh, whose short film *Dirty Bitch* forms the focus of this chapter, has used the short format on several occasions to challenge the constraints of public discourse in Singapore. Koh's *The Secret Heaven* (2002), which recounts the fantasies of a young girl wanting to escape her piano lessons, comments on the pressure put on Singaporean children by their parents to perform well. Another short made by Koh, *Bedroom Dancing* (2006), explores issues of isolation, voyeurism and lack of privacy in Singapore's public HDB (Housing Development Board) flats, and was inspired by a criminal case in which a man was arrested and fined S$6500 for masturbating in his own apartment. More recently, Koh has directed the short comedy film *Singapore Panda/New New Panda* (2013), as part of the omnibus collection *Letters from the South* (executive produced by Tan Chui Mui), and the short drama *The Secret Passion of Madam Tan Ah Lian* (2014). In

2018, Sun Koh produced a '360 film' entitled *Presence*, 'which places the viewer in the presence of a family witnessing the death of a loved one at home'.[3] Koh's innovative body of work includes music videos, TV movies, omnibus films and documentaries, although short films dominate.

The short film form has been especially embraced by queer Singaporean filmmakers – the higher profile of whom, including Loo Zi-han, Royston Tan and Boo Jun-feng – are men.[4] Although Singapore has to-date only produced one full length gay feature film, Loo Zi-han's *Solos* (2007), the short film form has afforded queer filmmakers a greater degree of artistic freedom in negotiating issues of censorship relating to sexuality, and several women filmmakers including Eva Tang (*Londres-London*, 2006) and Kirsten Han (Spudnik Productions) have had success with their queer-themed short films. The Substation, an arts centre founded in Singapore in 1990, has provided an important space for screening and nurturing the short film scene, in particular through its 'Short Circuit' programme and annual Singapore Short Film Awards (SSFA). The inaugural 'Short Circuit' film festival in October 2006 featured twelve short films that were either produced by lesbian, gay, bisexual and transgender (LGBT) individuals or featured a LGBT theme (R. Tan undated). In the context of the young and relatively small, i.e. minor, queer film scene in Singapore, this is a notable event.

Singapore is not the only Southeast Asian nation to become known for its short films. An article by producer Juan Foo entitled 'Mini cinema' suggests that 'A nation's cinema starts with shorts' (2002), emphasising the importance of this form to many of the smaller film industries in Southeast Asia. Writing on the contemporary short film movement in the Philippines, Nick Deocampo suggests that short films are a 'new' Philippines cinema, marking a period distinct from the 1970s commercial and independent cinema in the country. Deocampo notes that the format of the short film has been taken up fervently by the youth in the Philippines since the 1980s; however, the short still remains critically and popularly marginalised in relation to the commercial cinema. Deocampo (1985) characterizes the short film in the Philippines as a 'submerged cinema' that has always existed, but as the 'other' to the commercial cinema, with 'its own history, aesthetics, ideology, and practicing filmmakers' (viii). Deocampo argues that 'a counter-culture results from this tenacity to survive despite prevailing hindrances like rising costs, absence of a "professional system" to sustain film production and distribution, competition from commercial films and video, and an audience that has yet to be tapped' (viii). While Singapore's short filmmaking culture does not reflect the same avant-garde oppositional culture of the kind Deocampo notes in relation to the Philippines, the tenacity for commercial survival in Singapore underscores the short form as an integral mode of filmmaking especially, but not only, for emerging film industries in light of the economic realities of film production, distribution and exhibition today. For a minor film industry like Singapore, short films become an important entry into 'major' cinema circuits, including those of elite international film festivals.

Drawing from Gilles Deleuze and Félix Guattari's use of the term 'minor literature' in their study *Kafka: Toward a Minor Literature* (1975), Tom Gunning (1989–90) has noted the appearance of a new form of avant-garde cinema during the late 1980s which he calls 'minor cinema'. Gunning defines minor films as those that 'recognize their marginal identity and consciously maintain a position outside the major cinematic languages' (3). Minor films are 'creatively parasitic' and often oppositional, in the sense of not holding aspirations of a commercial breakthrough (Gunning 1989–90: 3). The relationship between the commercial and the creative is more fully emphasised in the context of Singapore's emergent film industry, where generous government funding does make demands (however implicit) for a 'return', making it a requirement for filmmakers to engage the 'minor' in cinema in ever more creative ways.

There have been valuable re-articulations of the concept of 'minor cinema' to account for the transnational circuits of women's cinema and queer cinema, highlighting the gendered dimensions of the term 'minor' and reclaiming the pejorative connotations associated with its gendering. These include Alison Butler's (2002) consideration of contemporary women's cinema as a form of 'minor cinema' and Patricia White's (2008) study of short-form commissioned works in her essay 'Lesbian minor cinema'. As with Gunning, both Butler and White draw from Deleuze and Guattari's notion of minor literature. Butler observes that women's cinema 'now seems "minor" rather than oppositional' and develops a connection between Deleuze and Guattari's notion of collective enunciation and her characterisation of women's cinema as a minor cinema (19). Butler (2002) writes that because a minor literature or cinema emerges from a de-territorialised group, it conjures up collective implications 'even in the absence of an active community' (20). Beyond a reconceptualisation of authorship that such an approach offers, Butler cautions on the continued need to engage the 'major' – issues of funding, production and distribution.

Paying particular attention to these questions of the global movement of capital and the reception of queer women's cinema, Patricia White (2008) considers how lesbian filmmakers deploy the notion of the minor in imaginative and generative ways. While White does not posit a direct equivalence between Deleuze and Guattari's notion of the minor and the concept of queer, she finds productive resonances between the two, understanding minor cinema 'most straightforwardly as making use of limited resources in a politicized way' (413). By embracing the 'minor' (for example, in the use of video rather than film, and by making short-format works instead of features), lesbian filmmakers demonstrate their resourcefulness in negotiating 'major' languages, genres and national cinemas from which their work might otherwise be excluded. White notes that short-format work in particular 'circumvents the commodity circulation and narrative boundedness of the feature film, crossing into other communities and contexts such as . . . festival networks' (413).

White (2015) suggests that 'regional, gendered dynamics in world film culture generate [what she refers to as] . . . network narratives' (134). 'The network as a spatial model with which to approach Asian women directors is meant to map local and national nodes as well as regional and global flows' (White 2015: 133–4). White notes that women's film festivals, such as the International Women's Film Festival in Seoul, are the most apparent example of a transnational feminist film network (2015: 134).

The important role played by film festivals in the exhibition of queer short films is especially pertinent to queer Asian cinema, which remains, as Helen Hok-Sze Leung (2003) notes, predominantly a festival category, unlike New Queer Cinema in the United States, which rapidly became mainstreamed. Leung argues that outside of the festival circuit, it is 'difficult to speak of the influence of these films as though they form a coherent body of work. The very notion of a "queer Asian Cinema" is in many ways a festival invention' (14). Queer Asian cinema produced by women filmmakers can be located between specialist queer film festivals and women's film festivals, and occasionally as part of elite art festivals. This particular distribution and exhibition framework presents a need to consider not only the transnational production of queer Asian cinema produced by women but also its reception.

Alison Butler (2002) notes that while comparative, cross-cultural analyses in film studies are still relatively new, in women's studies transnational critical practice is more widely accepted, and indeed, influential (119). Although transnational approaches in film studies may only be nascent, their uptake has nowhere been more fervent than in the context of Asian cinemas. As Will Higbee and Song Hwee Lim (2010) suggest, transnationalism is fast becoming a 'default concept' when discussing (East) Asian cinemas (15). Higbee and Lim argue for a 'critical transnationalism' in film studies that remains attuned both to the loose usage and to the over-valuation of the term transnationalism (7). Lingzhen Wang (2011) re-engages long-standing debates of transnational feminism, linking these to film scholarship in her collection *Chinese Women's Cinema: Transnational Contexts*. Wang writes, '[t]oday, feminist film studies must step outside the restrictive framework of the nation-state and critically resituate gender and cinema in a transnational feminist configuration that enables the examination of relationships of power and knowledge among and within cultures and nation-states' (2). Transnational film feminism, in its most critical form, does not privilege Western film feminisms or consider Asian film feminisms as temporally coming *after* Western film debates. The applicability of Western film feminisms to the Asian context is questionable, as the level of permeation and access to Western feminist theories, including feminist film theories, has at best been uneven, and at worst almost non-existent (Spakowski 2011). Rather, transnational feminism's relevance to Asian cinema is that it emphasises political links – links of a 'political rather than biological or cultural bases for alliance' (Mohanty 1991: 4). What emerges out of these connections is a rich network of women filmmakers and filmmaking practices, spanning short films, documentaries, animation and video work and not only a dominant narrative of nation states, or of prominent auteurs lauded at major international film festivals. By exploring these connections between women filmmakers and their work in Singapore and beyond, it is possible to rethink the notion of female authorship in relation to Asian cinema as something less individualised and more politicised. The short works of female directors in Singapore, including Sun Koh, Eva Tang, Jasmine Ng Kin-Kia, Kirsten Tan, Tan Pin Pin and Kaz Cai, need to be regarded as part of a wider, coterminous development of independent filmmaking by women in the Asian region. Considered in this light, women's filmmaking within Asian cinema, and in particular queer Asian cinema, can most accurately be described as a form of minor transnationalism.

Françoise Lionnet and Shu-mei Shih (2005) describe minor transnationalism as a specific intervention into dominant conceptions of transnationalism 'from above.' They write:

> Major discussions of transnationalism and globalization assume that ethnic particularity and minoritized perspectives are contained within and easily assimilated into the dominant forms of transnationalism . . . What is lacking in the binary model of above-and-below, the utopic and the dystopic, and the global and the local is an awareness and recognition of the creative interventions that networks of minoritized cultures produce within and across national boundaries. (Lionnet and Shih 2005: 7)

Not only does minor transnationalism consist of minority cultural articulations with a majority culture, but also minor-to-minor articulations within and across national borders (Lionnet and Shih 2005: 7). By examining the minor cinema of women's short filmmaking in Asia, the minor transnation-alism of queer Asian circuits is also foregrounded since it is queer Asian cinema produced by women filmmakers that is most routinely excluded from the feature film and auteurist terrain of major international film festi-vals. Through an analysis of Sun Koh's short film *Dirty Bitch*, I explore not only how Singapore's minor cinema engages with the 'major' circulations of elite international film festivals but also how the minor-to-minor trans-national connections between women filmmakers and queer film cultures in Asia enable a reimagining of traditional forms of film authorship.

Dirty Bitch (Sun Koh, 2009, 13:42 min)

After studying mass communication at Ngee Ann Polytechnic and working for several years as a director of television documentaries, dramas, info-tainment and commercials in Singapore, Sun Koh (born in 1977) made the transition from commercial to independent work. Her first short film, *The Secret Heaven* (2002), performed well internationally and was the first Singapore film to win a major award (the Silver Hugo) at the Chicago International Film Festival. Koh also won Best Director at the Fifteenth Singapore International Film Festival. Koh's later short, *Dirty Bitch*, was commissioned by the Rotterdam International Film Festival as part of its 'Meet the Maestro: Claire Denis' programme in 2009, screening alongside the premiere of Denis's *35 Rhums*, the only short to be so commissioned.

As Koh notes in the opening intertitles, *Dirty Bitch* was inspired by a violently censored VHS copy of Denis's *Nénette et Boni* (1996), which she found at Singapore's public performing arts library at the Esplanade. The film is both an homage to, and a whimsical reinterpretation of, Denis's gritty and poetic feature film, with Sun Koh's version, made over a decade after Denis' film, shifting the original Marseille setting to Singapore. The film has achieved a small measure of success locally and internationally through the film festival circuit, with critics praising its brazen visuals and unexpectedly comedic representation of youthful sexual desire and violence. Film critic Chris Fujiwara comments, '[a]t 14 minutes, the film has more ideas than most features'.[5]

Nénette et Boni, Claire Denis's tale of a fraught yet ultimately tender relationship between a brother and sister, is transplanted in *Dirty Bitch* from a run-down house in Marseille to a public housing flat in Singapore. Sexual imagery involving baguettes and coffee percolators in the Denis original finds substitution in a bowl of instant noodles, and brother-sister disagreements become physicalised as a (slow motion) sumo wrestling match. A young police constable, Chen Ming Jun (played by Kevin Tan), narrates (in Mandarin-language voice-over) his desire for a female colleague. He berates his sister, Chen Ming Zhen (played by Serene Chen), for returning to the family home, pregnant. Zhen is determined to keep the 'dirty secret' of her unwanted pregnancy from everyone and violently silences anyone who might expose her. In fantastical interludes, she pokes out her brother's eyes and cuts out the tongue of her gynaecologist (all of this is humorously portrayed, in vibrant colour and imagery and with exaggerated performances). Interspersed in the film is a musical segment featuring a dominatrix gynaecologist, played by Loretta Chen, who lip synchs an upbeat rap song in French (written and performed by Anne-Laure Sibon, winner of Pop Idol France). In an animated sequence accompanying the soundtrack, the Merlion (a Singapore landmark with the head of a lion and the body of a fish) spits out kewpie dolls into the Singapore River, and more dolls dance around other tourist landmarks. The gynaecologist tells Zhen that it is too late for her to have an abortion and proceeds to whip the pregnant girl's bottom. Finally, one of the kewpie dolls is flattened by a shoe and the animated musical segment ends as blood splatters and slowly drips away. In the final scene of the film, Zhen, now heavily pregnant, is being interviewed for entry into law school. Her interviewees (played by Fanny Kee, Ken Sun and Kenneth Paul Tan), begin asking her questions in English. As Zhen stumbles on her answers, music fades in and the interviewees rise from their seats and begin laughing, drinking beer and dancing in blood-splattered white bunny slippers as the film concludes.

Dirty Bitch has generally not been read or positioned as a queer text (it has not, for example, screened at any queer film festivals), but I read the film's queer potentiality in terms of how it provokes a rethinking of female authorship within a minor transnational network of women's short filmmaking and queer Asian cinema. *Dirty Bitch* resonates aesthetically and thematically with the early short films of one of Singapore's best known independent documentary filmmakers, Tan Pin Pin, arguably more so than it represents an homage to the stylistic qualities of Denis's original film. While Tan Pin Pin's short films and documentaries also do not explicitly reference queer subjectivity, two of her short fiction films can be read as queer through their deployment of a camp aesthetic and use of Barbie doll figurines in the tradition of Todd Haynes's *Superstar: the Karen Carpenter Story* (1987). Tan's *Lurve Me Now* (1999), a three-minute short that portrays the sexual fantasies of a Barbie doll, was banned by the Singapore government for its suggestive sexual content. *Microwave* (2000), a two and a half minute short film with the simple yet effective premise of a Barbie doll placed in a rotating microwave oven, is an even more condensed example of the unusual blend of comedy, camp and suppressed sexualised violence to which Sun Koh's *Dirty Bitch* pays tribute. Tan's films also do not circulate on queer film festival circuits; the 'queerness' of *Lurve Me Now* and *Microwave* is primarily a matter of interpretation and reading, although the films themselves are open, experimental, and invite multiple perspectives and interaction with audiences.

In reading *Dirty Bitch* and Tan Pin Pin's early short films as queer texts, I draw on Helen Hok-Sze Leung's (2001) notion of the 'queerscape'. Writing in the context of Hong Kong cinema, and the recent proliferation of works featuring new expressions of sexuality and sexual identity, Leung introduces the term 'queerscape' to avoid passing judgement on which representations should be regarded as legitimately 'queer', for example by essentialising a queer perspective or what might be considered authentic queer subjecthood. Leung writes:

> Queerscapes refer to the contingent and tangential uses of public space by sexual minorities and to public acts and expressions of desire, eroticism, and sexuality that momentarily disrupt what heterocentric ideology assumes to be an immutable, coherent relation between biological sex, gender, and sexual desire. (2001: 426)

Queerscapes are not equivalent to, but share theoretical resonances with, the much-debated term queer, referring 'not only to gay and lesbian spaces, but also to all spaces that challenge heteronormativity' (Leung 2001: 426). Leung's idea of 'queerscapes' introduces a more fluid definition of queer as a critical concept since it does not rely on the question of the identity of the film author or even of the film's subjects. Rather, queer becomes 'an analytical framework to look for what denaturalizes, disrupts, or resignifies the relation conventionally drawn between gendered embodiments, erotic desire, and sexual identities' (Leung 2008: 2). Within such a framework, it also becomes possible, and indeed useful, to align a queer spectatorial position and methodology with the minor transnationalism of women's filmmaking in Singapore and in the region beyond. It is this minor cinema of women's short filmmaking in Asia that in turn highlights and articulates with the minor transnational circuits of Singapore's cinematic queerscapes.

Instead of reproducing the kind of realist art house film privileged by the elite international film festival circuit (including the one for which it was commissioned, Rotterdam), as arguably Denis's film does, Koh has instead produced a short comedy 'about facing your inner bunny' (film tagline). Boni's pet rabbit in the Denis original has become, in Koh's version, a pair of blood-splattered fluffy white bunny slippers worn by the violent female protagonist, the 'Dirty Bitch' of the film's title.

In contrast to the film's provocative English title, the Chinese title, *Tu Nu* (兔女), translates literally as 'rabbit girl'. While the figure of the rabbit can be seen as a reference to the animal's perceived reproductive promiscuity ('breeding like rabbits'), rabbit also has another connotation: rabbit (*tuzi*) was a slang term for homosexuals used in late imperial China, and the term retains the connotation of homoeroticism in particular Fujian-speaking Chinese communities, where gay men are still sometimes referred to as 'rabbits' (Kang 2009: 37–8). The historical reference for this terminology is a folktale recounted in the *Zi Bu Yu*, a book written by Qing dynasty scholar and poet Yuan Mei, about a man named Hu Tianbao who became known as the Rabbit God. Hu Tianbao, as the story goes, fell in love with an imperial inspector of Fujian Province. He was caught spying on the inspector and when he confessed his infatuation he was sentenced to death. The judges of the underworld, learning that his crime was one of love, appointed him patron god of homosexuals and safeguarder of homosexual affections (Szonyi 1998). He was posthumously deified as Tu Er Shen, the Rabbit God, and a temple was dedicated to his worship in Yonghe, Taiwan. This historical reference is not commonly known outside Fujian-speaking communities or Chinese homosexual communities, highlighting the minor transnational circuits of queer Asian cultures in which the film circulates. *Dirty Bitch* combines this symbolism of the rabbit (in the film's Chinese title) with the reclamation of a word considered derogatory to women (in its English title). Although the folktale does not explicitly reference female homosexuality, I argue that the connotation of homosexuality carries over through the film's pervasive deployment of the rabbit symbolism.

In *Nénette et Boni*, point of view is aligned with the brother, Boni. Although the brother's heterosexual fantasy also frames the opening of Sun Koh's short, the film itself, as I argue, is pervasively queer (Doty 1993: xii). From the imagery of the camp dominatrix to the queer symbolism of the rabbit, *Dirty Bitch* can be read as a queer text that, as Teresa de Lauretis (2011) describes, 'not only works against narrativity, the generic pressure of all narrative toward closure and the fulfilment of meaning, but also pointedly disrupts the referentiality of language and the referentiality of images' (244). The loose narrative thread of Sun Koh's short film is overlaid with suggestive imagery and potent symbolism removed from their usual referents. Kewpie dolls make an appearance in the camp, kitsch musical sequence but are transformed from a symbol of European domesticity to one representing Asian cute culture.[6] As an icon of Zhen's unwanted baby, the kewpie doll also represents Zhen's tainted future (she says to her gynaecologist: 'Cut it out! I won't have it come out and disgrace me!').

As the central motif of the film, Zhen's pregnancy invokes Lee Edelman's (2004) critique in *No Future* of the figuring of the child as the Imaginary that secures the future, 'the emblem of futurity's unquestioned value' (4). José Muñoz (2009), arguing conversely of the possibility of queerness as a utopic future, posits that queerness is primarily the realm of futurity and hope' (11). Muñoz insists 'on the essential need for an understanding of queerness as collectivity' (11), invoking Alison Butler's comments on women's (minor) cinema as a form of collective enunciation. *Dirty Bitch* cleverly invites a play with these ideas: its heroine is a seemingly oppositional, isolated and violent individual but the film ultimately offers a celebration of the (queer) bonds between people. The fact that the film is inspired by Denis's film, but is also a 'love letter' to the Singapore censors, creates a multilayered sense of the remake, of a work that is 'reproductive' but also future oriented and open-ended.[7]

Dirty Bitch engages in (at least) two kinds of transnationalism: one is more explicit and comprehendible (that is, as a remake and commissioned homage to a 'major' French filmmaker and indeed an icon of women's cinema, Claire Denis); the other pertains to the film's circulation as part of a less visible, still not-yet-fully conceptualised *minor* transnationalism of women's filmmaking in Asia, particularly as it articulates with the minor transnational circuits of queer Asian cinema. To view *Dirty Bitch* as merely an homage to the Denis original is to risk celebrating only the 'major' transnational exchanges between 'West' and 'East' (France/The Netherlands and Singapore) and the institutional and funding structures that facilitate these dominant flows through elite film festivals such as Rotterdam, at the expense of the minor transnational networks of women's filmmaking and queer Asian cinema that the film also circulates within and that are arguably more (critically) productive. In addition to its debut at Rotterdam, *Dirty Bitch* also screened at the Women Make Waves Film Festival in Taiwan (2010) and at regional Asian film festivals including the Eleventh Cinemanila International Film Festival, Philippines, the Third Balinale International Film Festival, Bali, Indonesia, the Tenth Jeonju International Film Festival, South Korea, and the Fifth INDPanda International Short Film Festival, Hong Kong.

Implicit in a reading of the film as an example of minor transnationalism is a politics of affirmation that invites new collaborations to emerge out of what has come before. *Dirty Bitch* opens up precisely these critical investigations, using the future possibility of the child (figured through the protagonist's pregnancy) to engage women filmmakers' participation in (queer) Asian cinema as a form of potentiality. Rather than simply repeating or remaking Denis's film, Koh's film builds on it with references from Singapore cinema (especially Singapore women's filmmaking), queer

Asian cinema, as well as international art cinema, and in turn provides an invitation for others to respond to her film.

Sun Koh's ethic of collaboration is also evident in her other filmmaking projects, including the 'exquisite corpse' feature she executive produced in 2008. *Lucky 7* is directed by seven Singaporean filmmakers – Sun Koh, Brian Gothong Tan, Boo Junfeng, Ho Tzu Nyen, Tania Sng, K. Rajagopal and Chew Tze Chuan – four of whom are queer. The film consists of seven segments of 10–12 minutes in length. Each filmmaker is only permitted to watch the final minute of the previous segment before making his or her own; that is, building on what came before. The only element that cannot change with each new segment is the lead actor (played by Sunny Pang). Sun Koh says of the film:

> I wanted it to be a showcase of the filmmakers working in Singapore back then. Most important of all, it had to reflect the diversity. So the directors were chosen to be very different from each other. The directors also had to crew on each other's shoot, as a way of fostering active collaboration.[8]

Supporting collaboration was regarded as a circumstantial response to local conditions in the film industry:

> we Singaporean directors are too isolated, working on our own instead of with each other. In contrast with Malaysia's independent filmmakers, who serve on each other's sets and collaborate to a greater degree. The film is experimental, but this allows greater collaboration between the independent filmmakers, allowing them to share ideas as well as technical skills, to complete a feature length film. (Zee 2008)

Although this example occurs within an ostensibly 'national' film culture, this assumption belies the existence of a minor transnationalism at work not only within but also across national contexts. Koh is a strongly transnational filmmaker in the production, circulation and exhibition of her films; she has been highly awarded at festivals internationally and is an alumna of the Berlinale Talent Campus (2003), Busan International Film Festival's Asian Film Academy (2007), and Taiwan's Golden Horse Film Academy (2009). Koh is not unique among Singaporean directors in her international outlook. For a small nation, in geopolitical terms, Singapore necessarily looks outward, and this international orientation can be seen in the many efforts and campaigns of the government's Media Development Authority to attract international collaborators (for example, through the signing of bilateral co-production agreements in film and in sending local talents to be trained abroad before returning to work in the domestic industry). By invoking the collaborative nature of Malaysia's independent film scene, Koh also immediately raises comparisons between Singapore's independent filmmakers and their cross-straits counterparts.

Well beyond the national context, Sun Koh is reprising the 'exquisite corpse' format in a filmic collaboration with six women directors in Sweden, where she was based from 2011 to 2013. This film, entitled *Sweden 7/Sverige 7*, is a collaboration between Koh, Elisabet Gustafsson, Tove Krabo, Jenifer Malmqvist, Jessica Nettelbladt, Stina Bergman and Maja Borg. The first segment of the film was crowdfunded with the hope that the segment could then be used to obtain more funding from other 'official' (governmental and commercial) sources. From the success of her omnibus project in Singapore, Koh is able to facilitate a minor-to-minor cinematic network between small nation film industries and create an opportunity to engage Swedish funding sources. What these filmmaking initiatives of Sun Koh's reveal is a creative embrace of 'in-betweenness' as an attempt to create greater commercial opportunities from an otherwise 'independent' film project and to go beyond the national context to explore transnational connections among women filmmakers. In addition to the collaborative works already discussed, another example of a transnational collaborative film featuring the participation of women filmmakers both from within and outside Asia is *The Children of Srikandi* (2012), directed by the Children of Srikandi Collective and produced by Laura Coppens, Angelika Levi and co-directed by Yulia Dwi Andriyanti. *The Children of Srikandi* is an Indonesia/Germany/Switzerland co-production blending documentary, fiction and experimental elements. The film began as a workshop, which led to a collaborative film project reflecting the directors' lived experiences as queer women in Indonesia. Participants collectively worked as crew members or actresses in each other's film. A film mentioned in Chapter 3, *Vai* (2019) was collaboratively created by nine South Pacific filmmakers: Nicole Whippy, 'Ofa-Ki-Levuka, Guttenbeil-Likiliki, Matasila Freshwater, Amberley Jo Aumua, Mīria George, Marina Alofagia McCartney, Dianna Fuemana and Becs Arahanga. This follows a similar project titled *Waru*, directed by eight Maori filmmakers: Briar Grace-Smith, Casey Kaa, Ainsley Gardiner, Katie Wolfe, Renae Maihi, Chelsea Cohen, Paula Whetu Jones and Awanui Simich-Pene (2017, New Zealand). Collaborative projects like these effectively create a 'feature film' out of a number of collaborative shorts, redefining the meaning of authorship to incorporate emerging forms of transnational solidarity. By using the short film form in this way, Koh challenges the traditional meaning of female authorship, drawing on a minor transnational cinema network across Singapore and beyond.

Other women filmmakers in Singapore employing similar strategies of collaboration in order to develop their creative projects out of a 'minor' cinema include Kaz Cai, one of three female directors from Asia involved in the transnational omnibus film, *Breakfast, Lunch, Dinner* (together with Wang Jing from China and Anocha Suwichakornpong from Thailand, 2010), and Eva Tang, director of award-winning lesbian short *Londres-London*, who has reprised her collaboration with well-known local filmmakers Royston Tan and Victric Thng to make *Old Romances* (2013), a sequel their earlier *Old Places* (2010). Like Sun Koh, Eva Tang was born in Singapore but has lived and studied abroad, in Hong Kong, London and China, leaving a career in journalism to accept a scholarship from the Singapore Film Commission to study film in the United Kingdom. Her short film *While You Sleep* (2002) was shot in the UK, funded by both the British Council and the Singapore Film Commission, and features dialogue entirely in Japanese. Tang's career has also been shaped by success at major film forums: she was the first Singaporean filmmaker to have her student short selected by the Venice Film Festival in 2002 and has also been selected for the Berlinale Talent Campus (2009), Torino FilmLab (2010) and Taipei Golden Horse Film Academy led by Hou Hsiao-Hsien (2010). Yet the minor networks that exist alongside these major accolades are not to be dismissed as trivial or marginal; rather, they allow filmmakers from emergent, smaller film industries in Asia to negotiate limiting national cinema frameworks and to create transnational connections that cross commercial as well as geographical boundaries. Similarly, although Sun Koh's career received a boost after the Rotterdam commission of *Dirty Bitch*, she continues to make 'minor' works in collaboration with other women filmmakers alongside developing her first feature film.

While the active building of ties among women filmmakers in Asian cinema is nascent, it is occurring, building new opportunities and new potentialities beyond the dominant auteurism that feature film accolades at major international film festivals bring. Short films allow for a rethinking of authorship as part of this varied terrain of women's film culture in Asia and amidst the uncertainty of the commercial landscape of global filmmaking.

Conclusion

I have argued that in order to account for the participation of women filmmakers in contemporary Asian cinema using the short film form, we need to recognise the forms of in-betweenness within which these filmmakers exist, as well as the strategies of in-betweenness they employ as a matter of survival and as a means of visibility. As an example of the mode of 'in-betweenness' in which Asian women filmmakers operate, Sun Koh's *Dirty Bitch* reinterprets certain themes, symbols and techniques, not only from the Denis original but also across a minor-to-minor transnational circuit of women's filmmaking and queer Asian cinema. The symbolism of the rabbit employed in Koh's version produces an entirely different (and queer) connotation in the context of Chinese same-sex cultures than it does in Denis's film. Similarly, the use of the male voice-over, which appears in both *Nénette et Boni* and *Dirty Bitch*, is reinterpreted, in the latter, in the form of a Chinese woman lip synching to a French rap song, resulting in a completely altered political and enunciative act. In Sun Koh's 'exquisite corpse' projects, authorship is again reconfigured through an ethic of collaboration, a form of collective enunciation that is as much local as it is transnational.

It is not my intention to participate in a debate about 'Asian' collectivism against 'Western' individualism but rather to emphasise how short films such as Sun Koh's *Dirty Bitch*, and the segments of the omnibus projects discussed, engage strategies of both national *and* transnational connection. Although it is important to remain mindful of local specificities to gendered and sexual identities, there is also value in considering regional solidarities between women filmmakers in Asia (Sinnott 2010: 18). Women in Asia are actively working not only, or predominantly, within the feature film industry but also in a range of other minor film forms. Moreover, they are collaborating, in political as well aesthetic terms, transnationally – from inception and production, to circulation, distribution and exhibition. Thus, it is important to consider the minor transnational networks in which women's filmmaking in Asia exists beyond their national contexts, particularly as it is women's work that further foregrounds the minor transnational circuits of queer Asian cinema and the (double) exclusion of women's queer cinema from the feature and auteurist terrains of international art cinema. The queer film scenes within national contexts in Asia are also generally too small to allow us to think solely in local or national terms, or indeed only in terms of feature films.[9]

The cultural value associated with making a feature film continues to marginalise short film production, positioning the latter outside the realm of traditional 'authorship'. Thus it is necessary to find an analytical frame that can account for, and furthermore to value, this 'minor' form both in terms of practices of reading and as a mode of authorship, as I have sought to do in my reading of *Dirty Bitch* by placing it within a minor transnational network of women's filmmaking and queer culture in Asia.

Promisingly, access to short films from Asia continues to grow via a range of alternative modes of distribution and exhibition. Beyond the various festival circuits, short films are also increasingly being distributed via non-theatrical means including video-sharing sites such as YouTube and Vimeo, and regional examples such as Viddsee, as discussed in the previous chapter.

In an example from public broadcast television, online replays of *The Daughters of Bilitis*, an hour-long KBS (Korean Broadcasting System) drama about three generations of lesbian couples, were pulled three days after the drama aired in August 2011 due to public pressure. Full-length clips have since circulated online in a variety of subtitled forms produced by fans. The circulation of queer films (with subtitling) is even more limited. Through these alternate channels, there is a further possibility for short format works to circulate and to be consumed across and between borders, particularly as dedicated fans will often provide translations and subtitles to texts, anticipating transnational audiences. In the context of the growing regionalisation of Asian cinema and the consolidating inter-Asian circulations of production, distribution, exhibition and reception, it becomes increasingly important to consider changing notions of authorship as these affect women's filmmaking, and in particular to make visible the minor transnational circuits that function 'in-between' dominant modes of authorship.

Notes

1. Chapter 5 was originally published as 'The Minor Transnationalism of Queer Asian Cinema: Female Authorship and the Short Film Format' in *Camera Obscura* 85, 29:1, pp. 33–57. (c) 2014, Camera Obscura. Republished by permission of the copyrightholder, and the present publisher, Duke University Press.
2. The Singapore Film Commission's now defunct Short Film Grant supported over seventy short films in 2006, compared to only eleven in 1998. The definition of a short film for the purposes of the grant was any film under thirty minutes. In September 2011 Singapore's Media Development Authority overhauled its grants schemes, replacing them with five new schemes covering development, production, marketing, and talent assistance. Short films will now be funded under one of these schemes. See <https://www.imda.gov.sg/news-and-events/Media-Room/archived/mda/Media-Releases/2011/fact-sheet--mda-grant-schemes> (last accessed 15 September 2020).
3. See <https://www.objectifs.com.sg/ps_sunkoh/> (last accessed 15 September 2020).
4. All have made at least one film (feature length or short) with homosexual characters and/or themes: Royston Tan with his short film *Anniversary* (2009), Loo Zi-han's *Solos* (2007) and Boo Jun-feng's *Tanjong Rhu* (2008).
5. See <https://vimeo.com/72635260> (last accessed 19 September 2020).
6. The Kewpie doll is based on Rose O'Neill's illustrations for the *Ladies' Home Journal* in 1909. These dolls were first produced in Germany (made out of bisque and celluloid, and later hard plastic). The dolls are popular not only in Europe and America, but also in Asia, especially Japan, where they exist within local *kawaii* (cute) culture.

7. See   <https://www.berlinale-talents.de/bt/project/profile/54523>   (last accessed 19 September 2020).

8. See <http://www.fundedbyme.com/projects/2012/01/sweden-7-sverige-7/> (last accessed 14 September 2020).

9. To provide a sense of the size of the national queer film scenes within Asia, the following list provides a survey of feature length productions (over sixty minutes running time) with lesbian main characters made by women directors in Asia between 2000 and 2012, a period in which queer cinema in Asia was growing strongly – China: *Fish and Elephant/Yu he Daxiang* (Li Yu, 2002), *Lost in You/Lalala* (Zhu Yiye, 2006), *Love Mime/Xiaoshu de xiatian* (Zhu Yiye, 2008), *The Box/He zi* (Ying Weiwei, 2001, documentary); Hong Kong: *Butterfly/Hu Die* (Yan Yan Mak, 2004), *Ho Yuk: Let's Love Hong Kong/Ho Yuk* (Yau Ching, 2002); Taiwan: *Corners/Si Jiao-Luo* (Zero Chou and Hoho Liu, 2001), *Drifting Flowers/Piao lang qing chun* (Zero Chou, 2008), *Incidental Journey/Haijiao tianya* (Chen Jofei, 2001), *Love Me, If You Can/Fei yue qin hai* (Alice Wang, 2003), *Love's Lone Flower/Gu Lian Hua* (Tsao Jui-Yuan, 2005), *Spider Lilies/Ci qing* (Zero Chou, 2007); Japan: *Love/Juice* (Kaze Shindo, 2000). *Sugar Sweet* (Desiree Lim, 2001); Thailand: *She: Their Love Story/Ruang Rak Rawang Ther* (Sranya Noithai, 2012), *Yes or No? So, I Love You/Yak Rak Ko Rak Loei* (Sarasawadee Wongsompetch, 2010); Singapore: *Women Who Love Women: Conversations in Singapore* (Lim Mayling, 2007, documentary); Indonesia: *Children of Srikandi/Anak-Anak Srikandi* (The Children of Srikandi Collective, 2012, documentary/fiction hybrid). I have tried to be as exhaustive as possible in constructing this list but may have missed some titles. If the list were to include lesbian-themed films directed by men it would be much longer, and of course new films are being made every year. Not all of the directors listed are queer, although several are.

CHAPTER 6

Archiving Asian Cinema

This chapter explores issues of archiving and digital preservation in light of changing exhibition strategies, with a focus on the important roles played by the Southeast Asia-Pacific Audiovisual Archive Association (SEAPAVAA), the Asian Film Archive (AFA), and the Network for the Promotion of Asian Cinema (NETPAC). The issue of archiving is considered more broadly to encompass not only the physical preservation of films from across Asia in physical (and digital) archives, but also journals, societies and other forums that have sought to preserve scholarly interpretations of Asian films to provide a regional screen history. As mentioned in the Introduction, scholarship on Asian cinema as a regional cinema is scant prior to the 1990s. Studies of individual national cinemas and auteurs did exist; however, within the disciplinary context of film studies internationally, Asian cinema did not emerge as a relatively coherent disciplinary field until about thirty years ago. The seminal journal *Asian Cinema*, which provided a home for much of the early scholarship in the field, had been published since 1995 by the Asian Cinema Studies Society under the stewardship of John A. Lent. In 2012, *Asian Cinema* was transferred to British commercial publisher Intellect, marking a new era in the publication of Asian cinema scholarship. Around the same time, in 2011, the Busan International Film Festival (BIFF) held its inaugural Busan Film Forum, a unique academic and industrial forum focused on new developments in Asian cinema scholarship. What models of a shared film heritage are being afforded by these critical and institutional efforts at maintenance, preservation, education and scholarly discussion across Asia? How do newer developments, considered against longer-running associations such as NETPAC, which has been in existence for thirty years, mark the significant changes that have occurred in the advancement of Asian cinema, and Asian cinema studies, during the last three decades? What is at stake in archiving for the future of Asian cinema as a regional cinema?

The practical techniques of archiving (generally) are beyond the scope of this chapter. Instead, I focus on how archiving has played a part in the formation of a regional conception of Asian cinema. Asian film archives (and the archiving of scholarship, for example in the *Asian Cinema* newsletter and then journal) are shaping our sense of Asian cinema beyond a collection of distinct national cinemas. Previous chapters have explored issues of (co-)production, remaking, distribution and circulation of Asian cinema. In Chapter 4, I discussed how the Internet and streaming sites such as Viddsee function as an informal archive, especially for a cinema that is in digital and short form.[1] This chapter turns to consider the institutional consolidation of Asian cinema. It does this by tracing the changing scholarship on Asian cinema (including the growing currency of the term 'Asian cinema' to refer to a regional formation) as well as questions of how to archive a regional cinema outside of national film preservation strategies.

Film Archiving in Asia: Networking, Access and Preservation

Archives are repositories for the organisation and storage of media, from printed text to film and digital material. The archive itself is a medium – of storage – functioning both to preserve and to make available and accessible. Through its preservative function, an archive is distinct from a mere collection. Archives of Asian cinema have an important role to play in the preservation of the cinema at the same time as they help create awareness of the rich audiovisual histories of the region through access, outreach and education initiatives. A key issue is how archives can be forward-looking in shaping the future of Asian cinema at the same time as they preserve and memorialise sometimes fragile and lost histories of cinema. Marlene Manoff suggests that an archive simultaneously 'affirms the past, present, and future' (2004: 12) – preserving records from the past and embodying the promise of the future. It is these multiple functions, arguably in tension and certainly in constant negotiation, which Jacques Derrida has captured in his statement that every archive is by nature both revolutionary and conservative: '[an archive] is liberal in its general purpose as a repository, whose function is to serve (either society or some part thereof) . . . Its conservative character derives from its need to maintain order, and the inherent necessity of caution and protection against outside forces, decay, and entropy' (1996: 7). Derrida's notion of 'archivization' suggests that the 'methods for transmitting information shape the nature of the knowledge that can be produced' (Manoff 2004: 12). Thus archives hold an important part of the key in determining how much of Asian cinema, and which aspects of it, are available to audiences and therefore what can be viewed, discussed, and studied. As Derrida (Derrida and Prenowitz 1995) rightly points out, 'archivization produces as much as it records the event' (17). Where archives are located, what they hold, and how accessible they make themselves, are all important factors in a consideration of Asian cinema's regional identity.

Institutionalised film archiving began in the 1930s, and most film and television archives are located either in Europe or in North America (Edmondson 2000: 148). The first film archives in Asia were established in Iran (in 1949), China (in 1958) and India (in 1964) (Ho 2001: 2). Hong Kong, one of the most prolific film production centres in the world, only established its film archive in 1993. Film archives in Asia are on the whole much younger than their Euro-American counterparts, yet they have grown significantly in size and number over the last several years, due largely to the commitment of particular individuals and teams (Ho 2001). This growth of archives in the region can also be attributed to technological changes (notably access to digital technologies) that, while not specific to Asia, have certainly been felt intently in Asia.

Ray Edmondson, former Deputy Director of the Australian National Film and Sound Archive and founding president of SEAPAVAA, notes that there are several challenges that face the region in terms of archiving: from technical issues, to more philosophical and theoretical concerns. Preservation challenges to many of the archives in Asia are associated with 'climate, communication, resources, development and training' (Edmondson 1997: 2). These range from vinegar syndrome and rusty cans from the tropical weather to a need for skills growth.[2] All of these require co-ordinated efforts, for example through training and staff exchange, sharing of facilities (e.g. storing collection material on behalf of another archive), and complementation of resources and capabilities. The loss of Asia's film heritage, particularly before 1960, and the limited possibilities of its retrieval are a reality, but what of the future? Edmondson (2014) writes:

> Asia/Pacific is a large region and contact with each other is not always easy – let alone practical or economic. Isolation, and the fact that the international bodies in our field tend to be based in Europe, has inhibited development and networking in the region.

What emerges is the necessity for greater collaboration between Asia's film archives. A sign of the pressing need for collaborative approaches to archiving in Asia was born with the establishment of the Southeast Asia-Pacific Audiovisual Archive Association in 1996.

Southeast Asia-Pacific Audiovisual Archive
Association (SEAPAVAA)

The idea of forming a regional association for archiving was developed out
of a 'shared sense of need' (Edmondson 2014), first discussed at a workshop
on ASEAN Audio/Video and Film Retrieval, Restoration and Archiving
in Manila in 1993, and followed up at the ASEAN Training Seminar on
Film and Video Archive Management in Canberra in May 1995. Thus the
regional intergovernmental organisation of the Association of Southeast
Asian Nations (ASEAN), comprising Indonesia, Thailand, Singapore, the
Philippines, Malaysia, Vietnam, Brunei, Cambodia, Myanmar and Laos,
has been central to efforts to promote audiovisual archiving in the region.
Under the purview of the ASEAN, the collection, preservation and accessibility of audiovisual heritage from member countries are treated as collective
concerns, to be shared within a broader network.

SEAPAVAA was formally launched in Manila, the Philippines, in February 1996, with twenty founding members from across Southeast Asia and
Australasia (Edmondson 1997: 2).[3] The current president of SEAPAVAA
is Irene Lim of the National Archives of Singapore, who holds this post
from 2017 to 2020. The stated objectives of the Association are to 'provide
a regional forum for addressing common issues and concerns related to the
collection and preservation of, and provision of access to, the audiovisual
heritage of member countries', and specifically, to 'promote awareness and
development of audiovisual archiving at the national, regional and international levels'.[4] The Association also aims to establish 'regionwide standards, methods and procedures' and 'encourage communication and mutual
assistance, including the sharing of knowledge, skills, services, resources and
experiences among others' (SEAPAVAA Constitution, 'Article II: Objects').
Thus, SEAPAVAA provides a regional forum and network for the archives
in the region whereby the capabilities of individual member countries are
strengthened through shared research, training and technology. As Ray
Edmondson (1999) notes, 'the spirit of SEAPAVAA since it began . . .
[is] discovering how, by working collectively, we can achieve far more than
we could ever accomplish separately' (104).

The Association's collective approach to the region's film heritage is
achieved through a range of means, from annual conferences, to the provision of a Resource Centre, to the publication of books and articles, including
AV Archives Bulletin – the SEAPAVAA newsletter. SEAPAVAA's Resource
Centre services both professionals and the general public interested in
learning more about audiovisual archiving in Asia. A key book published
by the organisation is *Film in Southeast Asia: Views from the Region*, edited

by (now retired) film scholar David Hanan. The book was developed collaboratively, with two host archives, Vietnam and Australia, assuming the cost of publication, and authors and editors providing individual contributions and services (Hanan 2001: 26).

Annual conferences have been held by the Association where much of this kind of networking and sharing can take place regularly. Since its inauguration in Manila in 1996, member countries have taken turns hosting the Association's annual conferences. The conferences are not restricted to SEAPAVAA members and are open to all.[5] After the first conference in Manila there were meetings held in Jakarta and then Hanoi, and most recently in Bangkok in 2018 (on the theme 'AV Archiving Beyond Boundaries'), and in Noumea, New Caledonia, in 2019 (on the theme 'Memory, History, and Archives'). Publications and reports arising from annual conferences serve as important resources and references, and are sometimes printed in the local language as well as in English.[6] As Ray Edmondson (1997) notes, an annual meeting helps to develop relationships between member countries and encourages ongoing sharing of information and communication; it also has the 'strategic value of drawing attention to audiovisual archiving in the host city' (2).

There are economic, political and historical linkages that tie the member institutions together, enabling and facilitating greater sharing, co-operation, and the building of a professional community and communication network. Many member institutions are former European colonies, or have been under a period of American power (Edmondson 2000: 151). Most member countries have tropical climates, with implications for storing and preserving collections. However, there is also significant cultural, political, geographic and economic diversity in the region. A key limitation to data sharing and to other forms of communication between member institutions is that there is no shared language (besides the colonial language of English). Despite this challenge, SEAPAVAA has worked towards the adoption of region-wide standards and a shared cataloguing database:

> Multi-lingual cataloguing, which can be done at varying levels of complexity, is one approach that is being tried in archives within the ASEAN countries. Films are catalogued in the national language of the country concerned, and – selectively and at varying levels – in English, which is the official language of contact within ASEAN. This offers the potential of developing, over time, a regional database of archive holdings: and hence, of minimising duplication of work, and maximising the potential use of collections by the largest possible marketplace. (Edmondson 2014)

SEAPAAVA represents an important development in regional co-operation in relation to Asian cinema, addressing a lack of recognition of the archiving of films both in their home countries and internationally through greater regional co-operation and exchange. As a collective, the Association brings greater visibility to the issue of film archiving in Asia beyond the dominant Euro-American bias. While there may be vast differences between some member institutions in terms of state involvement, resourcing, and film culture, these differences can be seen as strengths when taking a broader regional perspective.

Edmondson (2008) asks:

> Were we right to set up SEAPAVAA? Yes. Why? The most important reason is prob-
> ably the least obvious one. In 1995 our region was more or less a black hole on the
> international landscape. The audiovisual archiving world knew little about our insti-
> tutions and our audiovisual heritage, and we weren't part of the agenda. We were
> below the radar. That's all changed now. Even if SEAPAVAA had done nothing else,
> it made our region visible. (29)

Asian Film Archive (AFA)

A newer archive taking a regional approach to Asian cinema is the Asian Film Archive (AFA), a non-profit organisation based in Singapore and founded by Bee Thiam Tan and Kirsten Tan following discussions at a Holland Village coffee shop in 2005. The AFA was born out of the question, '[w]here do Southeast Asian films go once they have completed their festival run?' (Tan 2015b: 41). In its first year, the AFA operated out of an office at the National University of Singapore and has since grown in size and influence.

The AFA has a high profile International Advisory Board, with Singaporean filmmaker Glen Goei the Chair of the Board.[7] Bee Thiam Tan remained the executive director of the AFA from its inception until 2010, when he was succeeded by Karen Chan, the current executive director. The Asian Film Archive became an institutional member of SEAPAVAA in 2015 and hosted the Nineteenth SEAPAVAA Conference with the theme 'Advocate, Connect, Engage'. In 2017 the AFA became the first Singaporean associate member of the International Federation of Film Archives (FIAF).

The AFA's mission is 'to save, explore and share the art of Asian Cinema'.[8] In particular, it 'develops, cares for, and interprets a collection that reflects the history, society, and the art of film amongst Asian countries and about Asians'.[9] Operating under four main principles, the Archive has a *preservation* and collection function, focusing on culturally important works of independent Asian filmmakers; a *promotion* function, to build cultural value and appreciation of Asian films through research, publications and education; an *access* function, opening up access to Asian film resources for educational (teaching and research) purposes; and a *nurturing* function, encouraging new audiences to appreciate Asian films through curated screenings and discussions.[10]

Given the broad remit of films the AFA could potentially collect, the Archive has developed guidelines around its collection of more than 2,100 titles, focusing on Asian 'classics' and contemporary independent films from Southeast Asia. The following guiding questions suggest the scope of the AFA's collecting policy:

1. Is the film shot in Asia or an Asian production?
2. Is the film about Asian societies, subject matters, or characters?
3. Does the film impact or show a relationship to any Asian peoples?
4. Does the film demonstrate a distinct style thought to be associated with Asian films?
5. Can the film be regarded as part of an Asian 'national cinema'?

Beyond scope, there are also questions of urgency (around the physical condition of the film, its format and number of available copies, and whether the film is preserved in any other archive), and a film's quality and significance (whether the film has historical, social, political, cultural or aesthetic significance to Asia).[11]

While the majority of films archived are from Singapore, the collection also includes titles from Malaysia, Indonesia, the Philippines and Vietnam, covering a gap for films that are not collected in other film archives in Southeast Asia.[12] The Archive also includes independent (underground) cinema from China that may not otherwise be collected elsewhere.[13] In her reflection on the Asian Film Archive after five years of its existence, Patricia Zimmerman (2010) notes that although many of the films in the Archive's collection

> receive accolades at internationally prominent film festivals like Berlin, Hong Kong, Oberhausen, Pusan, and Rotterdam, they survive almost exclusively at these festivals, excised from theatrical distribution and non-cinephile audiences. To solve this problem, AFA not only aggressively collects these films, but develops imaginative outreach strategies to expose the works to new audiences. They screen at schools, polytechnics, universities and museums. They partner with other institutions to do programming and run a variety of workshops on cinema literacy, archiving, film and culture, filmmakers, and the process of filmmaking. (3)

The AFA has developed strong partnerships with government agencies in Singapore including the National Archives of Singapore, the Singapore Film

Commission, the Media Development Authority, and the National Library Board. In 2014, the AFA became a subsidiary of the National Library Board, a move that academic and former Chair Kenneth Paul Tan characterised as a 'radical decision', but also a 'wise' one: '[t]oday, we worry much less about having to raise funds just to stay alive and do the basic work of an archive' (K. P. Tan 2015: 11). Of the films in its collection, more than 500 titles are available for public access at the library@esplanade and the National Library in Singapore, and through their online channel on Viddsee. Because the Archive began as a small, volunteer-run enterprise, these partnerships have afforded access to facilities, technology and space that would not otherwise have been possible for the Archive's work. Collaborations with other institutions, including universities and schools, have also allowed the AFA to raise awareness and attract donations (K. P. Tan 2015: 10).

Thus, beyond its preservation function, the Asian Film Archive has placed significant emphasis on access in order to increase audiences' appreciation of films from Asia. The Archive's outreach programmes encourage film literacy and seek to find new audiences for films in its collection. One of its key outreach programmes is Moving Minds, a programme that aims to increase film literacy among youth, and incorporate films from Asia into the school curriculum. The Educators' Workshop series, launched in 2006, has developed programmes such as CineOdeon (2008) that mentors students on film programming. The AFA also runs a 'salon series' of film screenings and panel discussions entitled *Reframe*, which encourages dialogue on issues surrounding cinema (topics covered include #nostalgia, examining the trend of nostalgia in Singaporean films, and issues of migration and transience), and *Alt Screen*, showing Asian documentaries with perspectives on global issues, in conjunction with the National Library Board.[14] The Archive runs additional film screenings at the National Archives of Singapore, including a screening of eight Asian horror films in April 2019 (including *Orang Minyak* (1958), starring P. Ramlee, and its Hong Kong remake, *Oily Maniac* (1976)).

An annual film festival run by the AFA, *Asian Restored Classics*, showcases classics of Asian cinema that have been restored for modern audiences. Its first edition in 2016 featured Akira Kurosawa's *Ran* (1985) and King Hu's *Dragon Inn* (1967). The AFA also houses the Cathay-Keris Malay Classics from the 1950s–1970s, which were inscribed into the UNESCO-funded 'Memory of the World' Asia-Pacific Regional Register in 2014, for films considered historically, culturally and artistically significant (UNESCO Bangkok 2017).[15]

Kenneth Paul Tan reflects on the naming of the Archive at its establishment, and considers whether 'Singapore' should have been included in its title as the first film archive based in the nation, or whether it was strategically more inclusive to refer to it as a 'Southeast Asian' or 'Asian' film archive, given Singapore's place within the region. Tan (2015) asks:

> By naming it the 'Asian Film Archive', who are the filmmakers and the archive's other research and institutional clientele that it is supposed to appeal to? What is the cultural and historical significance of archiving a film within the cultural rubric of 'Asian'? What categorical spaces does it open up, or close off? What kinds of material and financial support can such a moniker garner? What sort of future does an 'Asian' institution as such have? (40)

The founding members settled on the name 'Asian Film Archive' in the belief that it

> reflected the geographically and culturally expansive possibilities that the name signifies in this digital era of cinematic production, distribution, consumption, and preservation. It links the institution and the Singapore cultural scene to the larger networks of Southeast Asian, East Asian, diasporic Asian, and transnational Asian cinemas. (Tan 2015a: 40)

While Singapore remains the locus and hub of the Archive, it is very much a regionally oriented endeavour. Ray Edmondson, a member of the Asian Film Archive's International Advisory Board, notes that the AFA 'broke the established global mould' of archives, which are 'typically the creations of national governments or of cultural or educational institutions, like universities' (2015: 43). SEAPAVAA, for instance, consists mainly of government-created national archives, such as the Vietnam Film Institute, the Hong Kong Film Archive and the Thai Film Archive, with a predominantly 'national' collecting focus – of films about their own country or with a significant influence on the community's cultural memory. Whilst collectively SEAPAVAA has a regional focus, individual member institutions are still nationally oriented. Uniquely, the AFA:

> is not constrained by a national focus but by the word 'Asian' – a term that is clear but not precise, and which can therefore mean different things to different people. It has both cultural and geographic connotations without being obviously prescriptive. But it is prescriptive enough to mean something other than the European or American films which have traditionally dominated the global study of cinema. Hence, it claims its own cultural space . . . There is no European film archive. There is no American film archive. But there is an Asian Film Archive. Just ponder on the potential of that concept. (Edmondson 2015: 43)

While the AFA cannot be comprehensive and can only be selective, the key point is that 'it approaches its task from an Asian rather than a national mind set, and that in turn bears on the way it researches, contextualizes and presents films from its own, and other, collections' (Edmondson 2015: 43).

Through their symposia, publications, film screenings and critical discussions, film archives like SEAPAVAA and the AFA have also contributed to the scholarly debate and research of Asian cinema, beyond the physical and digital archiving, and promotion and appreciation of the films themselves.

Promotion and Scholarship: Network for the Promotion of Asian Cinema (NETPAC)

NETPAC is an organisation devoted to the promotion of Asian film, consisting of over twenty-nine member countries and involving filmmakers, academics, festival organisers, distributors and exhibitors. Its two current presidents are Ashley Ratnavibhushana and Philip Cheah.[16] NETPAC was founded by Aruna Vasudev in 1990 following a conference on Asian cinema held in New Delhi. At that time, Asian cinema was still fairly unknown in the region and internationally. NETPAC has a strong presence on the international film festival circuit and presents an award for Best Asian Film at film festivals in Busan, Singapore, Jeonju, Kerala and Kazakhstan in Asia, and outside Asia at Berlin, Locarno, Karlovy Vary, Rotterdam, Vesoul, Brisbane and Honolulu. Registered in Brisbane, Australia, with the Secretariat based in Sri Lanka, NETPAC encompasses the film cultures of East, Southeast, South and West Asia (Afghanistan, Iran), as well as Australia.

As part of its promotion of Asian cinema, NETPAC has published several books, including *Asian Film Journeys – Selections from Cinemaya 1988–2004*, edited by Rashmi Doraiswamy and Latika Padgaonkar (2010). It also features festival reports, articles, and other publications on its website.[17] The journal associated with NETPAC, *Cinemaya: The Asian Film Magazine*, was founded in 1988 in New Delhi by Aruna Vasudev. *Cinemaya* is a pioneering English-language resource on Asian cinema, and includes interviews, reports of Asian films at international festivals and reports of Asian film festivals. For sixteen years it was at the forefront of the promotion Asian filmmaking regionally and internationally. As Chris Berry (1990) notes, *Cinemaya* was not the only new Asian cinema journal or magazine. *East-West Film Journal* and *Asian Cinema* (which will be discussed next) also provided English-language forums that catered to the growing interest in films from Asia. However, *Cinemaya* was the only one of these journals to be published *in* Asia (and distributed internationally). Straddling *East-West Film Journal*'s focus on more scholarly publications, and *Asian Cinema*'s membership-based journal associated with the Asian Cinema Studies Society, which until 2013 was based mostly in North America, *Cinemaya*'s location within Asia meant that it was able to report the most recent happenings in the region as they occurred (Berry 1990). *Cinemaya* thus played a significant historical role in the publishing of scholarship on Asian cinema from within Asia, although the publishing centres of academic journals are mostly located in the UK/ Europe and North America, and this is where much of the scholarship on Asian cinema is published, even if it increasingly originates from Asia-based scholars.

Asian Cinema Journal

Asian Cinema began as a publication affiliated with the Asian Cinema Studies Society (ACSS), which was founded in 1984 by Mira Reym Binford at the annual meeting of the Association for Asian Studies (AAS) in 1984. The first Asian Cinema Conference, held in Athens, Ohio, in 1988 included scholars from AAS and the Society for Cinema Studies (SCS, now Society for Cinema and Media Studies, SCMS) working together under the ACSS banner (Lent 2011b: 3). Early publications associated with the society were first produced in the form of newsletters. Since 1995 the society began publishing *Asian Cinema* under the editorship of John A. Lent. For sixteen years it was published twice yearly. In an interview with Cherian George, Lent (2013) notes that in the early years of publication the journal was published very quickly, and without institutional support (with Lent investing his own money into the publication). From 1994 to 2012 the journal was published from Lent's home in Pennsylvania and the journal was not peer reviewed (Lent 2012b: 105). Given the nascency of the field, Lent notes, '[i]t's a young field of study and, until recently, to whom would I send the manuscripts? Now, I could. But when I started 15 years ago I would be hard-pressed to find people who would know about these areas. That's not the case now' (2013: 304). In 2012 the journal was passed on to UK publisher Intellect, with new editors Gary Bettinson and See Kam Tan overseeing reappointed editorial and advisory boards and a peer-review system for the journal. Past issues of the journal, before its move to Intellect, are now available electronically through Intellect's website (Bettinson and Tan 2012: 3).

At the Eleventh Asian Cinema Studies Society Conference, the theme of 'Post-Asia' was highlighted. Taking issue with the limitations imposed by regionalism, other approaches, such as genre and stardom, were foregrounded in the conference's themes. Ien Ang's keynote paper, 'Not yet post-Asian: paradoxes of identity and knowledge in transitional times', asserts that if the twenty-first century is one of burgeoning Asian supremacy, then Asia is 'still properly to come' (Ang 2014). In his report on the conference, Robert Hyland (2014) notes, '[w]hat is at stake in the notion of de-regionalized cinema is a reorientation and reconsideration of the relationship between the nation and the region, rather than denying the presence of both on the cultural products' (244). The archives discussed above, from SEAPAVAA to the Asian Film Archive, to publication forums focused on the study of Asian cinema, constantly keep this tension and relationship between nation and region in mind, using the advantages of a regional approach to interrogate and/or reinforce national film culture.

Conclusion: The Pasts and Futures of Archiving

As can be seen by the dates that these film journals and archives were launched, it was really only in the 1990s that Asian cinema as an institutional category began to be established, and even later that Asian cinema can be regarded as a regional cinema with interconnections and collaborations across the national industries that make up the region. Lent published *The Asian Film Industry* in 1990 and Dmitris Eleftheriotis and Gary Needham published *Asian Cinemas: A Reader and Guide* in 2006 (with Markus Nornes noting that the appearance of the Reader marked 'a sure sign that a field has taken root' (2013: 183)). Nornes (2013) adds:

> the publishing of regional studies has markedly intensified in subsequent years. A community has formed, if still marked by the subregionalizations of South, South East, and East. It is at these [conference] panels that one palpably senses an increasing integration of Asian cinema studies. At the same time, it is notable that most panels and books are configured in a national cinema mode. (183)

This is slowly changing. In spite of this rich field of criticism and debate, it is surprising that consolidated research on the changing landscape of Asian cinema scholarship that draws together historical and more recent developments in research and criticism is virtually non-existent.

Archiving is a key site in which we can see the formation of a regional Asian cinema through the organisation and storage of Asian films, as well as sharing and making accessible Asian cinema and media. Not only do archives preserve, it is equally important, if not more so, that they provide access to their collections. What has been integral to a regional view of Asian cinema is making films from the region more visible and accessible – not only to those in the region but also to the rest of the world.[18] As David Hanan (2001) notes, film archives 'keep a sense of film history alive' (23). They also (re)invigorate its futures.

Scholarship on Asian cinema has also grown, from seminal journals such as *Cinemaya* and *Asian Cinema*, with their changing fates and (re)incarnations functioning like a living, breathing archive, providing accessibility and a forum in which to consider, discuss, and debate. One of the more recent publications on Asian cinema to be produced is *Nang*, a glossy, limited run (ten-issue) magazine dedicated to films from Asia.[19] *Nang* is an independent publication, with Davide Cazzaro as the editor-in-chief. *Nang* relies heavily on visual imagery, and is published twice yearly over a period of five years, produced in South Korea and Italy and printed in Sweden 'on fine papers', in the English language. The journal promotes itself as being 'for knowledge, inspiration, and enjoyment . . . [aiming] to broaden the horizons of what the moving image is in Asia'.[20] Publications and scholarship on Asian cinema continue to diversify with the growing regional identity of the cinema and this requires new ways of recording its pasts and futures.

Notes

1. Kuhu Tanvir (2013) has described the network of pirated films (VCDs and DVDs) as a mobile, networked archive of cinema brought about by changes in digital technology (writing on Indian cinema specifically). Tanvir comments, '[t]he cinephile is at the centre of this archive, because he is one of several archivists contributing to this global phenomenon in productive or destructive ways. There is then a fundamental change in the constitution of the archivist and the archive, as the fluid, pirate, and networked archive of cinema poses a potent challenge to the contours of control wielded by a state-run archive' (116).

2. Vinegar syndrome refers to the process of cellulose triacetate degradation, which releases acetic acid, the key ingredient in vinegar and the cause of its characteristic smell. This process is hastened under hot, humid conditions, and therefore poses a particular concern in Southeast Asian nations.

3. See also https://seapavaa.net/history. SEAPAVAA's member institutions are Australia, Cambodia, China, Fiji, Hong Kong, Indonesia, Japan, Laos, Malaysia, New Caledonia, New Zealand, Papua New Guinea, Philippines, Singapore, South Korea, Thailand, Taiwan, and Vietnam. In the Association's Constitution, 'Southeast Asia-Pacific' refers to 'the geographic region embracing the members and observers of the Association of Southeast Asian Nations (ASEAN), Australasia, Melanesia, Micronesia and Polynesia'; 'audiovisual' refers to 'moving images and/or sounds, recorded on any medium including but not limited to, film, magnetic tape, or disc, and any other medium now known or yet to be invented'; and 'archive' refers to 'an organisation or unit of an organisation, which is focused on collecting, managing, preserving, and providing access to or making use of a collection of

audiovisual and related materials. The term includes any government, non-government, commercial, and cultural organisations which pursue these four functions.'

4. SEAPAVAA Objectives, available at <https://seapavaa.net/objectives/> (last accessed 12 September 2020).

5. SEAPAVAA Annual conferences, available at <https://seapavaa.net/annual-conferences/> (last accessed 12 September 2020).

6. English is the official language of the Association (SEAPAVAA Constitution).

7. The AFA's International Advisory Board includes filmmakers Apichatpong Weerasethakul and Hou Hsiao-Hsien, scholars Chris Berry, Chua Beng Huat, David Bordwell and Aruna Vasudev (President of NETPAC), and archivist Ray Edmondson among others; see <https://www.asianfilmarchive.org/people/> (last accessed 12 September 2020).

8. Asian Film Archive, <https://www.asianfilmarchive.org> (last accessed 12 September 2020).

9. Asian Film Archive, <https://www.asianfilmarchive.org/about/mission/>(last accessed 12 September 2020).

10. Asian Film Archive, <https://www.asianfilmarchive.org/about/mission/> (last accessed 12 September 2020).

11. Asian Film Archive, <https://www.asianfilmarchive.org/collection/collection-guidelines/> (last accessed 12 September 2020).

12. The AFA has over 2,100 titles in its collection today. About 55 per cent are Singaporean films while the rest come mainly from Malaysia, the Philippines and Indonesia. The AFA coordinates and shares resources with each nation's film archive organisation (Lui 2017).

13. The Archive also commissions films; in 2015, the AFA commissioned *Fragment*, a film anthology by Lav Diaz, U-Wei Haji Saari, Sherman Ong and others.

14. Asian Film Archive, <https://www.asianfilmarchive.org/programmes/> (last accessed 12 September 2020).

15. Bee Thiam Tan, former executive director of the AFA, stated that 'an archive is not a building. It is a memory institution' (cited in Zimmerman 2010). Former Chair of the AFA, Kenneth Paul Tan (2015), concurs: 'We have always viewed our archive as a living thing, not a tomb for well embalmed films' (7).

16. NETPAC website, <http://netpacasia.org/homepage> (last accessed 12 September 2020).

17. NETPAC's website has some search capabilities in Thai, Korean and Chinese; <https://netpacasia.org/homepage> (last accessed 12 September 2020).

18. The theme of the 2009 SEAPAVAA conference held in Bandung and Jakarta, Indonesia, was 'Collection and Access Development: Two Sides of the Same Coin'.

19. There is a limited print run of 1,500 copies of each issue with no reprints.

20. Nang magazine, <https://www.nangmagazine.com/about> (last accessed 12 September 2020).

CHAPTER 7

Asian Cinema in 3D: Regional Technical Innovation

This final chapter turns to the topic of 3D film technologies and, closer to my home, examines the question of whether, and how, Australia can be considered a part of the region Asia when it comes to taking a regional view on Asian cinema. As a European settler colony, Australia is generally considered a 'Western' country and has an uneasy relationship to the region Asia, even though film collaborations have long taken place between Australia and Asia (Khoo et al. 2013), with more recent official co-production agreements in place with Singapore, China and South Korea, and under negotiation with Malaysia and India.[1] I have spent much of my academic career exploring Asian and Australian connections in film but have largely avoided this question in this book thus far. Rather indulgently, this chapter provides a perspective on regional Asian cinema from the place from which I work and write.

It does not seem particularly innovative to say that the future of Asian cinema lies to a large degree on the regional development of new technologies. The use of digital technologies, from digital video (DV) cameras to social media and online streaming, 'make the production and sharing of moving images considerably easier than was the case under prior technological conditions' (Wagner et al. 2014: 11). Writing specifically on Chinese cinema, Wagner et al. (2014) refer to this contemporary period as 'iGeneration cinema'. The authors explore how Chinese cinema in the age of the digital is inscribed by personal experiences in and through technology, and how this is reinvigorating and re-inventing the cinema (16). As signalled throughout the book, I approach the word 'technology' expansively, in Chapters 2 and 3, to consider co-productions and omnibus films as technologies that can potentiate new forms of encounter and expression in the region, in Chapters 4 and 5 to examine online streaming and the circulation of short films, and in Chapter 6 to explore the digitisation of archiving and technologies of collaboration. This chapter continues to explore the ways in which technology shapes our understanding of the regional processes between Asia's film industries, in this case through changing consumer trends and audience experiences impacted upon by the development of digital film technologies.

From Wire Technology to Digital Interruptions: Histories of Computer-generated Imagery in Asian Cinema[2]

Each incarnation of a technological advancement in the cinema reveals a longer historical preoccupation cinema has had with technological effects. Digital cinema is arguably a return to one of cinema's earlier phantasms, animation (Manovich 1995). Computer animation – the process used to digitally create animated images for film, video games, television, art, and other media – is also commonly referred to as computer-generated imagery, or CGI for short. CGI is usually taken to refer to 3D computer graphics, although it can also refer to two-dimensional (2D) static or dynamic visual scenes. Hong Kong films in particular were famed for their earlier use of wire technology combined with green screen effects in martial arts films, spawning a genre in the 1980s and 1990s known as 'wire-fu' films (a combination of wire work and kung fu). Notable examples include *A Chinese Ghost Story/Sien lui yau wan* (Ching Siu-tung, 1987), *The Swordsman/Siu ngo gong woo* (Ching Siu-tung, 1990), *The Bride with White Hair/ Bak fat moh lui zyun* (Ronny Yu, 1993) and *Butterfly and Sword/ San Lau Sing Woo Dip Gim* (Michael Mak, 1993). The body is still viscerally present in these films, as a sometimes-clunky body jerking through the air, attempting to land, or alternatively as a graceful body floating majestically, and quite believably (within the story world), into the darkness of night. Other Chinese cinemas have also utilised the wire-work technique, including Ang Lee's *Crouching Tiger, Hidden Dragon* (2000), which elevated the art to the extent that it appeared effortless. This film was aided by significant developments in special effects and digital technology that was not available to most films until the late 1990s. From earlier wire-fu films (where most of the effects were created on-camera using wires and pulleys), there was a shift towards a predominance of post-production effects and computer-generated imagery.

Wire-enhanced choreography required the co-ordinated effort of a stunt team, stunt co-ordinator, and a star body to be manipulated, but the role of the computer has overtaken this human work in respect of an ever-increasing reliance on CGI in blockbusters. As Shelly Kraicer (1998) notes in a review of one of Hong Kong's earlier CGI-laden films, *The Storm Riders/Fung wan: Hung ba tin ha* (Andrew Lau, 1998), the special effects are responsible for 'displacing the dazzling acrobatics' that we have hitherto associated with martial arts cinema. This historical trajectory foregrounds a tension between the corporeal body and various technologies. This is perhaps most clearly encapsulated in *Crouching Tiger, Hidden Dragon*, where three generations of female martial artists have been cast, from Cheng Pei Pei to Michelle Yeoh to Zhang Ziyi. Each of these actresses embodies a different relationship to technology and to corporeal training and martial artistry.

In other films, the work of the human body has all but disappeared, replaced by computer-generated figures and special effects that threaten to overwhelm a film. For example, Jackie Chan's famous stunts and action sequences, while still present, were almost completely taken over by CGI effects in *The Myth/Shen hua* (Stanley Tong, 2005), in part a reflection of Chan's advancing age. *The Myth* takes place between modern-day Hong Kong and India, and travels back in time to Qin dynasty China. Chen Kaige's *The Promise/Wu ji* (2005), another pan-Asian blockbuster with stars from South Korea, Japan, Hong Kong and China, is also heavily reliant on CGI sequences. Both films appeared a few years after China's entry into the World Trade Organization in 2001, which ushered in a set of film industry reforms and enabled increased access to a global market of post-production, digital and visual effects (PDV) facilities. Digital technologies have not only transformed filmmaking at the level of technical process and operations; they have also transformed the ways in which we view, experience, and enjoy Asian films.

Tom Gunning's use of the term 'cinema of attractions' to describe early spectatorial relationships to pre-1907 cinema has been redeployed many times in the context of contemporary cinema.[3] Gunning (1990) acknowledged in his original essay that the cinema of attractions did not disappear with the dominance of narrative cinema but that it went 'underground, both into certain avant-garde practices and as a component of narrative films, more evident in some genres (e.g., the musical) than in others' (13). Because the history of Asian cinemas has not developed in parallel to American cinema, theories of the cinema of attractions and the impacts of special effects on American cinema, although useful, have their limits in relation to contemporary Asian cinema. Rather, I find it more productive to employ Lalitha Gopalan's (2002) notion of 'interruption', which she utilises in relation to Indian cinema, to describe the break in the traditional temporal and spatial relationships brought about or enabled by CGI technology in Asian cinema. Gopalan does not specifically discuss digital technologies, except in her conclusion, but her framework for reading popular Indian cinema provides some useful applications and allow us to think about a form of regionalism that emerges through these cinematic interruptions. Gopalan's theory also operates specifically in relation to

Indian action genres, which are more closely aligned to the genres I am describing in this chapter, providing a method for reading comparatively between different Asian cinemas.

Cinemas of Interruption

In *Cinema of Interruptions: Action Genres in Contemporary Indian Cinema*, Lalitha Gopalan (2002) identifies three main conventions that distinguish Indian cinema from other national cinemas: the song and dance sequences, the ten-minute interval halfway through a screening, and the tight control over censorship exercised by the Indian government. These three conventions represent what Gopalan calls a 'constellation of interruptions' that mark Indian cinema's uniqueness (2002: 13). Song and dance sequences, for example, work by delaying the development of the plot, distracting a viewer from the linear flow of the narrative and postponing the pleasure of narrative progression through this spatial and temporal disjunction. The ten-minute interval serves as 'a punctuation mark that continually directs our anticipation in surprising ways by opening and closing certain narrative strands', in effect producing two closings and two openings to every Indian film (Gopalan 2002: 19–20). Equally, censorship, both internalised and externally imposed, directs a filmmaker's subjects (and our viewing) towards a range of certain 'acceptable' narrative objects. Rather than viewing State intervention in film production as merely a form of control and interference, the Indian film industry has become very adept at negotiating codes of censorship and has worked this to its advantage; for example, the camera's tantalising withdrawal during a steamy love scene which produces its own 'crucial source of surplus pleasure' (21). Self-censorship therefore pre-empts the cuts that would otherwise be imposed, interrupting the flow of the narrative. As the preceding discussion illustrates, these three forms of 'interruptions' should not be seen in a purely negative light but should instead be analysed for how they 'both block and propel the narrative in crucial ways' (21). As Gopalan (2002) notes, '[j]ust as continuity in classical Hollywood narrative offers us both pleasure and anger, in this cinema, too, we find pleasure *in* these interruptions and not *despite* them. Indian cinema is marked by *interrupted pleasures*' (21).

Despite the particular configuration of these three elements of interrupted pleasures characterising the uniqueness of Indian *national* cinema, it is possible to see such an address as having *regional* resonances.[4] Importantly, Gopalan's theory aims to position a cinema that has been produced outside the Euro-American context out of which so much film theory has developed. Gopalan concedes that film theory has the ability to assume a 'trans-regional durability' despite its Euro-American foundations (9). This 'trans-regional durability', suggesting sustainability both across and beyond regions, seems especially useful in thinking about how Chinese cinema, for example, has managed to (re)define itself across national borders in order to find a regional audience. I argue that we can use the notion of 'interruption' as a critical space, or a point of rupture, against the notion of a singular 'Chinese national cinema', to consider instead the emergence of a regional cinematic imaginary and the development of a regional Asian cinema. In acknowledging how our viewing pleasure arises from these interruptions, that is, how temporal and spatial disjunctures structure a viewer's anticipation and pleasure, it is also important to consider the temporality of Asian regionalism.

In Asian films that heavily utilise CGI in the early 2000s, including *The Promise* and *The Myth*, it is possible to observe 'bad' CGI sequences that appear to stand out or apart from the 'official' narrative or story being told, causing our attention to break away from full absorption in the story world so that we instead contemplate the (failed/failing) technology. This 'time' of speculation and contemplation – an alternative temporality intruding on the film – is important as a kind of awakening to new realities and realisms. From time running backwards in *The Promise* to mythic time, immortality and suspension in *The Myth*, a distinct mode of spectatorship is produced through the use of new technologies that create sequences that interrupt our viewing. The spaces opened up by (obviously) 'bad' CGI sequences allow certain kinds of critical interruptions to occur, working against the forms of temporality offered by the films. What results is akin to a spectatorial return to early cinema, the 'animated cinema' described by Manovich (1995) or the 'cinema of attractions' by Gunning (1990), albeit punctuated by moments of 'unofficial' time, that is, unintended spectatorial contemplations created by the technology. In a related context, Laura Mulvey (2005) has reflected on the role technologies such as VCRs and DVD players have played historically in altering our perception of the image, allowing us to 'pause' or 'still' an image as a ghostly reminder of the celluloid image and strip. In her description of 'delayed cinema' (and the epistemology of delay in general), Mulvey describes the potential of being able to slow down the flow of a film to the point where we are able to notice some detail which has hitherto lain dormant but only now becomes perceptible. Mulvey's attempt to see cinema through delay is also possible through unintended 'breaks' in the narrative flow of the film, caused by technology that arrests the logical passage from image to image, sequence to sequence. These gaps open up a space for considering not only new possibilities of representation, which Mulvey is interested in, but also, in this context, new conditions of production and consumption for transnational Chinese films within a regional context.

There is, no doubt, a subjective quality to the effects that will interrupt or rupture one's otherwise absorbed viewing practices. However, as I will show through my film examples, there can be a shared reaction to certain sequences that are so poorly rendered (and hence unbelievable, even in the logic of the story world) that they effect a break from spectatorial immersion. Thus, I am not so much interested in CGI sequences that attempt to be 'perceptually realist' – an example of this would be the bamboo fighting sequence in *Crouching Tiger, Hidden Dragon*, which is seamlessly integrated into the logic of the film world and is hence believable in those terms, but in those sequences or moments that forcefully *interrupt*. That is, the flaunting (and/or poor execution) of special effects rather than its seamless blending with live animation. An acknowledgment that such a distinction exists marks a point of divergence from earlier studies of CGI that have hitherto aimed to situate CGI effects purely in terms of their potential for realism, in the sense of presenting an 'accurate' representation of reality. As Michele Pierson (2002) writes:

> film and cultural criticism of CGI effects has on the whole been preoccupied with demonstrating the extent to which the aesthetic dimensions of this imagery reflect the film and entertainment industries' obsession with realism, photorealism, simulation, and illusionism, terms that have increasingly come to be used interchangeably. (53)

Rather, by exploring the interruptions to cinematic realism, it is possible to consider how new imaginaries can be brought about. That is, by moving away from a model of classical cinema whereby spectatorship is characterised as a mode of absorption, we move to a way of viewing contemporary Asian blockbuster films through modes of interruption. This shift also marks a desire to move away from the use of predominantly Euro–American theories of cinematic spectatorship to consider an alternative model of comparative film studies that is inflected by different cinematic economies, histories and traditions.

Cinemas of Disappointment: Reading
The Promise and *The Myth*

The Promise made history by being China's most expensive film to date, costing some US$44 million. It stars some of Asia's most popular actors from Japan, Korea, China and Hong Kong. Hiroyuki Sanada plays General Guangming who, with his loyal slave Kunlun (Jang Dong-Gun), becomes embroiled in a love triangle over a princess, Qingcheng (Cecilia Cheung). Unbeknownst to both men, Qingcheng is fated to live a life full of riches but without love. In a pact she makes with the goddess Manshen (Hong Chen) as a young girl, she is destined to lose every man she falls in love with and the only way to break this promise is to turn back time itself. Fortunately for Qingcheng, Kunlun is from a race of people from the 'Land of Snow' who can run incredibly fast and, with enough will, can break the temporal barrier between the present and the past in order to 'remake' the past. Enlisting the assistance of the only other surviving member of the Land of Snow, Snow Wolf (Liu Ye), Kunlun tries to 'remake' Qingcheng's promise. To complicate matters, Snow Wolf is a slave bound to the villainous Duke Wuhuan (Nicholas Tse), who, as a child, was betrayed by Qingcheng. The film posits a struggle between epic, historical time, with the temporality of individual moments and of transient love that nevertheless strives to overcome its ephemerality.

The Promise opens with the vivid pink of a digitally enhanced crab apple tree, moving into a close-up of a computer-generated hummingbird as a filthy young girl grabs a bread roll from a dead soldier's hand. Directly after the opening sequence we encounter the first major 'interruption', which breaks us away from the blissful and idyllic surroundings of the beginning of the film. General Guangming is battling a tribe of barbarians outnumbering his army. He decides to purchase over a hundred slaves in order to divert the barbarians who have set a stampede of buffalo upon them. This sequence of the stampeding buffalo is the first in which we are introduced to the speed of the slave Kunlun. Kunlun at first stands completely still to avoid being stampeded but is then forced to run in order to rescue his master. The sequence is imaged using a number of swish pans that reduce it for the most part to an indistinguishable blur; however, we do get to glimpse at the operation of variable speeds at work – slow-motion shots punctuating Kunlun's rapid running as his foot hits the ground hard before lifting him into the air again. The General is so impressed with the slave's skill that he makes Kunlun his own. This sequence, far from being impressive to spectators, is one that *interrupts* our viewing pleasure. Even with its regional star power, *The Promise* was not the critical or popular success that had been hoped for, either in Asia or North America.

Despite the fact that the sequence aims for perceptual realism, the result is one of overt digital effects that nevertheless appears anachronistic because it is so poorly rendered. Monica Mak (2003) suggests that overt digital special effects are characterised by a disruption of narrative temporality through spatiality, in the sense that the space of the action takes over. According to Mak, spectators are encouraged to react to these overt CGI sequences at a pre-cognitive, pre-critical or affective level, rather than at a cognitive or critical level. Although audiences obviously perceive such sequences to be 'fake', in the sense of being digitally constructed, we nevertheless abandon any desire to rationalise about how they fit into the storyline and choose instead to enjoy the stimulation of our audiovisual senses:

> If we conceptualise these moments as spaces that momentarily interfere with narrative progression or that distract us temporarily from it, these instances, in a figurative sense, make 'time stand still' for us and therefore represent spatialities that disrupt temporality, in relationship to spectatorship. (Mak 2003)

On the contrary, I argue that the reaction of spectators to the sequences I am describing operates on a critical or cognitive level; time does stop, long enough for us to consider the failed technology and certainly long enough for us to critique it. What is promoted is not spectatorial immersion or absorption (as with simulationist CGI) but rather a close-up on the technology itself, received *cognitively*. As Tom Gunning (1994) explains for the early cinema of attractions, '[t]he spectator does not get lost in a fictional world and its drama, but remains aware of the act of looking, the excitement of curiosity and its fulfilment' (121). Instead of excitement and fulfilment, spectators experience disappointment at the fact that the big budget techno-futurist blockbuster they were expecting appears anachronistic.[5] Instead of moving forward, the film seems to take Asian cinema *backwards*. However, this kind of cognitive interruption can also be productive.

Writing on the Indian national cinema, Lalitha Gopalan (2002) notes that what results from spectatorial interruptions such as these is that 'the spectator's pleasure [is redirected] . . . towards and away from the state' (179). Fifth Generation Chinese directors such as Chen Kaige, whose films were previously banned by the Chinese government, are now making state-sanctioned blockbusters. Against the 'official' versions of these films, however, are individual stories that threaten to erupt, linked to other stories which cannot be contained within the national frame. In particular, these are love stories that cross temporal and spatial (geographical) borders (interestingly, the English translation of the film's Chinese title *Wu ji* is 'without limits').

Similarly, *The Myth* is marked by temporal and spatial boundary crossing. Two parallel times and places exist in the film, held together by the dream world of the modern-day archaeologist Dr Jack Chan (played by Jackie Chan). Jack, who lives in Hong Kong, is plagued by recurring dreams about a Qin era general, Meng Yi (also played by Jackie Chan), who falls in love with Princess Ok Soo (played by Korean actress Kim

Hee Seon). General Meng Yi has been entrusted with the task of escorting the Korean princess to the Emperor, where she is to be his concubine. Jack's best friend William (Tony Leung Ka-Fai) is a physicist, working to discover the secret behind anti-gravity. The answer to this mystery comes in the form of a gemstone in India that allows objects, including humans, to defy gravity. Part of the film takes place in Dasar, India, where Jack discovers an ancient sword from the Qin dynasty and William steals the gemstone that defies the force of gravity. These relics from the past eventually lead Jack and William to the mythical mausoleum of the Qin Emperor which is suspended in mid-air. Tying these two worlds together is a bilingual Jackie Chan, speaking both Cantonese (in present-day Hong Kong), and Mandarin (in Qin dynasty China). It is Jack's dreams, and static objects and images – paintings, a history book illustration, relics coming to life in the dream world – that trigger or compel the shift from one time and place to another, marking the transitions between present and past.

This constant back-and-forth movement is tiring for spectators, abruptly forcing us out of immersion from one storyline and into another; we are never given adequate time to ease into one story world before being thrust into the other. These narrative interruptions are also coupled with CGI interruptions, again through an attempt to use a transcendent love story between the Princess and Meng Yi to overcome spatial and temporal barriers. While this film is usually read in terms of the relationship between Hong Kong and China post-handover, what is often neglected are the *regional* elements that create this film, beyond the dyadic Hong Kong–China relationship. *The Myth* is a truly regional collaboration, including Korean, Indian as well as Hong Kong and mainland Chinese talent. Female stars from other parts of Asia, such as Kim Hee Seon and Bollywood actress Mallika Sherawat, have been employed to increase the film's regional appeal. There is a very strong South Asian connection and Jackie Chan's martial arts skills are pitted against those of martial arts exponent G. Sathyanarayanan, an expert in the traditional Indian martial art of Kalaripayattu, in the creation of a regional action genre film. As with *The Promise*, however, this regional imaginary failed to translate into wider success, despite Jackie Chan's major involvement in the film.

Between the backwards and forwards structure of the two worlds (the past and the present), together with the overarching desire for a transcendent immortality, another space emerges in this overt CGI sequence, a critical space of interruption. Instead of wonder at the boundaries of cinematographic possibility being extended in this sequence, we pause to question the film's narratological and technological motives. Just why is a Korean princess waiting endlessly for a Qin dynasty general to return? Technology, in particular CGI effects, is used in the service of this contemporary 'historical epic' to dream the future of Chinese cinema, albeit a future not clearly imagined or mapped out. What it does seem to rely on, however, is regional technological advancement. The disrupted temporalities or breaks in the narrative open up a critical space precisely because they appear anachronistic, a disappointment thrown back into the past, giving us cause to pause and to receive the scene critically and cognitively, rather than through affect (and this is despite the fact both films are tales of enduring love, across time and space).

Today, given the ubiquitous discourses of instantaneity and temporal compression confronting us in the form of digital technologies, how might 'interruptions' (created precisely through such technology) give us pause for thought? It is not that realism has been subsumed by CGI but that contemporary pan-Asian blockbusters have created increasingly unstable relations to realism, in their various forms, which have tended to dominate the cinema. Instead, these films seem to oscillate uneasily between realism and simulation/stimulation. Rather than consider how CGI and other digital effects *refer* to reality (in the form of realism), we should pay attention to how they communicate. As Sean Cubitt (2005) notes, '[d]igital media do not refer. They communicate'; '[t]hey not so much depict or falsify actuality but communicate aspiration' (250, 260). This aspiration of communication, of being understood, is intimately connected to the love story, which emerges as the dominant theme in blockbuster films including *The Myth* and *The Promise*. It is this form of communication between Asia's film industries that I have been discussing throughout this book: from co-productions between two or more national industries, to remakes in different local contexts in dialogue with the original, to omnibus collaborations, to regional co-operation in archiving. Considering how film technologies communicate is even more imperative when it comes to newer technologies such as stereoscopic 3D cinema that, while they aim to recreate reality in all its dimensions, arguably alienate and 'interrupt' audiences even further.

Stereoscopic 3D

Thomas Elsaesser (2013) notes that '[i]t cannot have escaped anyone's notice that the most remarked-upon phenomenon of mainstream cinema in recent years has been the publicity effort orchestrated by the film industry to launch digital 3-D cinema as a new attraction' (218). 3D cinema is, of course, not 'new' technology. Jones (2015) notes that the use of stereoscopic techniques predates film itself, and that 3D film was commonly used in the early 1950s and 1980s 'to entice audiences back to cinemas as television and VCRs, respectively, threatened the privileged position of the cinema' (53). Films have been made in 3D for over half a century (the first sound and colour stereoscopic feature, *Bwana Devil* (dir. Arch Oboler) was released in 1952); however, attraction for 3D filmmaking and viewing has come and gone, with the 1950s and 1980s representing periods of the most fervent interest (Hayes 1989; Mitchell 2004; Zone 2007).[6] A modern revival of the form took place throughout the 2000s, culminating in the phenomenal success of James Cameron's *Avatar* in 2009.[7] As Sarah Atkinson (2011) notes:

> in its previous iterations, discussions of S3D [stereoscopic 3D] film productions of the 1950s and 1980s have been reduced to their gratuitous and gimmicky assets . . . This early iteration of S3D was characterized by its accompanying meta-narratives and hyperbolic claims that implied that images from the screen would literally inhabit the audience and jump out of the screen. (145)

Atkinson (2011) suggests that while the use of gimmickry and gratuity continues into the current era of 3D films, especially in blockbuster films that sensationalise the 'spectacular' aspects of the form, we are also 'starting to see a rethinking and reconfiguration of the filmic form in a number of notable commercial releases' (149). *Avatar* is a major example of a film that uses 3D to create a mythical and immersive alternative film world. The effect of technology on aesthetics and storytelling possibilities provides a new dimension to the visual language of cinema, effectively altering the 'content' of a film in terms of the kind of stories that can be told and providing new means of telling them to global audiences. *Avatar* became one of the biggest global box office hits of all time, earning almost three billion dollars worldwide within six weeks of its release (Elsaesser 2013: 218). The film did exceptionally well in Asia, especially in mainland China, leading to a resurgence of interest in 3D cinema in the region.[8]

In what ways can we account for the popularity of 3D cinema in Asia? Critics such as Kristin Thompson have noted the technology's economic and critical failure in Hollywood (2009), although interest in 3D filmmaking in Asia does not appear to be abating. Adam Epstein (2017) notes that by the time of his article, most Americans audiences were 'over' the experience of watching 3D movies; however, Hollywood filmmakers continued to make 3D films for Asian (especially mainland Chinese) audiences. Epstein notes that '[i]n the US and Canada, 3D screens make up about 39% of all digital movie screens. In Asia-Pacific, however, 3D screens compose a whopping 78% of screens.' In China alone, 3D screens account for 85 per cent of screens (Global Times 2018). Asia has welcomed and celebrated the 3D format far more than any other cinema-going region. In an article for *Variety* (2011), Andrew Stewart suggests that certain markets support viewing films in 3D in a way other markets, including Hollywood, do not. Stewart remarks: '[t]o some degree, the divergence can be chalked up to a matter of preference – some cultures just like 3D more than others for reasons that can't be quantified, and big-budget f/x spectacles continue to draw big [audiences] overseas'. Singapore, South Korea and Hong Kong have invested heavily in 3D filmmaking, infrastructure and training to build regional technical centres in this area, attracting collaborations with Thailand, Taiwan and Australia (MDA 2010b). The Busan International Film Commission and Industry Showcase (Bifcom) held a focus on 'All That 3D' for its 10th anniversary celebrations in 2010, featuring international 3D experts to discuss technologies and trends in the region (Han 2010: 26).

In light of this interest and investment, what happens to audience responses and engagement when 3D films are not the technological marvels they strive to be? In a scathing review in *Variety* on China's 3D industries, written almost a decade ago now, Clifford Coonan (2011a) reports on China's lack of technical know how, with a lack of local expertise in post-production and special effects. Although there have been significant technological advances in this area in the last decade, the technology of some 3D films from Asia is still lagging.

There have been conversions of existing Asian blockbusters (such as *The Host 3D* (Bong Joon-ho, 2011), which adds 3D effects to the original 2006 film), although an increasing number of films from Asia are also being shot in 3D, often on comparatively low budgets for visual effects compared to their Hollywood counterparts. High-profile 3D films made in Asia in the period 2010 and 2012, following the release of *Avatar*, include *Amphibious* (Brian Yuzna, Indonesia/Netherlands, 2010), *A Fish* (Park Hong-min, 2011, Korea), *Persimmon* (Choo Sang-rok, 2011, Korea), *Sadako* (Tsutomu Hanabusa, 2012, Japan), *The Monkey King* (Cheang Pou-soi, 2012, Hong Kong) and *29 Februari*, Malaysia's first 3D movie (Edry Abdul Halim, 2012). The majority of these are horror films but martial arts and action films, animation and drama, also feature. *The Child's Eye* (Pang Brothers, 2010), part of the Pang Brothers' 'Eye' horror series, was Hong Kong's first 3D horror film. *The Flying Swords of Dragon Gate* (Tsui Hark, 2011, Hong Kong), starring Jet Li and a remake of *Dragon Gate Inn* (1966) and *New Dragon Gate Inn* (1992), was the first time 3D was used in a *wuxia* film, with 3D crew from China, Korea and Singapore.[9] *Don Quixote* (Ah Gan, 2010, China/Hong Kong) was promoted as 'China's first wholly 3D movie'.[10] Notable 3D animation films include *Legend of a Rabbit* (Sun Lijun, 2011, China) and *Little Ghostly*

Adventures of Tofu Boy (Gisaburo Sugii and Shimmei Kawahara, 2011, Japan), billed as the 'first fully 3D Japanese anime' (M. Lee 2011). *Dark Flight 407* (Issara Nadee, 2012, Thailand), a horror film, is the first Thai feature to be filmed in 3D, and was followed by *3AM* (2012), also produced by Thailand's Five Star Productions. *3AM* is an omnibus film, comprising three segments from established Thai directors, Patchanon Thammajira, Kirati Nakintanon and Isara Nadee. *My Dear Kuttichathan* (Jijo Punnoose, 1984), a Malayalam film, was the first 3D film to be made in India. The film was dubbed in Hindi in 1997 and titled *Chhota Chetan*. In 2010, further scenes were added in Tamil and it was released as *Chutti Chathan*. *Sex and Zen: Extreme Ecstasy* 3D (Christopher Sun, 2011), was touted as 'the world's first major 3D soft-porn movie' (Coonan May 2011a).[11] *Sex and Zen* is a period drama based on a classic Chinese erotic tale, *The Carnal Prayer Mat*. The film reworks the 1991 Hong Kong cult film *Sex and Zen* and features Japanese actresses Hará Saori and Suo Yukiko and Hong Kong star Vonnie Lui.[12] The many 'firsts' reported in this list of films demonstrates the nascency of this technology in Asia.

I will not be discussing 4D or 'D-Box' cinema technology, which is still underdeveloped as a technology across Asia (with the exception of South Korea), and more of a gimmick or theme park experience (and therefore a continuous 'interruption') than a fully immersive cinema-going experience. Torsten Hoffman (2012) notes that 'in Korea the 4D versions of many top blockbusters are available from day one of the release' because the market for 4D is fairly profitable. With motion (seat movement), smell, spraying water and fog synchronised to the action during a screening, the viewing experience is intensified, providing an affective experience of being 'in' a film (Yecies 2016: 23). Brian Yecies (2016) observes the contribution of Korean 4D film technicians to the growth of the format in China (23). The CJ Group, and its subsidiary CJ 4DXPlex, are among the largest to introduce 4D cinema across Asia. While this is a fast-growing area, 3D cinema is comparatively far more established as a format and has led to collaborations between industries in Asia.

I turn now to an Australia-Singapore 3D co-production, *Bait 3D* (Kimble Rendall, 2012), which has been selected because it represents a form of 'bad' 3D cinema in/from Asia, what Claire Perkins and Constantine Verevis (2014) have referred to as '[p]olarizing "event" films' (2). Beyond subjective questions of taste, Perkins and Verevis consider 'aesthetically and/or morally disreputable film work' that constitutes 'bad cinema', described as such in terms of its 'aesthetics, politics, and cultural value' (5). *Bait 3D*'s film effects are obvious, and clunky, returning us to Lalitha Gopalan's notion of cinematic interruptions. What is interesting is how the film's so-called 'failures' in technology provide interrupted modes of viewing that, through the gaps created in the film's realism, allow us to consider the possibility of an emergent regional cinematic imaginary between Australia and Asia.

Bait 3D (Kimble Rendall, 2012)

Bait 3D is a stereoscopic action thriller and the first feature film co-production made under the Australia-Singapore film co-production treaty signed in September 2007. The film opened theatrically in Australia on 20 September 2012 and in Singapore on 29 November 2012, with a delay in its projected release due to the earlier release of a similarly themed film, *Piranha 3DD* (John Gulager, 2012), a comedy-horror film and sequel to *Piranha 3D* (Alexandre Aja, 2010).

Although the film is a co-production with Singapore, *Bait 3D* tells a very *Australian* (horror) story. The film is a disaster-thriller about a freak tsunami that floods a resort community on the Queensland coast in northern Australia. The only survivors are trapped in an underground supermarket with a crazed gunman in their midst and two hungry great white sharks circling below. In the vein of recent Australian-made crocodile thrillers *Black Water* (David Nerlich, 2007) and *Rogue* (Greg McLean, 2007), or as a 3D companion to *Cane Toads: The Conquest 3D* (Mark Lewis, 2010), another pestilent animal-themed Australian film, *Bait 3D* glides over very familiar territory.

Perhaps because of its setting and storyline – the film is shot on the Gold Coast, with an Australian director and a mostly Australian cast[13] – very few references have been made in the Australian press to the fact that *Bait 3D* is a Singapore-Australia co-production. As discussed in Chapter 2, there are very attractive reasons for co-producing films with international partners but also certain drawbacks. Possibly the most significant of these for Singapore's developing film industry is the loss of cultural specificity, regarded in terms of stories, settings and themes that represent domestic audiences. Where Australia protects local content through its cultural policy, Singapore encourages production based in Singapore without necessarily having Singaporean representation on screen.[14] One way to regard Singapore's contribution to creativity beyond content defined narrowly in representational terms is to think through Singapore's development of 3D technology in the film. In *Bait 3D* it is the use of technology itself, in this case stereoscopic 3D technology, which is politicised as Singapore's 'creative' contribution to the international co-production. The 3D, visual and postproduction effects of *Bait 3D* were handled by Singapore companies Widescreen Media and Blackmagic Design.[15]

As Singapore's first stereoscopic 3D film, *Bait 3D* has been used to promote the latest developments in Singapore filmmaking, offered as a tourism artefact that itself represents Singapore talent and technology to the rest of the world. In comparison, the Chinese version of *Bait 3D* was re-edited to expand on certain storylines in the original film and introduced new characters (and Chinese actors) in order to resonate more with Chinese audiences. As a result of this targeted 'local' re-edit, *Bait 3D* performed extremely well in China, becoming the highest box office earner on its opening weekend and taking RMB 50 million (US$7.2 million) in three days.[16] While the size of the China market can justify an alternative edit of the film, in Singapore 'local content' requires an expanded definition that goes beyond representation in narrative terms to incorporate how film uses technology to develop new storytelling possibilities and new aesthetics of representation. *Bait 3D* does not entirely succeed in this attempt at storytelling through 3D, with stereoscopic effects still employed predominantly for sensationalism (for example, submerging viewers into a pool of water teeming with schools of fish or drawing them into the mouth of a shark). Nevertheless, the film provides an interesting example of Singapore's push into this area of media technology, and towards what Laikwan Pang (2012) has called 'the politicization of creativity' (17) in the context of China's cultural industries.

Singapore's Development of Stereoscopic 3D: the Politicisation of Technology

Singapore has been quick to capitalise on the growth in 3D in all its facets. In November 2008, Singapore established a S$10 million Stereoscopic 3D Film Development Fund to boost development of 3D filmmaking and build an industry of practitioners in the country. Under the S3D Film Development Fund, Singapore companies producing 3D content are eligible for up to 80 per cent of the production budget (up to S$350,000) in investment for a feature film of any genre, including documentaries. Singapore's Media Development Authority (MDA) has also supported workshops on 3D filming and technology at Ngee Ann Polytechnic and provided training in stereoscopic 3D subsidised at 50 per cent for Singaporeans and Permanent Residents (MDA 2010c). Even the National Day Parade in August 2010 was recorded in 3D (MDA 2010c).[17]

As a way of drawing international attention to Singapore's growing 3D capabilities, the country hosted the 3DX: 3D Film and Entertainment Technology Festival in 2008, the first festival dedicated to stereoscopic 3D content and technologies in the world. The festival was partly sponsored by the Singapore Tourism Board, a clear sign that the country seeks to establish a correlation between its technological developments in this area with a vision of the nation that it can project to the outside world; that is, of 'made-by-Singapore' technology providing a new global cinematic or entertainment experience. Christopher Chia, former Chief Executive Officer of the MDA, notes:

> The increased availability of 3D equipment and technology in Singapore allows local content providers to have greater access to a wider range of equipment to enable and expedite their development in 3D content and we are starting to see this bear fruit through quality made-by-Singapore 3D content. (MDA 2010b)

In this equation, 'local content' is defined through creativity; in particular, through the development of Singapore-made technology. The promotional rhetoric of film content being 'made-by-Singapore' has most recently shifted to a tagline of being 'made-with-Singapore' in the latest incarnation of the Singapore Film Commission's push towards greater internationalisation, and now, collaboration (2020).[18]

In July 2010 Singapore signed an international film co-production agreement with China (entering into force on 22 December 2010). Singapore is the sixth country and the first Asian country to sign with China.[19] One of the growth areas for collaboration is stereoscopic 3D productions (MDA 2010a). More recently, in December 2018, Singapore announced the Southeast Asia Co-Production Grant (SCPG), intended to provide funding of up to $250,000 per film for feature-length regional co-productions between Singaporean and Southeast Asian filmmakers.[20] As Singapore increases its collaborations with other film industries in Asia and elsewhere, the challenge may not be how to find ways of telling a story differently through technology but how to find the right partner to co-produce and co-create this vision. As the example of *Bait 3D* shows, the cultural politics involved in government-supported international co-productions requires a more complex understanding of what constitutes 'local content' in representing a film to domestic (and international) audiences. An expanded definition of local content that includes creativity in the form of the domestic development of technology has relevance in terms of accountability for government funded film projects but also, importantly, for fostering a sense of cultural nationalism through the cinema in light of wider efforts to regionalise and internationalise.

Conclusion

Through co-productions and pan-Asian film productions, from animation to live action, cinematic interruptions caused by obvious technological effects create a space for contemplation, allowing audiences to imagine a shared community of viewers across Asia. Lalitha Gopalan refers to interruptions in Indian cinema as opening up a critical space, or a point of rupture, against a singular notion of the national cinema. In the case of spectatorial interruptions caused by digital technology, other stories threaten to erupt that cannot be contained by the national frame. As local content becomes conjoined with the development of newer technologies, creativity itself becomes politicised. In this equation national imaginaries do not simply disappear; they persist in tension with emergent regional imaginaries. I end with a brief note on a recent children's animated film, *Abominable* (Jill Culton, 2019), to consider how national sentiments endure within the landscape of emergent regional cinematic imaginaries.

Abominable is a computer-animated children's adventure film produced by DreamWorks Animation and Pearl Studio, a Chinese film production company. The film recounts the adventures of a teenaged girl named Yi who finds an injured young Yeti on her rooftop in Shanghai. She dubs him 'Everest' and promises to return him to his family in the mountains. Chased by a wealthy businessman Mr Burnish and evil zoologist Dr Zara, Yi and two friends travel across China to reunite Everest with his family in the Himalayas. From the Gobi Desert to the Yellow River, and finally to Mount Everest, *Abominable* is a story of finding one's way home. The film caused controversy with a number of Southeast Asian countries due to a scene involving a map of the South China Sea region which included the Nine-Dash Line, a contested demarcation line used by China to lay claim over parts of the South China Sea. Because of the inclusion of this controversial Nine-Dash Line, *Abominable* was banned in several countries including Vietnam, the Philippines and Malaysia (BBC News 2019).[21] This seemingly innocuous and heart-rending children's animation about a friendship between a young girl and an imaginary creature, a Yeti, demonstrates how politically and culturally significant and persistent national imaginaries can be, as enacted through the cinema and in this case in relation to a long-standing dispute over a strategically significant regional area. The scene in *Abominable* featuring the contested map is very brief, almost an inconspicuous inclusion in an otherwise 'innocent' children's animated adventure. However, its insertion, causing both a cinematic interruption and an extra-textual political *eruption*, demonstrates how powerfully a regional imaginary that holds 'truth' for one country can be so very different from another's.

Notes

1. See <http://asianaustraliancinema.org/>; <https://www.screenaustralia. gov.au/funding-and-support/co-production-program/partner-countries> on Australia's co-production partner countries.

2. Parts of this chapter were originally published as 'Remaking the past, interrupting the present: the spaces of technology and futurity in contemporary Chinese blockbusters', in Olivia Khoo and Sean Metzger (eds), *Futures of Chinese Cinema: Technologies and Temporalities in Chinese Screen Cultures*, London: Intellect, 2009, pp. 241–62, and as '*Bait 3D* and the Singapore-Australia Co-production Agreement: From Content to Creativity through Stereoscopic Technology', *Transnational Screens*, 5:1, 2014, pp. 1–13.

3. See, for example, Strauven (2007).

4. Gopalan (2002) notes that these interruptions imbibe both global and local conventions, tending towards the possibility of globally recognisable genres in commercial cinema (20).

5. The visual effects in *The Promise* were headed by Frankie Chung of Centro Digital Pictures, a Hong Kong post-production, digital and visual effects company founded in 1985, which was also responsible for coordinating the visual effects for *Shaolin Soccer/Shaolin zuqiu* (Stephen Chow, 2001), *Kung fu Hustle/Gong fu* (Stephen Chow, 2004) and *The Emperor and the Assassin/ Jin ke ci qin qang* (Chen Kaige, 1998).

6. The first anaglyph (red–cyan) test reels were shown by Edwin S. Porter and William E. Waddell in June 1915; however, these reels were not further produced. In 1922 the first 3D feature film, *The Power of Love*, an American silent film directed by Nat G. Deverich and Harry K. Fairall, was shown in Los Angeles. The 3D version of *The Power of Love* is presumed lost. *Bwana Devil* is generally regarded as the film that sparked a craze in 3D filmmaking in the 1950s.

7. Home entertainment systems are also increasingly being built with 3D capabilities, including 3D television, 3D BluRay players and 3D mobile phones.

8. *Avatar* became the highest grossing film in China in 2010 and remained so until *Transformers: Age of Extinction*, another 3D blockbuster, four years later (Global Times 2018).

9. <http://ultimate3dmovies.blogspot.com.au/p/asian.html>.

10. <http://www.donquixote.com/film-ah-gan-3846329976-2010.html>.

11. Groves (2012) notes that *Sex and Zen: Extreme Ecstasy* was 'erroneously touted as the world's first 3D sex film when it was released in 2011. In fact, that honour belongs to Korean director Kyung-Jung Ju's *Natalie*, the tale of a playboy art professor and his hot-looking student, which came out in 2010.'

12. A sequel in 4D, *Sex And Zen: Slayer Of A Thousand From The Mysterious East*, was proposed in 2012 by China 3D Digital Entertainment, 'where your seat vibrates and gyrates in synchronisation with the film' (Kwok Kar Peng, 30 March 2012, The New Paper). Chinese audiences were required to travel to Hong Kong and Taiwan to see *Sex and Zen: Extreme Ecstasy* (Coonan 2011b: 5).

13. The film features a largely Australian ensemble cast starring Xavier Samuel, Julian McMahon, Sharni Vinson, Phoebe Tonkin and Lincoln Lewis, with two Singaporean actors, Adrian Pang and Yuwu Qi, joining the cast. Australian director Kimble Rendall replaced earlier director Russell Mulcahy, who wrote and developed the script, with Mulcahy remaining as executive producer.

14. This evacuation of local content can also be seen in recent Asian–Australia co-productions in animated children's television, which is another area in which collaborations have been increasing. The introduction of digital transmission to Australian television in 2001 resulted in a fragmentation of audience and advertising revenue, which was exacerbated by children's programming already being available on pay TV as well; over the decade that followed, this was further complicated by the rise to prominence of web-based streaming (YouTube) and on-demand services (such as Netflix). Children's content is expensive to produce and restrictions on advertising during children's programmes in Australia mean that the rate of return on a children's series is often unviable and there is little commercial incentive for Australian broadcasters to produce original children's content. One way Australian producers have tackled this obstacle is by reaching out to Asian screen industries for collaboration, as seen with *Zigby* (co-produced with Singapore and first airing in 2009); *Guess How Much I Love You* (co-produced with Singapore in 2012); *hoopla doopla!* (co-produced with China in 2014); and *Kuu Kuu Harajuku* (co-produced with Malaysia in 2015). With the exception of *hoopla doopla!*, which attempts to integrate Chinese characters, themes and cultural events, the other animated children's television series do not foreground local content relevant to domestic audiences in Singapore or Malaysia.

15. The film is a co-production between Arclight Films, Pictures in Paradise and Story Bridge Films in association with Screen Australia and Screen Queensland, and with Blackmagic Design and Singapore's Media Development Authority through its International Film Fund.

16. Screen Australia Media Release, available at <https://www.screenaustralia.gov.au/sa/media-centre/news/2012/10-16-bait-3d-box-office-china>. This is despite the fact that the film circulated on pirated DVDs prior to and during its release, demonstrating that 3D still offers a unique theatrical experience.

17. In 2016, Singapore's Media Development Authority (MDA) was renamed Infocomm Media Development Authority (IMDA). Throughout the chapter, I refer to the Authority as the Media Development Authority (MDA) for the purposes of consistency.

18. See <https://www.imda.gov.sg/for-industry/sectors/Media/Film> (Film Brochure).

19. Prior to this, in 2008, Singapore's Ministry of Information, Communication and the Arts and China's Ministry of Science and Technology signed a Memorandum of Understanding on bilateral collaboration in interactive digital media research and development. This resulted in the opening of the China-Singapore Institute of Digital Media in Singapore, and television programmes including *China Trend*, a thirteen-part series on modern China lifestyle, and *My China Destiny*, a series about foreigners settling in China. *Neon Sign*, directed by Korean Chinese Pil Gam-Sung, will be the first Singapore-China-Korean co-produced film.

20. See <https://www.imda.gov.sg/programme-listing/Southeast-Asia-Co-Production-Grant>.

21. The film was banned in Vietnam on 14 October 2019, ten days after its release. On 17 October 2019 Malaysia ordered the scene cut and when this was refused the film was banned (BBC News 2019).

Epilogue: New Regional Intimacies

I completed this book during unprecedented times, with the world gripped by the COVID-19 pandemic that will continue long after this manuscript is submitted. As countries around the world imposed lockdown conditions and physical distancing rules on their citizens, through social media – from the sharing of humorous cat memes to displays of small acts of kindness – we were reminded daily that even in our isolation there was an unbroken solidarity and connection.

With widespread disruption to film industries around the world caused by COVID-19 – cinemas and movie theatres shut down, international film festivals cancelled, postponed or moved online, and film production ground to a halt – a small glimmer of hope for the film and television industries could be seen in the rise of streaming services. In the first two months of 2020, usually the busiest period with the Lunar New Year, China's box office plunged 86 per cent compared to the corresponding period the year prior, representing a RMB15.194 billion (US$1.91 billion) loss (Clark 2020). South Korea lost approximately 60 per cent of its box office from January to March 2020, Hong Kong 35 per cent, and Singapore, the Philippines and Taiwan 30 per cent of its box office each (D'Alessandro 2020). Meanwhile, streaming sites throughout the Asia-Pacific reported significantly increased traffic as people stayed at home (Frater 2020; Screen Daily 2020). Netflix rose by almost 14 per cent since the beginning of 2020 (The Economist 2020; Trefis Team 2020), and ancillary services such as Netflix Party, Watch2gether, Rabbit and TwoSeven made it possible for viewers to watch films and videos simultaneously across distances, creating new practices of intimacy and digital co-presence through technology (Hjorth 2005). Thus, even as barriers between people and nations were erected to combat the virus, other boundaries to sociality were lowered or dismantled. Our forced 'locality' – to remain confined to our homes and neighbourhoods by a virus transmitted through close contact – was both a product of, and an impetus towards, greater global connectivity.

Throughout this book, I have attempted to document the myriad ways through which film industries in Asia have facilitated greater connections between and across national boundaries within (and beyond) the region. In this new landscape, irrevocably altered by the enduring traumas of a global pandemic, what is the continued status of the region? If, as Amitav Acharya (2013) notes, regions are 'not a given or fixed, but are socially constructed – they are made and remade through political, economic, social, and cultural interactions' (52), does Asia, as both a material space and an ideational space, still matter? In the Asia of this reconfigured land-scape, I suggest that new regional intimacies emerge in the (re)turn to new localisms and in the spaces between ever growing inter-nationalisms, and it is in the relationships forged through these intimacies that the region matters more than ever.

Darrell Davis and Emilie Yueh-yu Yeh (2008) refer to new localism as a trend emerging in East Asian screen industries post-2000, defined by 'local production employing resources specific to given markets, combined with key elements of global entertainment production' (38). The new localism 'revives interest in servicing local and regional audiences by area, and tar-geting specialised markets by genre or demographic' (Davis and Yeh 2008: 29). We can see this new localism at play in the domestic film remakes that are posited as an alternative to the pan-Asian blockbuster (Chapter 3), and in the form of locally-based 'regional' film festivals (Chapter 4), which assume importance as key meeting points or 'infrastructural node[s]' that allow for the creation of new networks and alliances (Iordanova 2011: 17). Davis and Yeh (2008) note that in some respects the new localism 'is not local at all; it is international, yet decentralised and Asia-specific' (38). In this sense, new localism in Asian cinema is in constant negotiation with ongoing tensions between the local, the regional and the international.

New localism also foregrounds the importance of form, for example in the case of a film called *Television* (2012). Directed by Bangladesh-based filmmaker Mostafa Sarwar Farooki, *Television* explores the increasing integration between local media forms, specifically cinema and television, in Bangladesh. In the context of this regional media convergence, the film considers how to negotiate audience requirements marked by a tension between a desire for very local forms of representation, what I have else-where referred to as 'slang images' (Khoo 2006), and the need to develop new regional vernaculars that will captivate and sustain larger audiences. In *Television*, members of a local community attempt to circumvent a fundamentalist dictate issued by their community leader that forbids the watching of television. (They are also directed to stop 'imagining' because of the negative effects of an infiltration of the mind, leading to a pervasive iconophobia). Farooki explains his inspiration for the film:

My father was deeply influenced by an Islamic belief that images are sinful. One fine morning, he asked me to stop watching TV and removed all photographs from the walls. I would sneak into neighbours' homes to watch TV and often get caught. I argued with my father and tried to reason with him that this was not correct. He would refuse to appreciate my views and I would stick to my belief. (Times of India 2013)

By the end of the film, it is television that allows the religious community leader to reach a transcendental state through a mediated (but still highly intimate) religious experience. Although *Television* has been hailed as 'a key exemplar of Bangladeshi new wave cinema' (Weissberg 2009), Farooki acknowledges the necessity of wider audiences for Bengali national cinema. On his desire for India and Bangladesh to open up their respective markets to Bengali films, Farooki is clear: '[t]o survive, our films need a bigger market' (Times of India 2013).

As for the inter-nationalisms that enmesh the region during these uncertain times, the hyphen in this phrase highlights the (re)strengthening of national boundaries, with the nation operating as the pre-eminent 'unit of global cultural encounters' (Iwabuchi 2013: 438). Koichi Iwabuchi cautions against what he refers to as 'banal inter-nationalism' – the marketing of the nation and national branding, which 'suppresses and marginalises multicultural questions within the nation' (2013: 439). From the diasporic contexts of Asian Canadian and Asian American publics, Christine Kim (2016a) foregrounds the displacement of conditions of race by multiculturalism itself, revealing what she refers to as the 'minor intimacies of race' in her book of the same title (5). These minor intimacies refer to the various conversations, gestures and events that define how collectives are mobilised, felt and expressed, however ephemeral or contingent, against more powerful displays of public social engagement.

While I have argued throughout this book for the value in seeing Asia as an intimately connected region that is nevertheless susceptible to outside forces as much as it impacts upon them, what the COVID-19 pandemic has brought into sharp relief – if it was not already glaringly obvious – is the towering asymmetry and economic disparity that remains both within the region and beyond. Arundhati Roy (2020), writing about the impact of the novel coronavirus on India and the world at large, describes the pandemic as a 'portal'. Roy urges us to think through new ways of being in the world in light of the current crisis:

Historically, pandemics have forced humans to break with the past and imagine their world anew. This one is no different. It is a portal, a gateway between one world and the next. We can choose to walk through it, dragging the carcasses of our prejudice and hatred, our avarice, our data banks and dead ideas, our dead rivers and smoky skies behind us. Or we can walk through lightly, with little luggage, ready to imagine another world. And ready to fight for it.

Of course, intimacy need not exist only amongst equals; intimacy's ambivalence means that while it promises safety and seeks stability and closeness, it also carries risk and a 'latent vulnerability' (Berlant 1998: 282). Lauren Berlant's (1998: 288) conceptualisation of intimate publics, of persons becoming public, and collective scenes becoming intimate spaces, provides a framework for understanding how place making and 'worlding' in the region might come to be structured post-pandemic.

On the inextinguishable human propensity to orient towards a brighter future in the face of immense difficulty, I am reminded of Chai Jing's self-financed documentary, *Under the Dome/Qiongding zhixia* (2015). Beginning with an emotive recounting of her first moments with her newborn daughter, taken away immediately after birth for surgery on a benign tumour, Chai, a former CCTV journalist, offers an intimately public, yet resolutely personal, introduction to a deeply critical documentary about China's air pollution problem.[1] *Under the Dome* was first released on 28 February 2015 on the website of the state-run *People's Daily* newspaper, before becoming available on Youku, Tudou and Tencent. Within forty-eight hours of being released online the documentary received more than 200 million views before it was removed from all major Chinese websites within China's Great Firewall around 7 March (Edwards 2015).[2] As an Internet sensation, gathering with it vast commentary on WeChat, the film demonstrates the spread by which films released online can gather momentum (I am reluctant to use the word 'viral' to describe the spread of the film; as Arundhati Roy (2020) notes, '[w]ho can use the term "gone viral" now without shuddering a little?'). Like *Okja* on Netflix, another film about how human manipulation of the natural environment brings horrifying consequences, *Under the Dome* achieved a 'transnational reaction' (Yang 2016) by 'flow[ing] across different fields of communication through digital channels' (Cui 2017: 30), illustrating the importance of a shared approach and collaborative effort towards regional environmental concerns.

This shared environmental ethos manifest in collaborative filmmaking can also be seen in Kirsten Tan's *Pop Aye* (2017), a Singapore-Thailand co-production and a 'road movie' (on foot) about a disillusioned Bangkok architect's journey home to Loei province, northeast Thailand, with his childhood companion, an elephant named Pop Aye. While the film is ostensibly focused on the mid-life crisis of the human protagonist, Thana, his animal companion, Pop Aye, catalyses a very local concern with a series of environmental issues in Thailand, from deforestation and habitat loss to water and air pollution, that can only be articulated indirectly in this film, through the voiceless figure of the elephant. Beyond commenting on issues of ecological concern in Thailand, the film also highlights environmental problems in Singapore through this transnational co-production, from land reclamation to the costs of rapid urbanisation. Playing with the genre of the road movie, the film uses the tropes of journeying and homecoming, between and across Singapore and Thailand, to create the beginnings of a filmic dialogue on shared environmental concerns in Southeast Asia.

In the face of increasingly inter-national encounters, and a (re)turn to new localisms, a comparative approach becomes ever more important. A critical comparative approach retains at its heart a collaborative ethos, 'transnationally extend[ing] our commitment to the local' while taking broader connections within Asia as a 'strategic focal point' (Iwabuchi 2016: 283). This ethos is central to the inter-Asia project and to the tactics of Asia as method. And, as I have tried to demonstrate in relation to cinema specifically, central to the project of comparative film studies. A critical comparative approach would also involve collaboration among film and media scholars where '[t]he final goal is not to create a globally unified discursive space of film studies, but to forge new networks and channels of communication' (Yoshimoto 2013: 60). As Prasenjit Duara (2010) notes, the region Asia 'has no external limits or territorial boundaries and does not seek to homogenize itself within' (981). To this extent, the region Asia in future imaginaries may far outstretch its current boundaries and embrace others as it seeks to establish new networks and channels of communication.

In her 2014 keynote address, uncannily entitled 'Not yet post-Asia: Paradoxes of identity and knowledge in transitional times', Ien Ang suggests that exploring 'the possibilities of a more genuinely post-Asian imaginary – in cinema and elsewhere – may be one way for us to navigate the brittle realities of these unsettling transitional times' (135–6).[3] I suggest that a 'genuinely post-Asian imaginary' does not do away with the region Asia; rather, it is a call to re-imagine Asia anew. From imperial conceptions of Asia, externally constructed and imposed, to anti-imperialist regionalisation projects, linked to rising Asian nationalisms prior to the Second World War, to more recent 'people-to-people interactions', migrations and movements (Duara 2010: 977), we are in the midst of a new phase that is marked as much by our separation as by our connectivity. The rich and varied examples of Asian cinema that permeate this book present a refracted image of what Asian cinema from a 'regional view' might look like, and collectively, what we might hope to expect for the future.

To write an epilogue for a book during a transitional time, and a time of crisis, is not to provide a 'conclusion', but to imagine anew amidst the uncertainty. When the dust settles and global relations realign, we will look again to what the space of this new Asia will be, and what it will mean.[4] How the region reimagines itself, rebuilds and reconstructs through its cinema, this will be our legacy.

Notes

1. China's air quality is reported to have improved with the social distancing and lockdown measures imposed in an effort to contain the COVID-19 outbreak (Monk 2020).
2. An English-subtitled version can still be found on YouTube, available at <https://www.youtube.com/watch?v=V5bHb3ljjbc>. See Edwards (2015), who reports 300 million clicks, while noting that clicks do not necessarily translate to discrete viewers who have necessarily watched the whole film, but that at least that number has viewed part of the film in a very short period of time.
3. Keynote address at the 'Post-Asia Film, Media and Popular Culture' conference at the University of Macau, 14–16 July 2014.
4. In an article in *Foreign Policy*, James Traub (2020) comments on the emergence of a 'post-pandemic cold war' between China and the United States and notes that in the subsequent realignment of global relations we will see that 'the future is Asian – but not Chinese'.

Bibliography

Ahn, SooJeong (2011), *The Pusan International Film Festival, South Korean Cinema and Globalization*, Hong Kong: Hong Kong University Press.

Ahn, SooJeong (2016), 'Film festivals and regional cosmopolitanism in cosmopolitan East Asia: the case of the Busan International Film Festival', in Koichi Iwabuchi, Eva Tsai and Chris Berry (eds), *Routledge Handbook of East Asian Popular Culture*, London and New York: Routledge, pp. 265–75.

Ang, Ien (2014), 'Not yet post-Asia: paradoxes of identity and knowledge in transitional times', *Asian Cinema* 25: 2, 125–37.

Acharya, Amitav (2013), 'Asia is not one', in Prasenjit Duara (ed.), *Asia Redux: Conceptualizing a Region for Our Times*, Singapore: ISEAS Publishing, pp. 51–68.

Atkinson, Sarah (2011), 'Stereoscopic-3D storytelling: rethinking the conventions, grammar and aesthetics of a new medium', *Journal of Media Practice* 12: 2, 139–56.

Bâ, Saër Maty and Will Higbee (eds) (2012), *De-Westernizing Film Studies*, London and New York: Routledge.

Baskett, Michael (2014), 'Japan's film festival diplomacy in Cold War Asia', *The Velvet Light Trap* 73, 4–18.

Baumgärtel, Tilman (2011), 'Imagined communities, imagined worlds: independent film from Southeast Asia in the global mediascape', *Transnational Cinemas* 2: 1, 57–71.

BBC News (2019), '*Abominable*: a DreamWorks movie, a map, and a huge regional row', 18 October 2019, <https://www.bbc.com/news/world-asia-50093028>.

Berkeley, Leo (2014), 'Tram travels: smartphone video production and the essay film', in Marsha Berry and Max Schleser (eds), *Mobile Media Making in an Age of Smartphones*, London: Palgrave Pivot, pp. 25–34.

Berlant, Lauren (1998), 'Intimacy: a special issue', *Critical Inquiry* 24: 2, 281–8.

Berry, Chris (1990), '*Cinemaya:* The Asian Film Magazine', *Continuum: The Australian Journal of Media and Culture* 4: 1, <http://wwwmcc.murdoch.edu.au/Readingroom/4.1/Berry2.html>.

Berry, Chris (2010), 'What is transnational cinema? Thinking from the Chinese situation', *Transnational Cinemas* 1: 2, 111–27.

Berry, Chris (2016), 'Sino-Korean screen connections: towards a history in fragments', *Journal of Chinese Cinemas* 10: 3, 247–64.

Berry, Chris, Nicola Liscutin and Jonathan Mackintosh (eds) (2009), *Cultural Studies and Cultural Industries in Northeast Asia: What a Difference a Region Makes*, Hong Kong: Hong Kong University Press.

Bettinson, Gary (2017), 'Posthandover Hong Kong cinema: co-production, censorship, and Chinese democracy: an interview with Johnnie To', *Cineaste* 42: 4, 25–7.

Bettinson, Gary and See Kam Tan (2012), 'Editorial', *Asian Cinema* 23: 1, 3.

Betz, Mark (2001), 'Film history, film genre, and their discontents: the case of the omnibus film', *The Moving Image: The Journal of the Association of Moving Image Archivists* 1: 2, 56–87.

Betz, Mark (2009), *Beyond the Subtitle: Remapping European Art Cinema*, Minneapolis: University of Minnesota Press.

Bhushan, Nyay (2018), 'Hallyu, Indian style: why Bollywood is betting on Korean remakes', *Hollywood Reporter*, 1 March 2018, <https://www.hollywoodreporter.com/news/hallyu-indian-style-why-bollywood-is-betting-korean-remakes-1069568>.

Bischoff, Paul (2014), 'Viddsee brands itself as a launchpad for Asian short films, adds Web series to boot', *Tech in Asia*, <http://www.techinasia.com/viddsee-brands-launchpad-asian-short-filmsadds-web-series-boot/>.

Bordwell, David (2009), 'Paolo Gioli's vertical cinema', August 2009, <http://www.davidbordwell.net/essays/gioli.php>.

Brzeski, Patrick, and Lee Hyo-won (2017), 'CJ Entertainment chief on South Korea's global film plan (despite China's ban)', *Hollywood Reporter*, 3 November 2017, <https://www.hollywoodreporter.com/news/cj-entertainment-chief-south-koreas-global-film-plan-chinas-ban-1054477>.

Budiey (Admin) (2013), 'Viddsee showcases selected nominated regional short films from ASEAN International Film Festival & Awards (AIFFA) 2013', <https://www.budiey.com/viddsee-showcases-selected-nominated-regional-short-films-from-aiffa-2013/amp/>.

Bui, Hoai-Tran (2019), 'Why the Korean company behind *Parasite* is developing English-language remakes of its own films', *Slash Film*, 5 July 2019, <https://www.slashfilm.com/cj-entertainment-english-language-remakes-of-korean-films/>.

Burgess, Jean and Joshua Green (2009), *YouTube: Online Video and Participatory Culture*, Cambridge: Polity Press.

Butler, Alison (2002), *Women's Cinema: The Contested Screen*, London: Wallflower.

Carter, David (2007), *East Asian Cinema*, Harpenden: Kamera.

Carter, Geoffrey V. and Sarah J. Arroyo (2011), 'Tubing the future: participatory pedagogy and YouTube U in 2020', *Computers and Composition* 28: 292–302.

Chan, Felicia (2011), 'The international film festival and the making of a national cinema', *Screen* 52: 2, 253–60.

Chan, Felicia, Angelina Karpovich and Xin Zhang (eds) (2011), *Genre in Asian Film and Television*, London: Palgrave.

Chan, Kenneth (2009), *Remade in Hollywood: The Global Chinese Presence in Transnational Cinemas*, Hong Kong: Hong Kong University Press.

Chang, Justin (2015), 'Office' review, *Variety*, 24 September 2015, <http://variety.com/2015/film/festivals/office-review-johnnie-to-1201601248/>.

Chang, Justin (2017), 'Bong Joon Ho on Netflix's *Okja*, the meatiest film of his career', *LA Times*, <https://www.latimes.com/entertainment/movies/la-ca-mn-okja-bong-joon-ho-20170622-story.html>.

Chen, Kuan-Hsing (2010), *Asia as Method: Toward De-imperialization*, Durham, NC: Duke University Press.

Chen, Kuan-Hsing and Chua Beng Huat (eds) (2007), *The Inter-Asia Cultural Studies Reader*, London and New York: Routledge.

Ching, Leo (2000), 'Regionalizing the global; globalizing the regional: mass culture and asianism in the age of late capital', *Public Culture* 12: 1, 233–57.

Choi, Jinhee and Mitsuyo Wada-Marciano (2009), *Horror to the Extreme: Changing Boundaries in Asian Cinema*, Hong Kong: Hong Kong University Press.

Chua, Beng Huat (2004), 'Conceptualizing an East Asian popular culture', *Inter-Asia Cultural Studies* 5: 2, 200–21.

Ciecko, Anne (ed.) (2006), *Contemporary Asian Cinema: Popular Culture in a Global Frame*, New York: Berg.

Clark, Travis (2020), 'China's box office is down nearly $2 billion as movie theatres remain closed amid Coronavirus concerns', *Business Insider*, 4 March 2020, <https://www.businessinsider.com.au/coronavirus-chinas-box-office-drops-by-nearly-2-billion-2020-3?r=USandIR=T>.

Coonan, Clifford (2011a), 'Filmmakers lack technical know-how', *Variety* 422: 13, 9 May, 13.

Coonan, Clifford (2011b), '3D could be B.O. Viagra for Asia porn', *Variety* 422: 10, 18–24 April, 5.

Cremin, Stephen (2014), 'Market share of South Korean films plummets', *Film Business Asia*, 8 July 2014, <https://web.archive.org/web/20140714075132/http://www.filmbiz.asia/news/market-share-of-south-korean-films-plummets>.

Crisp, Virginia (2012), 'Film distribution in the age of the Internet: East Asian cinemas in the UK', unpublished doctoral thesis, Goldsmiths, University of London.

Cubitt, Sean (2005), *The Cinema Effect*, Boston: MIT Press.

Cui, Shuqin (2017), 'Chai Jing's *Under the Dome*: a multimedia documentary in the digital age', *Journal of Chinese Cinemas* 11: 1, 30–45.

D'Alessandro, Anthony (2020), 'Coronavirus concern at the B.O.', *Deadline*, 4 March 2020, <https://deadline.com/2020/03/black-widow-f9-no-time-to-die-coronavirus-impact-on-box-office-1202874214/>.

Dalla Gassa, Marco and Dario Tomasi (2016), 'Festival and anti-festival: the Udine Far East Film Festival', *Journal of Italian Cinema and Media Studies* 4: 1, 127–38.

Dargis, Manola (2015), 'In *Office* by Johnnie To: the ups and downs of business', *New York Times*, 17 September 2015, <https://www.nytimes.com/2015/09/18/movies/review-in-office-by-johnnie-to-ups-and-downs-of-business.html>.

Davis, Darrell William and Emilie Yueh-yu Yeh (2002), 'Japan Hongscreen: pan-Asian cinemas and flexible accumulation', *Historical Journal of Film, Radio and Television* 22: 1, 61–82.

Davis, Darrell William and Emilie Yueh-yu Yeh (2008), *East Asian Screen Industries*, London: British Film Institute.

Davis, Rebecca (2019), 'China, Taiwan in film awards face-off with Roosters, Horses scheduled on same day', *Variety*, 20 November 2019, <https://variety.com/2019/film/news/china-roosters-awards-taiwan-horses-1203409619/>.

DeBoer, Stephanie (2014), *Coproducing Asia: Locating Japanese – Chinese Regional Film and Media*, Minneapolis: University of Minnesota Press.

DeBoer, Stephanie (2015), 'Working through China: scaled convergence and the contingencies of East Asian film production', *Screen* 56: 2, 214–33.

De Lauretis, Teresa (2011), 'Queer texts, bad habits, and the issue of a future', *GLQ* 17: 2–3, 243–63.

Deleuze, Gilles and Félix Guattari (1986), *Kafka: Toward a Minor Literature* (1975), trans. Dana Polan, Minneapolis: University of Minnesota Press.

Denison, Rayna (2014), 'Japanese and Korean film franchising and adaptation', *Journal of Japanese and Korean Cinema* 6: 2, 105–17.

Deocampo, Nick (1985), *Short Film: Emergence of a New Philippine Cinema*, Manila: Communication Foundation for Asia.

Deocampo, Nick (2017), *Early Cinema in Asia*, Bloomington: Indiana University Press.

Derrida, Jacques (1996), *Archive Fever: A Freudian Impression*, Chicago: University of Chicago Press.

Derrida, Jacques and Eric Prenowitz (1995), 'Archive fever: a Freudian impression', *Diacritics* 25: 2, 9–63.

Deshpande, Shekhar and Meta Mazaj (2018), *World Cinema: A Critical Introduction*, London and New York: Routledge.

Diffrient, David Scott (2012), '*If You Were Me*: human rights discourses and transnational crossings in South Korean omnibus films', *Transnational Cinemas* 3: 1, 107–28.

Diffrient, David Scott (2014a), *Omnibus Films: Theorizing Transauthorial Cinema*, Edinburgh: Edinburgh University Press.

Diffrient, David Scott (2014b), '*The Sandwich Man:* history, episodicity and serial conditioning in a Taiwanese omnibus film', *Asian Cinema* 25: 1, 71–92.

Dissanayake, Wimal (ed.) (1994), *Colonialism and Nationalism in Asian Cinema*, Bloomington: Indiana University Press.

Donovan, Barna William (2008), *The Asian Influence on Hollywood Action Films*, Jefferson: McFarland and Co.

Doraiswamy, Rashmi and Latika Padgaonkar (2010), *Asian Film Journeys – Selections from Cinemaya 1988–2004*, Delhi: NETPAC and Wisdom Tree Publishers.

Doo, Rumy (2017), 'CJ E&M aims to become global film production studio', *Korea Herald*, 13 September 2017, <http://www.koreaherald.com/view.php?ud=20170913000777>.

Doty, Alexander (1993), *Making Things Perfectly Queer: Interpreting Mass Culture*, Minneapolis: University of Minnesota Press.

Duara, Prasenjit (2010), 'Asia redux: conceptualizing a region for our times', *Journal of Asian Studies* 69: 4, 963–83.

Duara, Prasenjit (2015), *The Crisis of Global Modernity*, London: Cambridge University Press.

Economist, The (2020), 'Covid-19 is a short-term boon to streaming services', *The Economist*, 27 March 2020, <https://www.economist.com/graphic-detail/2020/03/27/covid-19-is-a-short-term-boon-to-streaming-services>.

Edelman, Lee (2004), *No Future: Queer Theory and the Death Drive*, Durham, NC: Duke University Press.

Edwards, Dan (2015), '300 million clicks: *Under the Dome* and the Chinese documentary context', Issue 76, September 2015, <http://sensesofcinema.com/2015/documentary-in-asia/under-the-dome-chinese-documentary/>.

Edwards, Graham (2015), 'Vertical cinema', *Cineflex*, 7 April 2015, <http://cinefex.com/blog/vertical-cinema/>.

Edmondson, Ray (1997), 'An introduction to SEAPAVAA', *Oral History of Australia Journal* 19, 92–3.

Edmondson, Ray (1999), 'Opening speech of the Fourth Annual SEAPAVAA Conference, April 1999', *Journal of Film Preservation* 58–9, 104–5.

Edmondson, Ray (2000), 'Archiving "Outside the Frame": audiovisual archiving in Southeast Asia and the Pacific', *Film History* 12, 148–55.

Edmondson, Ray (2008), 'Southeast Asia-Pacific: focus on SEAPAVAA', *International Preservation News* 46, December, 29–30.

Edmondson, Ray (2014), 'AV archiving: changes, choices and challenges', *Screening the Past*, <http://www.screeningthepast.com/2014/12/av-archiving-changes-choices-and-challenges/>.

Edmondson, Ray (2015), 'Asian Film Archive at 10', Singapore: Asian Film Archive.

Eistenstein, Sergei (1930), 'The dynamic square', in J. Leyda (ed.), *Film Essays and a Lecture*, New York: Praeger, pp. 48–65.

Eleftheriotis, Dimitris and Gary Needham (eds) (2006), *Asian Cinemas: A Reader and Guide*, Edinburgh: Edinburgh University Press.

Elsaesser, Thomas (2013), 'The "return" of 3-D: on some of the logics and genealogies of the image in the twenty-first century', *Critical Inquiry* 39, 217–46.

Epstein, Adam (2017), 'Americans are over 3D movies, but Hollywood hasn't got the memo', *Quartz*, 24 March 2017, <https://qz.com/940399/americans-are-over-3d-movies-but-hollywood-hasnt-got-the-memo/>.

Ezra, Elizabeth and Terry Rowden (eds) (2006), *Transnational Cinema: the Film Reader*, London and New York: Routledge.

Fang, Karen (ed.) (2017), *Surveillance in Asian Cinema: Under Eastern Eyes*, London and New York: Routledge.

Fernández Labayen, Miguel and Ana Martín Morán (2019), 'Manufacturing proximity through film remakes: remake rights representatives and the case of local-language comedy remakes', *Communications: The European Journal of Communication Research* 44: 3, 282–303.

Foo, Juan (2002), 'Mini cinema', *FilmsAsia*, December 2002, <http://www.filmsasia.net/gpage77.html>.

Frater, Patrick (2019a), 'Local production drive sees CJ Entertainment unveil dozen international titles', *Variety*, 19 March 2019, <https://variety.com/2019/film/asia/local-production-drive-sees-cj-entertainment-unveil-dozen-international-titles-1203166576/>.

Frater, Patrick (2019b), 'Rescued from bankruptcy, Fortissimo Films set for sales and PR comeback in Berlin', 28 January 2019, <https://variety.com/2019/film/news/fortissimo-films-sales-pr-comeback-berlin-film-festival-1203120314/>.

Frater, Patrick (2020), 'Coronavirus gives 60% boost to mobile streaming in Southeast Asia', *Variety*, 20 April 2020.

Frater, Patrick and Sonia Kil (2019), 'Asian film awards to relocate from Hong Kong to Busan', *Variety*, 4 October 2019, <https://variety.com/2019/film/asia/asian-film-awards-relocate-busan-1203358608/>.

Gates, Philippa and Lisa Funnell (eds) (2012), *Transnational Asian identities in Pan-Pacific Cinemas: the Reel Asian Exchange*, London and New York: Routledge.

Global Times (2018), 'Chinese filmmakers choosing 2D over 3D for their films', 22 January 2018, <https://www.globaltimes.cn/content/1085981.shtml>.

Goh, Teck Fann (2020), 'Japanese film festivals and cultural diplomacy in the Asia-Pacific', unpublished PhD dissertation, Monash University, Australia.

Gopalan, Lalitha (2002), *Cinema of Interruptions: Action Genres in Contemporary Indian Cinema*, London: BFI.

Grossman, Andrew (ed.) (2000), *Queer Asian Cinema: Shadows in the Shade*, Binghampton, NY: Haworth Press.

Groves, Don (2012), 'Italy takes first stab at soft sex in 3D', *SBS*, 13 February 2012, <https://www.sbs.com.au/movies/blog/2012/02/13/italy-takes-first-stab-soft-sex-3d>.

Gunning, Tom (1989–90), 'Toward a minor cinema', *Motion Picture* 3: 1–2, 2–5.

Gunning, Tom (1990), 'The cinema of attraction: early film, its spectator and the avant-garde', in Thomas Elsaesser (ed.), *Early Cinema: Space, Frame, Narrative*, London: BFI.

Gunning, Tom (1994), 'An aesthetic of astonishment', in Linda Williams (ed.), *Viewing Positions: Ways of Seeing Film*, New Brunswick, NJ: Rutgers University Press.

Han, Sunhee (2010), '3D drives mart meet', 420: 8, October: 26.

Hanan, David (ed.) (2001), *Film in Southeast Asia: Views from the Region – Essays on Film in Ten Southeast Asia-Pacific Countries*, Manila: Southeast Asia-Pacific Audiovisual Archive Association.

Hans, Simran (2017), '*I Am Not Madame Bovary* review: slow boat from China', *The Guardian*, 28 May 2017, <https://www.theguardian.com/film/2017/may/28/i-am-not-madame-bovary-review-china-kafkaesque>.

Hayes, R. M. (1989), *A History and Filmography of Stereoscopic Cinema*, Jefferson, NC: McFarland.

Higbee, Will and Song Hwee Lim (2010), 'Concepts of transnational cinema: towards a critical transnationalism in film studies', *Transnational Cinemas* 1: 1, 7–21.

Higson, Andrew (2000), 'The limiting imagination of national cinema', in Mette Hjort and Scott Mackenzie (eds), *Cinema and Nation*, London and New York: Routledge, pp, 63–74.

Higson, Andrew (2011), *Film England: Culturally English Filmmaking Since the 1990s*, London: I. B. Tauris.

Hillenbrand, Margaret (2010), 'Communitarianism, or how to build an East Asian theory', *Postcolonial Studies* 13: 4, 317–34.

Hjorth, Larissa (2005), 'Locating Mobility: practices of co-presence and the persistence of the postal metaphor in SMS/MMS mobile phone customization in Melbourne', *The Fibreculture Journal* 6, <http://six.fibreculturejournal.org/fcj-035-locating-mobility-practices-of-co-presence-and-the-persistence-of-the-postal-metaphor-in-sms-mms-mobile-phone-customization-in-melbourne/>.

Ho, Sam (2001), 'Fragile heritage and promising outlook: Asian Film Archives look ahead while looking back', *Journal of Film Preservation* 62, 2–9.

Hou Hsiao-Hsien (2003), 'In search of new genres and directions for Asian cinema', trans. Lin Wenchi, *Rouge 1*, <http://www.rouge.com.au/1/hou.html>.

Hoffman, Torsten (2012), 'Travel report: 3D (and *Avengers* 4D) in Korea', *3D Content Blog*, 19 May 2012, <https://3dcontentblog.wordpress.com/?s=4d+korea>.

Hunt, Leon and Leung Wing-Fai (eds) (2008), *East Asian Cinemas: Exploring Transnational Connections on Film*, London: I. B. Tauris.

Hwang, Yun Mi (2012), 'Trans-action: epic tensions and ethics of memory in East Asian co-productions', in Philippa Gates and Lisa Funnell (eds), *Transnational Asian Identities in Pan-Pacific Cinemas: The Reel Asian Exchange*, New York: Routledge, pp. 115–29.

Hyland, Robert (2014), 'Conference report: first past the post: 11th Asian Cinema Studies Society International Conference Roundup, Post-Asia Film, Media and Popular Culture, University of Macau, 14–16 July 2014', *Asian Cinema* 25: 2, 239–46.

Iordanova, Dina (2011), 'East Asia and film festivals: transnational clusters for creativity and commerce', in Dina Iordanova and Ruby Cheung (eds), *Film Festival Yearbook 3: Film Festivals and East Asia*, St Andrews: St Andrews Film Studies, pp. 1–33.

Iordanova, Dina and Ragan Rhyne (eds) (2009), *Film Festival Yearbook 1: The Festival Circuit*, St Andrews: St Andrews Film Studies.

Iordanova, Dina and Ruby Cheung (eds) (2010), *Film Festival Yearbook 2: Film Festivals and Imagined Communities*, St Andrews: St Andrews Film Studies.

Iordanova, Dina and Ruby Cheung (eds) (2011), *Film Festival Yearbook 3: Film Festivals and East Asia*, St Andrews: St Andrews Film Studies.

Ito, Mizuko, Misa Matsuda and Daisuke Okabe (eds) (2005), *Personal, Pedestrian and Portable: Mobile Phones in Japanese Life*, Cambridge, MA: MIT Press.

Iwabuchi, Koichi (2002), *Recentering Globalization: Popular Culture and Japanese Transnationalism*, Durham, NC and London: Duke University Press.

Iwabuchi, Koichi (ed.) (2004), *Feeling Asian Modernities: Transnational Consumption of Japanese TV Dramas*, Hong Kong: Hong Kong University Press.

Iwabuchi, Koichi (2010), 'De-Westernization and the governance of global cultural connectivity: a dialogic approach to East Asian media cultures, *Postcolonial Studies* 13: 4, 403–19.

Iwabuchi, Koichi (2013), 'Against banal internationalism', *Asian Journal of Social Science* 41, 437–52.

Iwabuchi, Koichi (2014), 'De-Westernisation, inter-Asian referencing and beyond', *European Journal of Cultural Studies* 17: 1, 44–57.

Iwabuchi, Koichi (2016), 'Trans-East Asia as method', in Koichi Iwabuchi (ed.), *Routledge Handbook of East Asian Popular Culture*, London and New York: Routledge, pp. 276–84.

Jackson, Andrew, Michael Gibb and Dave White (eds) (2006), *How East Asian Films are Reshaping National Identities: Essays on the Cinemas of China, Japan, South Korea, and Hong Kong*, New York: Edwin Mellen.

Jin, Dal Yong and Dong-Hoo Lee (2007), 'The birth of East Asia: cultural regionalization through co-production strategies', *Spectator* 27: 2, 31–45.

Jin, Dal Yong and Wendy Su (eds) (2019), *Asia-Pacific Film Co-productions: Theory, Industry and Aesthetics*, London and New York: Routledge.

Jones, Nick (2015), 'Variation within stability: digital 3D and film style', *Cinema Journal* 55: 1, 52–73.

Kang, Wenqing (2009), *Obsession: Male Same-Sex Relations in China, 1900–1950*, Hong Kong: Hong Kong University Press.

Khoo, Olivia (2006), 'Slang images: on the foreignness of contemporary Singaporean films', *Inter-Asia Cultural Studies* 7: 1, 81–98.

Khoo, Olivia, Belinda Smaill and Audrey Yue (2013), *Transnational Australian Cinema: Ethics in the Asian Diasporas*, Lanham, MD: Lexington.

Kil, Sonia (2015), 'CJ Entertainment at 20: still remaking movie markets', *Variety*, 13 May 2015, <https://variety.com/2015/film/spotlight/cj-entertainment-korean-cinema-1201494678/?jwsource=cl>.

Kil, Sonia (2017), 'Korea's CJ Entertainment targets global production', 13 October 2017, <https://variety.com/2017/film/asia/cj-entertainment-targets-global-production-1202589106/>.

Kim, Christine (2016a), *The Minor Intimacies of Race: Asian Publics in North America*, Champaign: University of Illinois Press.

Kim, Chunhyo (2016b), *Samsung, Media Empire and Family: A Power Web*, London and New York: Routledge.

Kim, Darae, Dina Iordanova and Chris Berry (2015), 'The Busan International Film Festival in crisis or, What should a film festival be?', *Film Quarterly* 69: 1, 80–9.

Kim, Soyoung (2005a), 'Genre as contact zone: Hong Kong action and Korena Hwalkuk', in Meaghan Morris, Siu Leung Li and Stephen Ching-kiu Chan (eds), *Hong Kong Connections: Transnational Imagination in Action Cinema*, Hong Kong: Hong Kong University Press, pp. 97–110.

Kim, Soyoung (2005b), '"Cine-mania" or cinephilia: film festivals and the identity question', in Chi-Yun Shin and Julian Stringer (eds), *New Korean Cinema*, New York: New York University Press, pp. 79–94.

Kim, Soyoung (2008), 'Postcolonial film historiography in Taiwan and South Korea', *Inter-Asia Cultural Studies* 9: 2, 195–210.

Kim, Soyoung (2013), 'Comparative film studies: detour, demon of comparison and dislocative fantasy', *Inter-Asia Cultural Studies* 14: 1, 44–53.

Knee, Adam (2006), 'Thailand in the Hong Kong cinematic imagination', in Gina Marchetti and See Kam Tan (eds), *Hong Kong Film, Hollywood and the New Global Cinema: No Film is an Island*, London and New York: Routledge, pp. 77–106.

Knee, Adam (2009), 'Film festival downsizing: a tale of two Southeast Asian cities', *Asian Cinema* 20: 1, 219–25.

Korea Bizwire (2017), 'CJ E&M to open "Hallyu" channels in Malaysia, Vietnam, Hong Kong', 3 April 2017, <http://koreabizwire.com/cj-em-to-open-hallyu-channels-in-malaysia-vietnam-hong-kong/79425>.

Kraicer, Shelly (1998), '*The Stormriders* and the future of Hong Kong cinema: a polemic', <http://www.chinesecinemas.org/stormriders.html>.

Kraicer, Shelly (2017), 'Small things and big things: Feng Xiaogang's *I Am Not Madame Bovary*', *CinemaScope* 70, <http://cinema-scope.com/features/small-things-and-big-things-feng-xiaogangs-i-am-not-madame-bovary/>.

Kwok, Kar Peng (2012), 'He wants to shake things up in 4-D', *The New Paper*, 30 March 2012, <https://www.asiaone.com/News/Latest%2BNews/Showbiz/Story/A1Story20120328-336325.html>.

Lange, P. M. (2010), 'Achieving creative integrity on YouTube, reciprocities and tensions', <http://enculturation.camden.rutgers.edu/achieving-creative-integrity>.

Lau, Jenny Kwok Wah (ed.) (2003), *Multiple Modernities: Cinemas and Popular Media in Transcultural East Asia*, Philadelphia: Temple University Press.

Leary, Charles (2004), 'Fulltime cinema: an interview with Johnnie To', *Off-Screen* 8: 6, <http://offscreen.com/view/johnnie_to>.

Lee Hyo-won (2017), 'CJ Entertainment to expand slate of overseas productions', *Hollywood Reporter*, 13 September 2017, <https://www.hollywoodreporter.com/news/cj-entertainment-expand-slate-overseas-productions-1038381>.

Lee Hyo-won (2018), 'South Korea's CJ Entertainment launches genre label 413 Pictures', *Hollywood Reporter*, 27 July 2018, <https://www.hollywoodreporter.com/news/south-koreas-cj-entertainment-launches-genre-label-413-pictures-1130260>.

Lee, Hyung-sook (2006a), *Between Local and Global: the Hong Kong Film Syndrome in South Korea*, Ann Arbor, MI: University of Michigan Press.

Lee, Hyung-sook (2006b), 'Peripherals encounter: the Hong Kong film syndrome in South Korea', *Discourse* 28: 2 and 3, 98–113.

Lee, Maggie (2011), '*The Little Ghostly Adventures of Tofu Boy*: movie review', *Hollywood Reporter*, 18 April 2011, <https://www.hollywoodreporter.com/review/little-ghostly-adventures-tofu-boy-179442>.

Lee, Nikki J. Y. (2012), 'Asianization and locally customized "Kor-Asian" movies: *Goodbye, One Day* (2010) and *Sophie's Revenge* (2009)', *Transnational Cinemas* 3: 1, 81–92.

Lee, Nikki J. Y. (2011), '"Asia" as regional signifier and transnational genre-branding: the Asian horror omnibus movies *Three* and *Three . . . Extremes*', in Vivian P. Y. Lee (ed.), *East Asian Cinemas: Regional Flows and Global Transformations*, New York: Palgrave Macmillan, pp. 103–17.

Lee, Nikki J. Y. and Julian Stringer (2012a), 'Counter-programming and the Udine Far East Film Festival', *Screen* 53: 3, 301–9.

Lee, Nikki J. Y. and Julian Stringer (2012b), 'Ports of entry: mapping Chinese cinema's multiple trajectories at international film festivals', in Yingjin Zhang (ed.), *A Companion to Chinese Cinema*, Oxford: Wiley-Blackwell, pp. 239–61.

Lee, Sangjoon (2017), 'The Asia Foundation's motion-picture project and the cultural Cold War in Asia', *Film History* 29: 2, 108–37.

Lee, Vivian P. Y. (ed.) (2011a), *East Asian Cinemas: Regional Flows and Global Transformations*, New York: Palgrave Macmillan.

Lee, Vivian P. Y. (2011b), '"Working through China" in the Pan-Asian film network: perspectives from Hong Kong and Singapore', in Vivian P. Y. Lee (ed.), *East Asian Cinemas: Regional Flows and Global Transformations*, London: Palgrave, pp. 235–48.

Lent, John A. (1990), *The Asian Film Industry*, Austin: University of Texas Press.

Lent, John A. (2011a), 'A rundown of 16 years of publication', *Asian Cinema* 22: 1, 1–2.

Lent, John A. (2011b), 'One recollection of the beginnings of Asian Cinema Studies Society and *Asian Cinema*', *Asian Cinema* 22: 2, 1–19.

Lent, John A. (2012), 'The history of the Asian Cinema Studies Society and *Asian Cinema* – continued: 1994–2012', *Asian Cinema* 23: 1, 105–11.

Lent, John A. (2013), 'Institutional approach can stifle scholarship', *Media Asia* 40: 4, 300–5.

Leung, Helen Hok-Sze (2001), 'Queerscapes in contemporary Hong Kong cinema', *positions: east asia cultures critique* 9: 2, 423–47.

Leung, Helen Hok-Sze (2003), 'Queer Asian cinemas', in Lisa Daniel and Claire Jackson (eds), *Bent Lens: A World Guide to Gay and Lesbian Films*, New York: Alyson Books.

Leung, Helen Hok-Sze (2008), *Undercurrents: Queer Culture and Postcolonial Hong Kong*, Hong Kong: Hong Kong University Press.

Li, Jinhua (2011), 'Transnational remakes: gender and politics in Chinese cinemas and Hollywood (1990–2009)', unpublished dissertation, Purdue University, Indiana.

Lijano, Ed (2018), 'NETPAC Festival Report 2018', <http://netpacasia.org/blogpost183-Vesoul-International-Film-Festival-of-Asian-Cinema-FICA-2018>.

Lim, David and Yamamoto, Hiroyuki (eds) (2011), *Film in Contemporary Southeast Asia: Cultural Interpretation and Social Intervention*, New York: Routledge.

Lionnet, Françoise and Shu-mei Shih (2005), *Minor Transnationalism*, Durham, NC: Duke University Press.

Lo, Kwai-Cheung (2009), 'Hong Kong ghost in the Japanese shell? Cross-racial performance and transnational Chinese cinema', in Olivia Khoo and Sean Metzger (eds), *Futures of Chinese Cinema: Technologies and Temporalities in Chinese Screen Cultures*, Bristol: Intellect, 2009, pp. 95–110.

Lo, Kwai-Cheung (2014), 'Rethinking Asianism and method', *European Journal of Cultural Studies* 17: 1, 31–43.

Lodderhose, Diana (2017), '*Okja* director hopes Netflix controversy becomes a "signal flare" in establishing new rules on day-and-date streaming', *Deadline*, 14 June 2017, <https://deadline.com/2017/06/okja-bong-joon-ho-netflix-controversy-becomes-signal-flare-in-establishing-new-rules-for-day-and-date-streaming-tilda-swinton-jake-gyllenaal-1202113040/>.

Lu, Sheldon (1997), *Transnational Chinese Cinemas: Identity, Nationhood, Gender*, Honolulu: University of Hawaii Press.

Lui, John (2017), 'The Life interview with Karen Chan: guardian of old films', *Straits Times*, 13 November 2017, <https://www.straitstimes.com/lifestyle/the-life-interview-with-karen-chan-guardian-of-old-films>.

Magnan-Park, Aaron Han Joon, Gina Marchetti and See Kam Tan (eds) (2018), *The Palgrave Handbook of Asian Cinema*, London and New York: Palgrave Macmillan.

Mak, Monica (2003), 'Keeping watch of time: the temporal impact of the digital in cinema', paper presented at the 'Life By Design: Everyday Digital Culture' symposium, University of California, Irvine, 10–12 April 2003, <http://www.humanities.uci.edu/visualstudies/everyday/papers/Mak.pdf>.

Manoff, Marlene (2004), 'Theories of the archive from across the disciplines', *Portal: Libraries and the Academy* 4: 1, 9–25.

Manovich, Lev (1995), "What is digital cinema?" <http://manovich.net/index.php/projects/what-is-digital-cinema>.

Marchetti, Gina (2008), 'Asian film and digital culture', in Robert Kolker (ed.), *The Oxford Handbook of Film and Media Studies*, London: Oxford University Press, pp. 414–21.

Marketing-Interactive (2018), 'Korean firm CJ E&M and mm2 join forces to up SEA film content quality', 11 May 2018, <https://www.marketing-interactive.com/korean-content-firm-cj-em-and-mm2-join-forces-to-up-sea-film-content-quality/>.

Marks, Laura U. (2000), *The Skin of the Film: Intercultural Cinema, Embodiment and the Senses*, Durham, NC: Duke University Press.

Media Development Authority (MDA) (2010a), Singapore, 'China and Singapore sign film co-production agreement', 23 July 2010, <http://www.mda.gov.sg/NewsAndEvents/PressRelease/2010/Pages/23072010.aspx>.

Media Development Authority (MDA) (2010b), Singapore, 'Singapore to showcase stereoscopic 3d and animation capabilities at 10th MIPCOM Expedition', 28 September 2010, <http://www.mda.gov.sg/NewsAndEvents/PressRelease/2010/Pages/28092010.aspx>.

Media Development Authority (MDA) (2010c), *Media Fusion E-Newsletter*, issue 32.

Millward, Steven (2013), 'New startup makes Southeast Asian short films more social and accessible', *Tech In Asia*, <http://www.techinasia.com/new-viddsee-for-southeast-asian-short-films/>.

Mitchell, Rick (2004), 'The tragedy of 3-D cinema', *Film History* 16: 3, 208–15.

Mohanty, Chandra Talpade (1991), 'Cartographies of struggle – third world women and the politics of feminism', in Chandra Talpade Mohanty, Ann

Russo and Lourdes Torres, (eds), *Third World Women and the Politics of Feminism*, Indianapolis: Indiana University Press, pp. 1–50.

Monk, Paul (2020), 'Coronavirus: lockdown's effect on air pollution provides rare glimpse of low-carbon future', *The Conversation*, 15 April 2020, <https://the-conversation.com/coronavirus-lockdowns-effect-on-air-pollution-provides-rare-glimpse-of-low-carbon-future-134685>.

Morris, Meaghan, Siu Leung Li and Stephen Ching-kiu Chan (eds) (2005), *Hong Kong Connections: Transnational Imagination in Action Cinema*, Durham, NC and Hong Kong: Hong Kong University Press, pp. 1–18.

Muñoz, José Esteban (2009), *Cruising Utopias: The Then and Now of Queer Futurity*, New York: New York University Press.

Murthy, C. S. H. N. (2013), 'Film remakes as cross-cultural connections between north and south: a case study of the Telugu film industry's contribution to Indian filmmaking', *Journal of International Communication* 19: 1, 19–42.

Mulvey, Laura (2005), *Death 24 x Second*. London: Reaktion Books.

Naficy, Hamid (2001), *An Accented Cinema: Exilic and Diasporic Filmmaking*, New Jersey: Princeton University Press.

Naficy, Hamid (2008), 'For a theory of regional cinemas: Middle Eastern, North African and Central Asian cinemas', *Early Popular Visual Culture* 6: 2, 97–102.

Nagib, Lucia (2017), 'The horizontal spread of a vertical malady: cosmopolitanism and history in Pernambuco's recent cinematic sensation', in Maria Delgado and Stephen Hart and Randal Johnson (eds), *A Companion to Latin American Cinema*, New Jersey: Wiley-Blackwell, pp. 343–56.

Neves, Joshua (2012), 'Media archipelagos: inter-Asian film festivals', *Discourse* 34: 2–3, 230–9.

Neves, Joshua and Bhaskar Sarkar (eds) (2017), *Asian Video Cultures: In the Penumbra of the Global*, Durham, NC and London: Duke University Press.

Noh, Jean (2016), '*Sweet 20* breaks Vietnamese box office record', *Screen Daily*, 20 February 2016, <https://www.screendaily.com/news/sweet-20-breaks-vietnamese-box-office-record/5100682.article>.

Nornes, Abé Mark (2013), 'The creation and construction of Asian cinema redux', *Film History* 25: 1–2, 175–87.

O'Falt, Chris (2019), 'Building the *Parasite* house: how Bong Joon Ho and his team made the year's best set', *Indiewire*, 29 October 2019, <https://www.indiewire.com/2019/10/parasite-house-set-design-bong-joon-ho-1202185829/>.

Pang, Laikwan (2007), 'Postcolonial Hong Kong cinema: utilitarianism and (trans)local', *Journal of Postcolonial Studies* 10: 4, 413–30.

Pang, Laikwan (2010), 'Hong Kong cinema as a dialect cinema', *Cinema Journal* 49: 3, 140–3.

Pang, Laikwan (2012), *Creativity and its Discontents: China's Creative Industries and Intellectual Property Rights Offenses*, Durham, NC: Duke University Press.

Peng, Weiying (2016), 'Sino-US film coproduction: a global media primer', *Global Media and China* 1: 4, 295–311.

Perkins, Claire and Constantine Verevis (2014), *B Is for Bad Cinema: Aesthetics, Politics, and Cultural Value*, New York: SUNY Press.

Pierson, Michele (2002), *Special Effects: Still in Search of Wonder*, New York: Columbia University Press.

Pugsley, Peter (2013), *Tradition, Culture and Aesthetics in Contemporary Asian Cinema*, London: Ashgate.

Pugsley, Peter (2015), *Exploring Morality and Sexuality in Asian Cinema: Cinematic Boundaries*, London: Ashgate.

Rajadhyaksha, Ashish and Kim Soyoung (2003), 'Introduction: imagining the cinema anew', *Inter-Asia Cultural Studies* 4: 1, 7–9.

Racoma, J. A. (2013), 'Viddsee launches mobile web app, looks to grow community', *Floost*, <http://e27.co/viddsee-launches-mobile-web-app-looks-to-grow-community/>.

Ramachandran, Naman (2018), 'Women directors drive new Japanese omnibus film', *Variety*, 7 October 2018, <https://variety.com/2018/film/asia/women-directors-japan-omnibus-film-1202971470/>.

Roy, Arundhati (2020), 'The pandemic is a portal', *Financial Times*, 4 April 2020, <https://www.ft.com/content/10d8f5e8-74eb-11ea-95fe-fcd274e920ca>.

Roxborough Scott and Patrick Brzeski (2018), 'Why local-language remakes are thriving at the global box office', *Hollywood Reporter*, 16 February 2018, <https://www.hollywoodreporter.com/news/berlin-why-local-language-remakes-are-thriving-at-global-box-office-1085701>.

Russell, Jon (2013), 'Viddsee is a place for Southeast Asia's top short filmmakers to showcase their work', *The Next Web*, 6 February 2013, <http://thenextweb.com/asia/2013/02/06/viddsee-southeast-short-films/>.

Sakai, Naoki (2000), '"You Asians": on the historical role of the West and Asia binary', *South Atlantic Quarterly* 99: 4, 789–817.

Schleser, Max (2014), 'Connecting through mobile autobiographies: self-reflexive mobile filmmaking, self-representation and selfies', in Marsha Berry and Max Schleser (eds), *Mobile Media Making in an Age of Smartphones*, London: Palgrave Pivot.

Screen Daily (2020), '*Lost In Russia* racks up 600m views as Chinese streaming platforms flourish during virus outbreak', *Screen Daily*, 30 January 2020, <https://www.screendaily.com/news/chinese-streaming-platforms-flourish-during-virus-outbreak/5146713.article>.

Shim, Ae-Gyung and Brian Yecies (2012), 'Asian interchange: Korean-Hong Kong co-productions of the 1960s', *Journal of Japanese and Korean Cinema* 4: 1, 15–28.

Shim, Doobo (2012), 'Korean cinema industry and cinema regionalization in East Asia', in Nissim Otmazgin and Eyal Ben-Ari (eds), *Popular Culture Co-Productions and Collaborations in East and Southeast Asia*, Singapore: NUS Press, pp. 52–67.

Shim, Doobo (2016), 'Hybridity, Korean Wave, and Asian media', in Koichi Iwabuchi, Eva Tsai and Chris Berry (eds), *Routledge Handbook of East Asian Popular Culture*, London and New York: Routledge, pp. 34–44.

Sinnott, Megan (2010), 'Borders, diaspora, and regional connections: trends in Asian 'queer' Studies', *Journal of Asian Studies* 69: 1: 17–31.

Sitney, P. Adams (ed.) (1970), *The Film Culture Reader*, New York: Praeger Publishers.

Smith, Iain Robert and Constantine Verevis (2017), *Transnational Film Remakes*, Edinburgh: Edinburgh University Press.

Sobchack, Vivian (1989), 'Cities on the edge of time: the urban science fiction film', *East-West Film Journal* 3: 1, 4–19.

Soh, Kai and Brian Yecies (2017), 'Korean-Chinese film remakes in a new age of cultural globalisation: *Miss Granny* (2014) and *20 Once Again* (2015) along the digital road', *Global Media and China* 2: 1, 74–89.

Spakowski, Nicola (2011), '"Gender" trouble: feminism in China under the impact of Western theory and the spatialization of identity', *positions: east asia cultures critique* 19: 1, 31–54.

Srinivas, S. V. (2003), 'Hong Kong action film in the Indian B circuit', *Inter Asia Cultural Studies* 4: 1, 40–62.

Stewart, Andrew (2011), 'Global 3D biz looks blurry', *Variety*, 22 August 2011, <https://variety.com/2011/digital/features/global-3d-biz-looks-blurry-1118041659/>.

Straubhaar, Joseph (1991), 'Beyond media imperialism: assymetrical interdependence and cultural proximity', *Critical Studies in Mass Communication* 8: 1, 39–59.

Strauven, Wanda (2007), *Cinema of Attractions Reloaded*, Chicago: Chicago University Press.

Stringer, Julian (2008), 'Film festivals in Asia', in Marijke de Valck, Brendan Kredell and Skadi Loist (eds), *Film Festivals: History, Theory, Method, Practice*, London and New York: Routledge.

Sweeney, R. Emmet (2015), 'Review: *Office*', *Film Comment*, 14 September 2015, <https://www.filmcomment.com/blog/review-office/>.

Szeto, Mirana and Yun-Chung Chen (2012), 'Mainlandization or Sinophone translocality? Challenges for Hong Kong SAR New Wave cinema', *Journal of Chinese Cinema* 6: 2, 115–34.

Szonyi, Michael (1998), 'The cult of Hu Tianbao and the eighteenth-century discourse of homosexuality', *Late Imperial China* 19: 1, 1–25.

Takeuchi, Yoshimi (2005), 'Asia as method', in Richard F. Calichman (ed. and trans.), *What is Modernity? Writings of Takeuchi Yoshimi*, New York: Columbia University Press, pp. 149–66.

Tan, Elizabeth (2013), 'Watch the best of Singapore's short films on Viddsee and hear from their co-founder', *Singapore News*, 21 February 2013, <http://sg.news.yahoo.com/watch-best-singapore-short-films-viddseehear-co-050730745.html>.

Tan, Kenneth Paul (2015a), 'Asian Film Archive at 10', Singapore: Asian Film Archive.

Tan, Kirsten (2015b), 'Asian Film Archive at 10', Singapore: Asian Film Archive.

Tan, Roy (n.d.), 'Singapore Gay Films', *sgWiki*, <http://sgwiki.com/wiki/Singapore_gay_films>.

Tanvir, Kuhu (2013), 'Pirate histories: rethinking the Indian Film Archive', *BioScope* 4: 2, 115–36.

Taubin, Amy (2016), '*Too To*', *Art Forum*, 25 March 2016, <http://artforum. com/film/id=58957>.

Teo, Stephen (2008), '*Promise* and *Perhaps Love*: Pan-Asian production and the Hong Kong-China interrelationship', *Inter-Asia Cultural Studies* 9: 3, 341–58.

Teo, Stephen (2009), 'Asian film festivals and their diminishing glitter domes: an appraisal of PIFF, SIFF and HKIFF', in Richard Porton (ed.), *Dekalog 3 – On Film Festivals*, London: Wallflower Press, pp. 109–121.

Teo, Stephen (2012), *The Asian Cinema Experience: Styles, Spaces, Theory*, London and New York: Routledge.

Thompson, Kristin (2009), 'Has 3D already failed?', 28 August 2009, <http:// www.davidbordwell.net/blog/2009/08/28/has-3-d-already-failed/>.

Tiffany, Kaitlyn (2017), '*Okja* is the first great Netflix Movie – here's why that matters', 26 June 2017, <https://www.theverge.com/2017/6/26/15747466/ netflix-okja-bong-joon-ho-snowpiercer-cannes-hollywood>.

Times of India (2013), 'TV created audience for mature films, Mostofa Sarwar Farooki says', *Times of India*, 16 November 2013, <https://timesofindia. indiatimes.com/entertainment/events/kolkata/Star-cast-of-Hanuman-com- at-a-restaurant-launch-in-Kolkata/articleshow/25831382.cms>.

Trefis Team (2020), 'Netflix stock up 14% in 2020 at $375 despite COVID-19; is it sustainable?', *Forbes*, 2 April 2020, <https://www.forbes.com/sites/ greatspeculations/2020/04/02/netflix-stock-up-14-in-2020-at-375-despite- covid-19-is-it-sustainable/#7df82eed30e4>.

Traub, James (2020), 'The future is Asian – but not Chinese', *Foreign Policy*, 27 April 2020, <https://foreignpolicy.com/2020/04/27/the-future-is-asian- but-not-chinese-coronavirus-pandemic-china-korea-singapore-taiwan/>.

Uhde, Yvonne Ng and Jan Uhde (2000), *Latent Images: Film in Singapore*, Singa- pore and New York: Oxford University Press.

Uhde, Jan and Yvonne Ng Uhde (2004), 'Singapore cinema: spotlight on short film production', *Spectator* 24: 2, 18–26.

UNESCO Bangkok: Asia and Pacific Regional Bureau for Education (2017), 'Media advisory: preserving Southeast Asia's cinematic heritage through UNESCO's memory of the world programme', 6 June 2017, <https://bangkok.unesco. org/content/media-advisory-preserving-southeast-asia%E2%80%99s-cine- matic-heritage-through-unesco%E2%80%99s-memory-world>.

Vasudev, Aruna, Latika Padgaonkar and Rashmi Doraiswamy (eds) (2002), *Being and Becoming, the Cinemas of Asia*, India: Macmillan.

Verevis, Constantine (2006), *Film Remakes*, Edinburgh: Edinburgh University Press.

Vick, Tom (2007), *Asian Cinema: From Iran to Thailand, India and Japan – An Expedition Through the Dynamic World of Asian Film*, New York: HarperCollins.

Voci, Paola (2012), *China on Screen: Smaller-Screen Realities*, London and New York: Routledge.

Wagner, Keith B., Tianqi Yu and Luke Vulpiani (2014), 'Introduction – China's iGeneraton cinema: dispersion, individualization and post-WTO moving image practices', in Wagner, Keith B., Tianqi Yu, Luke Vulpiani and Matthew

D. Johnson (eds), *China's iGeneration Cinema and Moving Image Culture for the Twenty-First Century*, London: Bloomsbury, pp. 1–20.

Wagner Keith B., Tianqi Yu, Luke Vulpiani and Matthew D. Johnson (eds) (2014), *China's iGeneration Cinema and Moving Image Culture for the Twenty-First Century*, London: Bloomsbury.

Wang, Lingzhen (2011), *Chinese Women's Cinema: Transnational Contexts*, New York: Columbia University Press.

Wang, Yiman (2013), *Remaking Chinese Cinema: Through the Prism of Shanghai, Hong Kong, and Hollywood*, Honolulu: University of Hawaii Press.

Weissberg, Jay (2009), 'Third person singular number', *Variety*, 2 November 2009, <https://variety.com/2009/scene/reviews/third-person-singular-number-1200477629/>.

Whissel, Kristen (2014), *Spectacular Digital Effects: CGI and Contemporary Cinema*, Durham, NC: Duke University Press.

White, Patricia (2008), 'Lesbian minor cinema', *Screen* 49: 4, 410–25.

White, Patricia (2015), *Women's Cinema, World Cinema: Projecting Contemporary Feminisms*, Durham, NC: Duke University Press.

Willemen, Paul (2002), 'Detouring through Korean cinema', *Inter-Asia Cultural Studies* 3: 2, 167–86.

Willemen, Paul (2005), 'For a comparative film studies', *Inter-Asia Cultural Studies* 6: 1, 98–112.

Willemen, Paul (2013), 'Introduction to *Subjectivity and Fantasy in Action: For a Comparative Film Studies*', *Inter-Asia Cultural Studies* 14: 1, 96–103.

Wong, Cindy Hing-Yuk (2007), 'Distant screens: film festivals and the global projection of Hong Kong cinema', in Gina Marchetti and Tan See Kam (eds), *Hong Kong Film, Hollywood and the New Global Cinema: No Film is an Island*, London and New York: Routledge, pp. 177–92.

Wong, Cindy Hing-Yuk (2011), *Film Festivals: Culture, People, and Power on the Global Screen*, New Brunswick, NJ: Rutgers University Press.

Wong, Kenneth (2013), 'Watching Southeast Asian short films with Viddsee', *Pop Culture Online* 34, <http://www.popcultureonline.net/pop-corn/watching-southeast-asian-short-films-viddsee>.

Xu, Gang Gary (2005), 'Remaking East Asia, outsourcing Hollywood', *Senses of Cinema* 34, February, <http://sensesofcinema.com/2005/feature-articles/remaking_east_asia/>.

Xu, Terry (2015), 'Singapore startup Viddsee streams regional short films for the social Web', *Online Citizen*, 1 October 2015, <https://www.onlinecitizenasia.com/2013/04/24/singapore-startup-viddsee-streams-regional-short-films-for-social-web/>.

Yang, Fan (2016), '*Under the Dome*: "Chinese" smog as a viral media event', *Critical Studies in Media Communication* 33: 3, 232–44.

Yau Shuk-ting, Kinnia (2009), 'The early development of East Asian cinema in a regional context', *Asian Studies Review* 33, 161–73.

Yau Shuk-ting, Kinnia (2010), *Japanese and Hong Kong Film Industries: Understanding the Origins of East Asian Film Networks*, London and New York: Routledge.

Yau Shuk-ting, Kinnia (2011), *East Asian Cinema and Cultural Heritage: From China, Hong Kong, Taiwan to Japan and South Korea*, London: Palgrave Macmillan.

Yecies, Brian (*2016*), 'Transnational collaboration of the multisensory kind: exploiting Korean 4D cinema in China', *Media International Australia* 159: 1, 22–31.

Yecies, Brian and Ae-Gyung Shim (2015), *The Changing Face of Korean Cinema: 1960 to 2015*, London and New York: Routledge.

Yeh, Emilie Yueh-Yu and Darrell Davis (2002), 'Japan Hongscreen: Pan-Asian cinemas and flexible accumulation', *Historical Journal of Film, Radio and Television* 22: 1, 61–82.

Yeh, Emilie Yueh-yu (2010), 'The deferral of Pan-Asian: a critical appraisal of film marketization in China', in Michael Curtin and Hemant Shah (eds), *Re-Orienting Global Communication: Indian and Chinese Media Beyond Borders*, Indianapolis: University of Illinois Press, pp. 183–200.

Yonhap (2018), 'China screens first Korean films since ban on Korean content during THAAD feud', *Korean Herald*, 6 April 2018, <http://www.koreaherald.com/view.php?ud=20180406000645>.

Yoshimoto, Mitsuhiro (2003), 'Hollywood, Americanism and the imperial screen: geopolitics of image and discourse after the end of the Cold War', *Inter-Asia Cultural Studies* 4: 3, 452–9.

Yoshimoto, Mitsuhiro (2006), 'National/international/transnational: the concept of trans-Asian cinema and the cultural politics of film criticism', in Paul Willemen and Valentina Vitali (eds), *Theorising National Cinema*, London: British Film Institute, pp. 254–61.

Yoshimoto, Mitsuhiro (2013), 'A future for comparative film studies', *Inter-Asia Cultural Studies* 14: 1, 54–61.

Yue, Audrey (2014), 'Contemporary Sinophone cinema: Australia-China co-productions', in Audrey Yue and Olivia Khoo (eds), *Sinophone Cinemas*, London: Palgrave Macmillan, pp. 185–202.

Zee (2008), 'Sun shines on Singapore queer cinema', *Fridae*, 26 March 2008, <http://www.fridae.asia/newsfeatures/2008/03/26/2026.sun-shines-on-singapore-queer-cinema>.

Zimmermann, Patricia R. (2010), 'Asian Film Archive at 5', *Afterimage* 37: 6, 3.

Zone, Ray (2007), *Stereoscopic Cinema and the Origins of 3-D Film, 1838–1952*, Lexington, KY: University Press of Kentucky.

Index